The Complete Book of Freezer Cookery

BOOKS BY ANN SERANNE

The Art of Egg Cookery

Your Home Freezer

The Complete Book of Home Preserving

The Complete Book of Home Baking

Delectable Desserts

The Complete Book of Desserts

The Epicure's Companion (WITH JOHN TEBBEL)

Happy Living (WITH EVELYN ENRIGHT)

The Complete Book of Freezer Cookery

With Eileen Gaden

The Blender Cookbook

The Best of Near Eastern Cookery

The Church and Club Woman's Companion

The Sandwich Book

The Complete Book of Freezer Cookery

ANN SERANNE

Formerly published as
THE COMPLETE BOOK OF HOME FREEZING

DOUBLEDAY & COMPANY, INC., GARDEN CITY, NEW YORK

Contents

Can Foods Be Stored at Zero?, Can You Refreeze Foods?, Care of Purchased Frozen Foods, Equivalent Weights of Frozen and Fresh Foods, Fifteen Basic Rules for Freezing.

Recipes for items printed in small capitals can be located by consulting the Index.

Introduction

The Complete Book of Freezer Cookery is exactly that. It's as complete as any book can be on one subject. Whether you live on a farm or in the heart of a large city, this book will help you make the most out of your freezer.

If the home freezer is used intelligently and with a plan in mind, it can save many hours of work in the daily preparation of food for the table, and can miraculously transform you from cook to hostess when you entertain.

The book is divided into two sections: the first is an entirely new approach to the home freezing of prepared dishes, from everyday meat loaves, stews, and casseroles to delicious gourmet dishes, such as fillet of sole in white wine sauce, chicken Bordelaise, beef in red wine; savory appetizers, delicate cakes, homemade breads, frothy chiffon pies, and velvety desserts. The second part is a revision of *Your Home Freezer,* published by Doubleday in 1953. At that time most people bought a freezer to preserve the excess produce from garden, orchard, and pasture.

Today, the emphasis of the home freezer is on the freezing of prepared dishes so that this has now become the most important part of the book. The first section is, I hope, for people who like to cook and don't begrudge spending time in the kitchen to give the pleasure that only good food can give to family and friends. If you have an adequate freezer, you must like to cook—otherwise why do you have it? Not to store great quantities of raw foods when there is a frozen-food counter right around the corner! There are exceptions to this, of course, for the home freezer is a great asset to the avid hunter or fisherman who wants to preserve his catch and to farm folk who live in isolated areas, far from a shopping center. But for the average homemaker, for the working wife, and for the career girl, the freezer is a boon, because it allows you to cook when you have the time and are in the mood, enables you to put better quality and greater variety on your table and to entertain with confidence and ease.

The provident homemaker will devote a couple of mornings or one day each week to cooking for the freezer. This is a happy time spent in the kitchen, for you know that the hours put in today will give you many dividends of free time in the future. You may decide to have a morning for bread making, another for sauce making, or you might prefer preparing in one day all the dishes you will need for the week.

If you can't put aside a day for freezer cooking, then you can double up on recipes when preparing a family meal. Never make a single dish of anything: double or triple it; eat one portion and freeze the rest for a week or two later. It's just as easy to make twice or three times the quantity of a stew, ragout, or chowder as it is to make a small-quantity recipe, and just as simple to make and bake two or three pies as one. You save fuel, preparation time, and dishwashing. By freezing what you don't eat, you can have a free weekend or a free week out of every two.

Most of the recipes in this book are for 12 servings. If yours is a family of six, divide the finished dish in half. If only a family of four, then divide it into thirds. Eat one portion and freeze the rest. You may have to invest in some large saucepans and a Dutch oven, if you don't have one, a few extra pie plates and casseroles, but it is well worth the investment.

The recipes in this book are not the kind usually found in cookbooks. It wouldn't make much sense to fill up the recipe section with recipes for chicken croquettes, salmon loaf, Swiss steak, and so on. Most homemakers have their favorite recipes for these dishes and, if they don't, can easily find a good one in any one of a dozen basic cookbooks. So I have tried to give you unusual and unusually delicious recipes that you will be proud to serve to family and guests. Any one can be considered a "party" dish and all are excellent for intimate sit-down dinners or for buffet suppers. I have also tried to make the recipes reflect the various types of dishes that take kindly to freezing, so that you will know that if you follow your special recipe for creamed or curried chicken it will freeze as well as mine.

Every time I write a book, I can't help talking about phyllo pastry (pronounced feel-o), in the hope that I can interest a few more people each time in one of the great pastries of the world.

It is available in the frozen-food compartments of some supermarkets and in every Greek store from coast to coast—Greek, naturally, because it was the Greeks who invented this pastry, brought it to perfection, and now freeze it for store distribution. Phyllo pastry is paper-thin sheets of pastry that look like tissue paper, in which you wrap a variety of fillings for appetizers, main dishes, and desserts. Wonderful little cheese-filled turnovers, cheese and spinach pies, and innumerable honey-drenched desserts made of phyllo pastry all freeze beautifully. The only trouble with the pastry is that it takes time to work with it and fashion it into the various dishes. The technique is fully described in a recent Doubleday book, *The Best of Near Eastern Cookery,* and I recommend it to anyone interested in learning the intricacies of phyllo pastry. It's such a specialized technique that I did not feel I could afford the space to deal with it in this book.

Before getting to the recipes, here are a few quick freezer tips:

Don't store foods too long. While most prepared dishes will keep for 4 to 6 months, the sooner they are eaten the more they will be enjoyed. For best use of your freezer and for the best quality in frozen fare, try not to keep any cooked foods longer than 1 month.

For special occasions, freeze a few perfect strawberries, with the hulls left on. Freeze first on a baking sheet, each one separated from the other. When frozen, package and return to the freezer.

To dress up beverages, slip a sprig of mint, a twist of lemon or orange, or a strawberry into each section of an ice-cube tray before freezing. When frozen, remove and package in polyethylene bags.

Freeze garden-fresh herbs as follows and you can have a constant supply of your favorites all year round: Pack tiny containers (empty baby-food jars are perfect) tightly with tarragon leaves, sweet basil, dill, or other herb. Seal and cook in boiling water for 30 minutes. Cool and store in the freezer. Use what you want for a recipe and return the jar to the freezer.

Don't let partially used cans of food mold in the refrigerator. I'm thinking particularly of tomato purée and tomato paste. Freeze them right in the cans. Either cover or wrap in aluminum foil.

And did you know that coconut stays fresh, brown sugar doesn't lump, marshmallows never get dry, and potato chips remain crisp in the freezer?

You have a freezer—use it wisely and well!

ANN SERANNE

Part One

PREPARED DISHES FOR THE FREEZER

CHAPTER 1

Appetizers

It's good to have a variety of appetizers and a few packages of canapés in the home freezer for emergency, but since many appetizers are quick to make, and the kinds of canapés that freeze well are limited, it is best not to devote too much space to this category of prepared foods.

In the event of a cocktail party, the freezer can be pressed into service to preserve those appetizers that take kindly to freezing. You may wish to make some a week or two in advance so that you do not crowd your refrigerator on the day of the event.

Mayonnaise, salad dressings, hard-cooked egg mixtures, and raw vegetables cannot be used in appetizers or canapés for the freezer. Apart from these limitations, don't be afraid to experiment with your favorite appetizers. Appetizers and canapés should not be kept longer than 1 month in the freezer.

DIPS

Dips made of cottage cheese, cream cheese, Cheddar cheese, clams and sour cream, and liver spreads all freeze well, but these take so little time to prepare, especially if you have an electric blender, that there is little reason to freeze them in any quantity. If you do freeze them, package in cup or pint containers; defrost for 5 to 6 hours at room temperature.

BAKED CHEESE STRAWS, TINY BISCUITS, AND PUFFS

Freeze baked cheese straws or tiny herbed or cheese-flavored baking-powder biscuits in freezer cartons, separating layers with freezer paper. Freeze miniature baked cream puffs, unfilled, on baking sheets, then pack in freezer cartons. To defrost: bake in a very slow (250° F.) oven for 10 to 15 minutes. Serve cheese straws warm; split and butter the biscuits while warm; cool and fill the cream puffs.

PASTRY APPETIZERS

Tiny, RICH PASTRY turnovers filled with meat or cheese or with minced cooked chicken in curry sauce are one of the best cocktail appetizers for the freezer. Freeze them, unbaked, on baking sheets. Then pack in freezer cartons, separating layers with freezer paper. To defrost and cook: bake in a preheated 400° F. oven for 15 to 20 minutes, or until hot and golden brown. Serve hot.

Mushroom turnovers

3 tablespoons butter
1 medium onion, finely
 chopped
½ pound mushrooms,
 finely chopped
2 tablespoons flour

¼ teaspoon thyme
½ teaspoon salt
Freshly ground black
 pepper
¼ cup cream
RICH PASTRY

In skillet heat butter and in it sauté onion until lightly browned. Add mushrooms and cook for about 3 minutes, stirring frequently. Stir in flour, thyme, salt, and pepper. Gradually stir in cream and cook, stirring, until mixture is thick. Cool.

Place 1 teaspoon of the mushroom filling in center of 3-inch round of pastry. Fold dough over and press edges together with tines of a fork. Freeze unbaked on baking sheets, then pack in freezer cartons, separating layers with freezer paper. To defrost and cook: bake in a preheated 400° F. oven for 15 to 20 minutes, or until browned. Serve hot.

Piroshki
(Makes 3 dozen)

1 cup (2 sticks) butter	*2 tablespoons sour cream*
8 ounces cream cheese	*1 cup cooked rice*
¼ cup heavy cream	*1 teaspoon dry dill weed*
2½ cups all-purpose flour	*½ teaspoon salt*
1 teaspoon salt	*¼ teaspoon freshly ground*
2 onions, chopped	* black pepper*
¼ cup butter	*1 egg*
¾ pound ground beef	*1 tablespoon water*

Cream together the 1 cup butter and cheese and beat in cream. Blend in flour and salt and chill well.

Sauté onions in the ¼ cup butter until transparent.

Add beef and cook, stirring, until meat loses color.

Remove from heat and stir in sour cream, rice, dill weed, salt, and pepper.

Roll out dough very thinly between waxed paper, and cut 3-inch rounds or squares.

Put 1 teaspoon filling on one side of each pastry cutout. Combine egg and water. Moisten edges of dough with egg mixture. Fold dough over filling, forming crescents or triangles. Seal edges. Arrange on baking sheet and brush with remaining egg mixture.

Freeze on baking sheet, then package, label, and store.

To bake fresh or frozen

Make a small hole in center of each piroshki to allow steam to escape. Bake in preheated 400° F. oven for 15 to 20 minutes, or until golden brown. Serve hot or cold.

PIGS IN BLANKETS

Tiny cocktail franks, wrapped in RICH PASTRY, freeze well. Freeze unbaked on baking sheets, then pack into freezer cartons, separating layers with freezer paper. To defrost and cook: bake in a preheated 400° F. oven for 10 to 15 minutes.

BACON ROLL-UPS

Wrap olives, cooked chicken livers, stuffed prunes, or cooked mussels in strips of bacon, and secure with toothpicks. Freeze on baking sheets, then pack into freezer cartons, separating layers with freezer paper. To defrost and cook: broil until bacon is crisp on all sides. Serve hot.

Bacon and liver roll-ups

Combine 1 cup chopped cooked chicken livers, 1 tablespoon chopped chives or grated onion, 1 tablespoon butter, 1 teaspoon brandy, and salt and pepper to taste. Spread mixture on strips of bacon. Roll up and fasten with toothpicks. Freeze as above. To defrost and cook: broil until bacon is crisp on all sides. Serve hot.

SANDWICH ROLL-UPS

Thin slices of buttered bread, spread with filling and rolled up like tiny jelly rolls, freeze well. Freeze on baking sheets, then pack in freezer cartons. To serve cold, simply thaw in the cartons at room temperature for 1 hour. To serve hot, place the frozen rolls on baking sheet and bake in a preheated 400° F. oven for 10 to 15 minutes, or until bread is toasted.

Anchovy sandwich roll-ups

Spread thin slices of trimmed bread with butter mixed with anchovy paste. Place a cooked asparagus tip in center of each slice and roll up. Freeze. Serve hot.

Cheese sandwich roll-ups

Melt 1 pound Cheddar cheese with 3 tablespoons chili sauce, 3 tablespoons butter, and 2 tablespoons catsup. Spread mixture on thinly sliced trimmed bread and roll up. Freeze. To serve, slice rolls 1 inch thick, place on baking sheet, and bake in a preheated 400° F. oven for 10 minutes. Serve hot.

MEAT ROLLS AND DECKERS

Almost any kind of cold meat, spread with filling, rolled, stacked, or shaped into cornucopias, is a good appetizer for the freezer. Freeze on baking sheets, then pack in freezer cartons, with freezer paper between the layers. To defrost: defrost without opening package for 1 hour at room temperature.

Bologna rolls

Spread thinly sliced bologna with cream cheese seasoned with Worcestershire sauce. Roll and fasten with toothpicks. Freeze and serve as above.

Ham or salami deckers

Put 6 slices ham or salami together with softened cream cheese between. Wrap in aluminum foil and freeze. Defrost for 1 hour at room temperature in the foil, then cut into pie sections or small squares. Serve on picks.

COCKTAIL BALLS

This is another good item for the freezer. Almost any kind of meat, chicken, or fish, made into tiny bite-size balls, can be preserved in the freezer. Freeze, uncooked, on trays, then package in freezer cartons, separating the layers with a piece of freezer paper. To defrost and cook: deep-fry in hot cooking oil (350° F.) until golden brown. Drain and serve hot.

Spiced meat balls

Combine 1½ pounds ground round steak, 2 eggs, beaten, ½ cup fresh bread crumbs, 1 medium onion, minced, 1 tablespoon chopped parsley, 1 tablespoon chopped fresh mint, ¼ teaspoon cinnamon, ¼ teaspoon allspice, ¼ teaspoon cayenne, and 1½ teaspoons salt. Mix thoroughly. Form into bite-size balls and freeze; cook and serve as above.

CANAPES

Not all canapés freeze well. Avoid using hard-cooked egg mixtures or raw vegetables. Spread bread or toast rounds with butter, not mayonnaise. Sliced or ground meats, meat spreads, fish, cheese, peanut butter, and crisp bacon are all good, but the best canapés for the freezer are those that are served hot. Freeze canapés on baking sheets, then package in freezer containers in layers with freezer paper between each layer. To serve cold: thaw in unopened packages for about 1 hour at room temperature. To serve hot: arrange canapés on baking sheet and bake in a preheated 350° F. oven for 5 to 10 minutes, or heat and brown under the broiler.

Salmon and cheese canapés

Combine 1 cup shredded Cheddar cheese, ½ cup flaked salmon, 1 tablespoon sherry, and freshly ground pepper to taste. Spread on squares of toast and freeze. Serve hot.

Deviled sardine canapés

Mash the contents of a can of skinless, boneless sardines with enough of the oil from the can to moisten. Season with lemon juice, Tabasco, and freshly ground black pepper. Spread on buttered toast fingers and freeze. Serve hot.

Curried cheese canapés

Combine 3 ounces soft cream cheese, 8 pitted ripe olives, chopped, ¼ teaspoon curry powder, and 1 tablespoon minced parsley. Spread on toast rounds and freeze. Serve cold.

Clam and cheese canapés

Combine 1 cup shredded Cheddar cheese, 1 (8-ounce) can minced clams, drained, 1 tablespoon each minced parsley and chives, and a pinch of cayenne. Spread on toast rounds and freeze. Serve hot.

Parmesan canapés

Cook 2 slices bacon until brown and crisp. Drain, cool, and crumble. Mix with ½ cup grated Parmesan, ¼ cup heavy cream, and 1 teaspoon Worcestershire sauce. Spread on toast rounds and freeze. Remove from freezer, top each with a slice of stuffed olive, and bake in a preheated 350° F. oven for 5 to 10 minutes. Serve hot.

Roquefort and anchovy fingers

Chop a 2-ounce flat can of anchovies and mix with ¼ cup soft, sweet butter, and 4 tablespoons crumbled Roquefort or blue cheese. Stir in ½ teaspoon curry powder. Spread on toast fingers and freeze. Serve hot.

Bacon and cheese canapés

Shred ½ pound Cheddar cheese and mix with 6 slices chopped raw bacon and 1 teaspoon onion juice. Pile lightly on bread rounds and freeze. Serve hot.

Crab-meat canapés

Mix 1 (7½-ounce) can Alaska King crab meat, flaked, with 8 ounces soft cream cheese and a dash of Tabasco. Spread on rounds of toast or bread and freeze. Serve hot.

FIRST COURSE APPETIZERS

Following are a group of special appetizers that freeze well.

CHINESE EGG ROLLS
(Makes 28 rolls)

*28 crêpes, freshly made
 or from freezer
½ cup chopped water
 chestnuts
4 green onions, sliced
2 pieces canned bamboo
 shoots, chopped
2 stalks celery, minced*

*4 eggs, lightly beaten
2 tablespoons soy sauce
1 teaspoon salt
2 pounds cooked shrimp,
 shelled, deveined, and
 chopped
2 tablespoons flour
2 tablespoons water*

In mixing bowl combine water chestnuts, green onions, bamboo shoots, and celery. Stir in eggs, soy sauce, and salt. Mix in shrimp.
Place 1 tablespoon of the filling on one half of each crêpe.
Mix flour and water to a paste. Moisten edges of crêpe with the flour paste. Fold sides of crêpe toward center and roll up, enclosing filling. Place on baking sheet and freeze. When frozen, package, label, and store.

To finish fresh or frozen egg rolls

Fry in deep fat heated to 365° F. for about 5 minutes, or until golden brown. Drain on absorbent paper. Serve very hot with plum sauce and hot mustard.

CRAB-MEAT ROLLS
(Makes 36 rolls)

36 PANCAKE SKINS, *freshly baked or frozen*
2 (7½-ounce) cans Alaska King crab meat, flaked
2 teaspoons cornstarch
1 teaspoon salt
1 teaspoon sugar
2 tablespoons soy sauce
2 tablespoons cooking oil
4 green onions, sliced

2 cups soybean sprouts
2 cups coarsely shredded raw spinach
8 dried mushrooms, soaked for 30 minutes in hot water, drained and flaked
2 pieces preserved ginger, minced
½ cup chopped water chestnuts

Make or defrost pancake skins.

Mix flaked crab meat with cornstarch, salt, sugar, and soy sauce. In skillet heat oil and in it sauté green onions lightly.

Add remaining ingredients and sauté for 2 minutes. Add crab-meat mixture, mix lightly, and cook for 2 minutes longer. Cool and chill.

Place 1 tablespoon filling on one half of a skin. Flip remaining skin on that side up over the filling. Flip the two side pieces of skin over filling, then roll up to far side of skin. Seal edge with a little beaten egg.

To freeze

Freeze prepared rolls on baking sheet, then package in serving portions, label, and freeze.

To finish fresh or frozen rolls

Heat about 1 inch cooking oil in a skillet to 365° F. and in it fry the rolls, fresh or frozen, for about 5 minutes, or until brown on all sides, turning once. Drain on absorbent paper. Serve hot with hot Chinese mustard and, if desired, plum sauce.

PARTY QUICHE LORRAINE
(Makes 2 tarts. Each serves 6 for a hot appetizer)

*Pastry for 2 (9-inch)
pie shells
1 pound sliced bacon
½ pound diced Gruyère
cheese
½ pound diced Swiss
cheese
12 egg yolks (save
whites for an
angel-food cake)*

*4 cups heavy cream
½ teaspoon salt
½ teaspoon dry mustard
¼ teaspoon freshly ground
black pepper*

Line two (9-inch) pie plates with pastry, trim edges, and crimp. Cover pastry with waxed paper, partially fill with dry rice or beans, and bake in a preheated 450° F. oven for 8 minutes. Remove paper and beans or rice (save the beans and rice especially for baking pie shells. They can be used over and over again) and continue to bake the pastry for 3 minutes longer. Remove from oven. Reduce oven temperature to 350° F.

Sauté bacon until crisp. Drain on absorbent paper. Crumble bacon into pastry shells. Mix the cheese and divide into pastry shells.

Combine egg yolks, cream, and seasoning and divide into the pastry shells.

Bake in the preheated oven for 35 minutes. Remove 1 quiche to cool for freezer. When cool, wrap, label, and freeze.

To finish 1 quiche

Continue to bake for 10 minutes longer, or until nicely browned. Cut into wedges and serve hot or warm.

To defrost and serve frozen quiche

Bake in preheated 350° F. oven for 15 to 20 minutes, or until lightly browned. Serve as above.

CREPES DE FROMAGE
(Serves 12 for appetizer; 6 for luncheon dish)

12 frozen CRÊPES
  WITHOUT SUGAR
½ cup dry white wine
2 cups (½ pound)
  shredded Swiss cheese
2 teaspoons cornstarch

1 tablespoon milk
¾ cup HOLLANDAISE
  SAUCE, *freshly made or*
  defrosted
½ cup heavy cream,
  whipped

Remove crêpes from freezer to defrost.

In saucepan combine wine and cheese. Cook over low heat until cheese is melted and mixture is smooth. Dissolve cornstarch in the milk and stir into cheese mixture and cook, stirring, until mixture comes to a boil. Keep warm over hot water.

Arrange defrosted crêpes on worktable. Spread each with about 1½ tablespoons of the cheese mixture and roll up. Arrange in buttered baking dish.

Bake in a preheated 425° F. oven for about 8 minutes, or until hot. Meanwhile combine hollandaise sauce and whipped cream.

Remove crêpes from oven and spoon a ribbon of sauce over each. Return to the hot oven for 1 to 2 minutes, or until sauce is lightly browned.

CAPONATINA (*Eggplant Appetizer*)
(6 to 8 servings)

1 large eggplant
2 teaspoons salt
¾ cup olive oil
2 medium onions,
*   chopped*
2 cloves garlic, minced
1 (1-pound 12-ounce)
*   can Italian plum*
*   tomatoes, drained*

4 stalks celery, sliced
½ cup pitted green olives
¼ cup capers
1 tablespoon pine nuts
2 tablespoons wine
*   vinegar*
Salt and pepper to taste

Wash eggplant but do not peel. Cut into 1-inch cubes, sprinkle with salt, and let stand for 2 hours. Squeeze out excess moisture and dry on absorbent paper.

In saucepan heat olive oil and in it sauté eggplant until soft, turning occasionally to brown eggplant on all sides. Remove eggplant from pan with slotted spoon.

To oil remaining in pan add onions and garlic and cook over moderate heat for 8 minutes, or until onions are cooked but not browned.

Add tomatoes, celery, and olives. Simmer for 15 minutes, or until celery is tender. Add eggplant, capers, nuts, and vinegar. Add salt and pepper to taste. Cook over low heat for 20 minutes, stirring occasionally to prevent mixture from sticking. Serve hot or cold.

To freeze

Cool, pour into freezer container, seal, label, and freeze.

To defrost

Remove from freezer about 6 hours before serving and let defrost in refrigerator. Or heat over simmering water until defrosted and serve hot, or chill to serve cold.

When those long, pale-green Italian peppers are in the market, buy a quantity and prepare this wonderful hot appetizer for your freezer.

CHILIS RELLENOS CON QUESTO

Wash peppers and roast in a hot oven (500° F.) for 7 to 8 minutes. Remove from oven and wrap in a towel to steam. When cool, peel off thin outer skin.

Slit peppers lengthwise, remove seeds, and rinse out insides. Fill with chunks of cheese—use a soft cheese such as Mozzarella, or a semisoft such as Bel Paese or Gruyère (in California and Texas, Monterey Jack is used). Chill or freeze on baking sheets. When frozen, package, label, and return to freezer.

To finish

Roll stuffed peppers in flour, dip in batter (see below), and fry in skillet containing 1 inch fat heated to 365° F. until nicely browned. Drain on absorbent paper, sprinkle with salt, and serve hot.

Frying batter for 8 stuffed peppers

Make batter just before frying peppers.

> 4 eggs, separated
> 4 tablespoons flour

Beat egg yolks until thick and pale in color.
Beat egg whites until stiff.
Fold egg yolks and flour into the beaten egg whites.

Grape leaves, preserved in brine, are available at stores specializing in Greek or Near Eastern foods.

STUFFED GRAPE LEAVES
(Makes about 60 rolls)

2 cups olive oil	12 green onions, including
6 large onions, chopped	tender green part,
2 teaspoons salt	minced
½ teaspoon pepper	Juice of 4 lemons
2 cups raw rice	5 cups water
2 tablespoons chopped	1 (1-pound) jar grape
fresh dill, or 2	leaves in brine
teaspoons dry dill weed	Stems from bunch of
1 cup chopped parsley	parsley

In saucepan heat half the olive oil and in it sauté the onions until they are transparent. Add salt, pepper, and rice and cook for 10 minutes, stirring occasionally. Add dill, parsley, green onions, half the lemon juice, and 1 cup water. Cook for 10 minutes, or until liquid is absorbed.

Rinse grape leaves, separate, and place shiny side down on worktable. Put 1 teaspoon filling on each leaf near base. Starting at the base, fold over. Fold over sides, then roll tightly toward the tip.

In a large casserole arrange rolls in layers with stems of parsley between. Add remaining olive oil and lemon juice and 2 cups water. Weight rolls down with a heavy plate, bring liquid to a boil, and simmer for 25 minutes. Add remaining water and simmer for 30 minutes longer. Cool rolls, arrange on baking sheets, and freeze. When frozen, package in serving portions, label, and freeze.

To defrost and serve

Remove from freezer about 4 hours before serving. Serve cold with lemon wedges and freshly ground pepper.

CHAPTER 2

Soups

Four types of soups in the freezer are invaluable aids to meal planning and to cooking. The first is those wonderful long-simmering stick-to-the-ribs soups made from beans, lentils, and split peas that are a meal in themselves when served with French bread, hot corn bread, or baking-powder biscuits. The second is fragrant fish stews and chowders, which do not take long to cook, but are time-consuming to prepare. If you live near a shore where clams, mussels, and scallops are abundant, or if you happen to have a fisherman for a husband, you'll want to make fish chowders frequently and in sufficient quantity to have some for the freezer.

The third type of soup for the freezer is vegetable soup bases, made from leftover vegetables from an evening dinner. Rather than freeze the vegetables as leftovers, it takes only a few minutes to convert them into a vegetable purée and freeze the purée for a cream of vegetable soup for a nourishing lunch or as a first course to dinner. If a dab of cooked potatoes is left over, you can use this as a thickener, otherwise you can use a little flour.

The fourth and, perhaps, most important type of soup for those who love to cook and appreciate fine dishes is beef, chicken, and fish stocks, which may be said to be the starting point of good cooking. They are the bases of most sauces, and add flavor to stews, casseroles, and braised dishes of all kinds. They make a stimulating beginning to a meal. Serve them hot with croutons or a garnish of finely chopped parsley, dill, or celery leaves, or add a small quantity of cooked vegetables, rice, or noodles. Beef and chicken stocks are available in cans, and are adequate, but can never take the place of a well-flavored homemade broth which has simmered for hours to distill the essence from bones and vegetables. If you use these stocks to any great extent, you'll find it much cheaper and most rewarding to make them yourself. While fish stock is comparatively simple to make, you can't buy it, but you can always have a supply in your freezer. Stocks may be concentrated, if desired, to save freezer space. Strain the cooked stock, return it to the heat, and cook until it is reduced to half its original quantity. To use, add equal parts of concentrated stock and water.

All soups freeze well, except those containing diced potatoes or macaroni. These become soggy when the soup defrosts. Simply omit them from any recipe specifying them as an ingredient. They can always be cooked separately and added to a soup just before serving.

To freeze soups and stocks

Cool soups thoroughly and quickly.
Package soups in quantity suitable for family use.
Package stocks in cup, pint, and quart containers.
Use wide-top freezer containers, and leave 1 inch head space.
To save freezer space, leave out last-minute additions of cream or milk.
Seal and label. Include on label any instructions for finishing the soup, if it was not completed before freezing.

To serve hot soup from freezer

Set container into a saucepan of hot water just long enough to loosen soup from container. Empty into saucepan and cook over low heat, for about 30 minutes, or until thawed and hot, stirring occasionally. Make last-minute additions if necessary.
Correct seasoning and serve.

To serve cold soup from freezer

Defrost overnight in refrigerator, or at room temperature for about 3 hours. To speed defrosting, set container into a saucepan of hot water. Renew hot water when necessary and stir occasionally. As soon as soup is defrosted, but is still very cold, put in refrigerator until ready to serve.

WHITE OR CHICKEN STOCK (*Fond Blanc*)
(Makes 3 quarts lightly salted)

1 (5-pound) roasting or
stewing chicken, ready
to cook
1 pound veal knuckle,
cracked
2 carrots, quartered
1 large onion, quartered
2 stalks celery with leaves

4 cloves
¼ teaspoon peppercorns
2 teaspoons salt
Small bunch parsley
¼ teaspoon thyme
1 bay leaf
5 quarts cold water

Put all ingredients into a large soup kettle.
Bring water to a boil, skimming surface frequently.
Reduce heat and simmer for 3 hours.
Remove chicken and use chicken meat for another dish.
Boil stock rapidly for 30 minutes.
Strain through a sieve or colander lined with cheesecloth.
Cool and remove fat from surface.

BROWN OR BEEF STOCK (*Fond Brun*)
(Makes 3 quarts lightly salted)

3 pounds shin of beef
2 pounds veal knuckle,
cracked
¼ pound lean raw ham,
diced
2 tablespoons cooking oil
3 carrots, sliced
2 onions, sliced
2 stalks celery with leaves,
sliced

2 cloves garlic
5 quarts water
Small bunch parsley
½ teaspoon thyme
2 bay leaves
½ teaspoon peppercorns
2 teaspoons salt

Preheat oven to very hot (475° F.).
In large shallow baking pan spread the beef, veal knuckle, and

ham. Sprinkle with cooking oil and bake in the hot oven for 45 minutes, stirring occasionally.

Sprinkle meat with carrots, onions, and celery. Add garlic and bake for 15 minutes longer.

Transfer meat and vegetables to a large soup kettle. Rinse baking pan with a little of the water and add to kettle. Add remaining water and ingredients.

Bring water to a boil, skimming surface frequently.

Reduce heat and simmer for 3 hours.

Cool, remove fat from surface, and strain through a sieve or colander lined with cheesecloth.

FISH STOCK (*Fond de Poisson Blanc*)
(Makes 2 quarts)

2½ pounds bones and
*   trimmings of*
*   white-fleshed fish*
2 medium onions, sliced
Small bunch parsley

¼ teaspoon peppercorns
1 teaspoon salt
Juice of ½ lemon
2½ quarts water

Put all ingredients into soup kettle.
Bring water to a boil, skimming surface frequently.
Simmer for 30 minutes.
Strain stock through a sieve or colander lined with cheesecloth.

MEAT AND VEGETABLE SOUP (*Petite Marmite*)
(Makes 3 quarts)

2½ pounds shin of beef
1 roasting chicken, cut
*   into parts*
Chicken giblets
3 teaspoons salt
½ teaspoon peppercorns
5 quarts water

2 stalks celery, sliced
3 carrots, sliced or cut
*   into thin strips*
3 leeks (white part only),
*   sliced*
2 white turnips, cut into
*   thin strips*

In large soup kettle put beef, chicken, giblets, salt, peppercorns, and water. Bring water to a boil, skimming surface frequently.
Reduce heat and simmer for 3 hours.
Remove soup from heat. Remove meat and chicken.
Strain stock through a sieve or colander lined with cheesecloth.
Return strained stock to heat and add vegetables.
Bring to a boil and simmer for 15 minutes.
Cut meat and chicken into thin strips and add to soup.
Correct seasoning with salt and pepper.
Simmer for 2 minutes, and serve with hot French bread.

MINESTRONE
(12 servings)

1 tablespoon olive oil
¼ pound salt pork, diced
2 cloves garlic, chopped
2 medium onions, chopped
2 leeks (white part only), diced
½ teaspoon orégano
2 tablespoons tomato paste
½ cup water
6 medium tomatoes, peeled, seeded, and chopped, or 6 whole canned tomatoes, chopped

2 cups chopped celery with leaves
3 carrots, sliced
2 small white turnips, peeled and diced
½ small cabbage, shredded
4 zucchini or summer squash, sliced
3 quarts water
Salt to taste
½ teaspoon freshly ground black pepper

In large kettle put olive oil and salt pork, garlic, onions, leeks, and orégano. Cook over moderate heat until pork is lightly browned and vegetables are tender.

Add tomato paste mixed with the ½ cup water, and simmer for 5 minutes.

Add tomatoes, celery, carrots, turnips, cabbage, zucchini or summer squash, water, salt, and pepper.

Bring to a boil, cover, and simmer for 45 minutes.

Set aside half to cool for freezer. When cool, package and freeze.

To finish half the soup (6 servings)

1 cup diced cooked
potatoes
1 cup elbow macaroni
1 cup canned chick-peas,
drained

Chopped parsley
Grated Parmesan cheese

Return remaining soup to heat.

Add potatoes and simmer for 10 minutes.

Add macaroni and chick-peas and simmer for 10 minutes longer.

Correct seasoning, pour into heated bowl, and sprinkle with chopped parsley.

Serve with grated Parmesan cheese.

ONION SOUP
(12 servings)

1 cup (2 sticks) butter
3 pounds onions (9
medium), sliced
2 cloves garlic, minced
8 cups beef consommé
or stock

½ teaspoon freshly ground
black pepper
Salt to taste

In large saucepan melt butter.

Add onions and garlic and cook over low heat so the vegetables stew for about 20 minutes, or until soft, without browning.

Add consommé or stock and bring to a boil.

Add pepper and salt to taste and simmer for 30 minutes.

Set aside half to cool for freezer. When cool, package and freeze.

To finish half the soup (6 servings)

½ cup Port wine
6 slices French bread, toasted
¾ cup grated Swiss or Gruyère cheese

Return remaining soup to heat.
Stir in Port wine.
Divide into 6 individual earthenware casseroles.
Top each serving with a slice of toasted French bread and sprinkle each slice with about 2 tablespoons grated cheese.
Bake in a preheated, moderately hot oven (375° F.) for 10 minutes, or until cheese melts and becomes crusty.

Any leftover vegetable, or a combination of leftover vegetables, may be quickly made into the base of a wonderfully nourishing and flavorful cream soup. It's a much better use of leftovers than storing dibs or dabs in freezer or refrigerator. Use your freezer for finished or nearly finished dishes, not for odds and ends.

CREAM OF VEGETABLE PUREE
(Makes 3 cups purée)

1 small onion, minced
4 tablespoons butter
4 tablespoons flour, or ½ cup cooked leftover potatoes

1 cup cooked leftover vegetables
1½ cups chicken broth
½ teaspoon celery salt

Cook onion in butter over low heat for 10 minutes, or until onion is tender.
Stir in flour or add potatoes.
Add vegetables, chicken broth, and celery salt.
Bring to a boil and simmer for 10 minutes.
Purée in food mill or blend in electric blender until smooth.
Finish for immediate service, or cool, package, and freeze.

To make the purée into soup (4 to 6 servings)

1 cup light cream
2 tablespoons chopped parsley or shredded celery leaves

Place pureé over simmering water, or defrost over simmering water.
Stir in cream and heat to serving temperature.
Correct seasoning. Sprinkle each serving with parsley or celery leaves.

One of the most delicious vegetable soups in the world is a cream of sorrel soup. Sorrel is a sour herb, commonly known as sour grass, which is available in many Italian markets in early spring months. This is when it is tender and at its best. With a home freezer you can enjoy sorrel soup the year round. Let your freezer preserve those food products which are unobtainable during a great part of the year.

CREAM OF SORREL SOUP
(8 servings)

2 pounds fresh sorrel leaves
½ cup minced onion
½ cup (1 stick) butter
2 cups chicken broth

Wash and pick over sorrel leaves. Drain well. Remove coarse center stem from larger leaves. Shred the sorrel thinly. In saucepan cook onion in butter over low heat for 10 minutes, or until onion is tender.
Add sorrel and cook for 5 minutes, stirring until sorrel is wilted.
Add chicken broth, bring to a boil, and simmer for 5 minutes. Set aside half to cool for freezer. When cool, package and freeze.

To finish half the soup (4 servings)

2 cups chicken broth
Salt and pepper to taste
½ cup heavy cream
1 egg yolk

Return remaining soup to heat.
Add chicken broth and bring to a boil.
Season to taste with salt and pepper.
Remove from heat. Combine cream and egg yolk with ½ cup of the hot soup. Stir into soup gradually and cook over low heat for 2 minutes, stirring rapidly and being careful not to let the soup boil. Serve immediately.

CREAM OF MUSHROOM SOUP
(8 servings)

1 pound fresh mushrooms   *1 quart chicken broth*
6 tablespoons butter   *½ teaspoon salt or to*
1 medium onion, finely   *taste*
  chopped   *¼ teaspoon white pepper*
6 tablespoons flour

Wash mushrooms and trim stem ends. Slice caps and mince stems. In saucepan melt butter and in it cook onion over low heat until onion is tender. Add mushrooms and continue to cook over low heat for about 10 minutes, or until mushrooms are cooked, turning mushrooms frequently.

Stir in flour. Gradually stir in chicken broth, salt, and pepper, and simmer for 30 minutes.

Set aside half to cool for freezer. When cool, package and freeze.

To finish half the soup (4 servings)

1 cup heavy cream
2 tablespoons dry sherry

Return remaining soup to heat. Stir in cream and sherry and heat to serving temperature.

CARROT POTATO SOUP
(12 servings)

4 cups peeled diced
  potatoes
2½ cups sliced carrots

2 leeks (white part only),
  sliced
6 cups chicken stock or
  broth

In saucepan combine potatoes, carrots, leeks, and chicken stock. Bring to a boil and simmer for 25 minutes, or until vegetables are tender.

Purée in food mill or blend 2 cups at a time for 30 seconds at high speed in electric blender.

Pour half into freezer container to cool. When cool, label and freeze.

To finish half the soup (6 servings)

1 teaspoon salt or to taste
Pinch of white pepper
1 cup heavy cream

Season remaining soup with salt and pepper. Stir in cream. Serve hot or cold, with topping of chopped chives.

CUCUMBER SOUP
(12 servings)

4 cucumbers
4 tablespoons butter
2 leeks (white part only),
  sliced

1 bay leaf
2 tablespoons flour
6 cups chicken stock
2 teaspoons salt

Peel cucumbers and slice. Sauté in butter with leeks and bay leaf for 20 minutes, or until tender, but not browned.

Stir in flour.

Add chicken stock and salt, bring to a boil, and simmer for 30 minutes.

Purée in food mill or blend 2 cups at a time for 20 seconds at high speed in electric blender.

Pour half into freezer container to cool. When cool, label and freeze.

To finish half the soup (6 servings)

1 cucumber, peeled,
   seeded, and grated
1 cup heavy cream
Juice of ½ lemon

2 teaspoons finely chopped
   fresh dill or mint
Salt and pepper to taste
Sour cream

Cool remaining soup over ice until very cold. Add cucumber, cream, lemon juice, and dill or mint. Correct seasoning with salt and pepper and serve cold in bowl of crushed ice. Top each serving with a dab of sour cream.

When home-grown tomatoes are vine-ripened and flavorful, make a quantity of this soup for your freezer.

FRESH CREAM OF TOMATO
(12 servings)

8 large ripe tomatoes,
   sliced
2 medium onions, sliced
1 teaspoon minced garlic
½ cup water

Salt and freshly ground
   pepper to taste
2 tablespoons tomato
   paste
6 tablespoons flour
3 cups water

Put tomatoes, onions, garlic, and the ½ cup water into a saucepan. Cover and cook over low heat for 15 minutes. Season with salt and pepper and stir in tomato paste. Combine flour with ½ cup of the water and stir into the hot soup. Stir in remaining 2½ cups water. Bring to a boil, stirring constantly.

Purée in food mill or blend 2 cups at a time for 30 seconds at high speed in electric blender and strain.

Pour half into freezer container to cool. When cool, label and freeze.

To finish half the soup (6 servings)

1½ cups cream
1 tablespoon finely chopped chives or fresh dill

Cool remaining soup over ice until very cold. Stir in cream and chives or dill. Serve cold in bowl of crushed ice.

CHEESE SOUP
(8 servings)

5 cups chicken stock
1 cup dry white wine or beer
2 leeks (white part only), chopped
2 stalks celery with leaves, chopped
1 medium onion, chopped

4 tablespoons cornstarch
4 tablespoons cold water
2 cups shredded Cheddar cheese, firmly packed
¼ teaspoon white pepper
¼ teaspoon nutmeg
Salt to taste

In saucepan combine chicken stock and white wine.

Add leeks, celery, and onion. Bring to a boil and simmer for 30 minutes. Strain into clean saucepan.

Combine cornstarch and water and stir into the hot stock. Cook, stirring, until stock is slightly thickened.

Add cheese, pepper, and nutmeg and cook, stirring, until cheese is melted. Season with salt if necessary.

Pour half into freezer container to cool. When cool, label and freeze.

To finish half the soup (4 servings)

1 egg yolk
½ cup heavy cream

Combine egg yolk and cream with ½ cup of the hot soup. Pour mixture gradually into soup, stirring rapidly, and cook over low heat for 2 minutes, without letting soup boil. Serve hot.

FISH AND SEA-FOOD CHOWDER
(12 servings)

1 (4-pound) or
  2 (2-pound) fresh fish
1 pound fresh shrimp
3 quarts water
½ teaspoon thyme
½ teaspoon peppercorns
1 bay leaf
1 teaspoon salt
½ cup olive oil
2 carrots, finely chopped
4 leeks (white part only),
  finely chopped

2 cloves garlic, minced
2 ripe tomatoes, peeled
  and chopped
½ teaspoon saffron
24 mussels, scrubbed and
  debearded
24 cherrystone clams in
  shells, scrubbed
Salt and pepper

Fillet the fish and put head and bones into a large saucepan.
Cut fillets into thick slices.
Shell shrimp and remove intestinal vein that runs down back.
Add shrimp shells to fish bones. Add water and bring to a simmer.
Add thyme, peppercorns, bay leaf, and salt. Simmer for 15 minutes.
Set aside.
In large kettle heat olive oil.
Add carrots and leeks and cook over low heat for 10 minutes, stirring frequently. Add garlic and tomatoes and cook for 5 minutes longer.
Strain hot stock from fish bones and shrimp shells into the kettle.
Add saffron. Bring to a rapid boil.
Add fish fillets, cover, and cook for 5 minutes.
Add shrimp, cover, and cook for 5 minutes.
Add mussels and clams. Cover and cook for 10 minutes, or until bivalves have opened.
Correct seasoning with salt and pepper.

Serve with hot French bread.

Cool what isn't used for the meal: discard clam and mussel shells, freezer-pack, and freeze.

DEFROST over simmering water until hot. Do not boil.

NEW ENGLAND CLAM CHOWDER
(12 servings)

24 chowder clams or
    quahogs
4 stalks celery with leaves,
    diced
2 medium onions, diced
2 cloves garlic, minced
1 bay leaf
6 sprigs parsley

3 quarts cold water
¼ pound salt pork, minced
2 small onions, minced
2 stalks celery, sliced
1 leek (white part only),
    sliced
6 tablespoons flour

Wash and scrub clams. Put them into a large kettle with 4 stalks celery, the 2 medium onions, garlic, bay leaf, parsley, and cold water. Bring to a boil, cover, and simmer 10 minutes. Remove clams and continue to simmer the stock for 20 minutes. Strain stock.

Discard shells from clams. Peel back outer sheath from the inner soft belly of each clam and cut away connecting cord. Dice bellies and mince or grind the tough outer sheaths. Cover with a little hot stock and set aside.

In large saucepan put salt pork, minced onions, sliced celery, and leek. Cook over low heat for 15 to 20 minutes, or until vegetables are tender and salt pork is browned.

Stir in flour.

Add the hot stock and cook, stirring, until soup is slightly thickened. Cook over low heat for 15 minutes.

Set aside half the chowder to cool for freezer. When cool, add half the clams, package, and freeze.

To finish half the soup (6 servings)

1 cup hot light cream
1 cup diced cooked potatoes

To remaining soup add remaining clams, cream, and potatoes. Heat, without boiling, and serve.

To defrost and finish

Defrost over simmering water. Just before serving, transfer to direct heat. Add cream and potatoes. Heat and serve.

LOBSTER CHOWDER
(8 servings)

2 pounds fish heads,
  bones, and trimmings
1 onion, thinly sliced
6 sprigs parsley
¼ teaspoon peppercorns
1 teaspoon lemon juice
1 cup dry white wine
2½ quarts cold water
2 (1½-pound) lobsters,
  halved
½ cup cooking oil

2 stalks celery, chopped
1 medium onion, chopped
1 large carrot, chopped
2 cloves garlic, minced
1 cup flour
2 tablespoons tomato
  purée
1 teaspoon salt
½ teaspoon pepper
4 tablespoons butter

Into soup kettle put the fish heads, bones, and trimmings, the sliced onion, parsley, peppercorns, lemon juice, white wine, and water. Bring to a boil and simmer for 30 minutes. Strain.

Makes 2 quarts fish stock.

Crack lobster claws and cut body halves into 2 or 3 pieces each.

In large saucepan heat oil until very hot. Add lobster and cook over high heat, stirring, until shell turns red.

Add celery, the chopped onion, carrot, and garlic and cook over moderate heat for 15 minutes, stirring occasionally.

Remove lobster to cool.

To liquid remaining in saucepan, stir in flour and cook, stirring, until flour is well blended. Stir in tomato purée, salt, and pepper.

Gradually stir in the hot fish stock and cook, stirring, until soup boils.

Remove lobster meat from shells and set aside. Add shells to saucepan, cover, and cook over low heat for 1½ hours.

Strain soup and stir in butter.

Pour half the soup into a 1-quart freezer container and cool. Dice lobster meat and add half to the cooled soup to be frozen. Label and freeze.

To finish half the soup (4 servings)

1 cup heavy cream

To remaining soup add remaining diced lobster. Stir in cream and heat to serving temperature, but do not boil.

CASSEROLE BOUILLABAISSE
FOR THE FREEZER
(4 servings)

½ cup olive oil
2 medium onions, finely chopped
3 cloves garlic, minced
2 large ripe tomatoes, peeled, seeded, and chopped, or 3 whole canned tomatoes
½ cup chopped parsley
2 cups fish stock
1 bay leaf
½ teaspoon thyme
2 cups dry white wine, heated

½ teaspoon saffron
1 tablespoon hot water
Salt to taste
Freshly ground pepper to taste
4 serving pieces red snapper, striped bass, or cod
8 pieces eel, about 3 inches long
4 small fillets flounder or lemon sole

In saucepan heat olive oil. Add onions and cook over moderate heat for 10 minutes, or until onions are soft, but not browned. Add garlic and tomatoes. Mix well and simmer for 8 minutes. Add parsley, fish stock, bay leaf, and thyme. Bring to a boil. Add wine.

Soak saffron in hot water for 5 minutes. Add saffron and salt and pepper to taste. Simmer 15 minutes longer to blend flavors. Cool, then chill well.

Butter a large ovenproof casserole. In bottom place the red snapper, striped bass, or cod. Add eel and then the flounder or sole.

Pour the cold bouillon over the fish. Freeze, then cover casserole tightly with casserole cover or with aluminum foil.

To finish

2 (*1-pound*) *lobsters, cut into pieces*
12 *or more fresh mussels, cleaned and debearded*

Defrost overnight in refrigerator.

Put casserole into a preheated 375° F. oven. When the bouillon starts to boil, cover and cook for 10 minutes. Add lobsters and mussels, cover, and cook for 10 minutes longer.

Serve in soup plates with lots of toasted French bread.

If you live near a seashore where mussels are abundant, you will want to serve this delicious soup often.

BILLI BI
(8 servings)

4 *pounds mussels, well*
   scrubbed
4 *shallots or green onions,*
   coarsely cut
1 *medium onion, sliced*
6 *sprigs parsley*
¼ *teaspoon freshly ground*
   black pepper

Pinch of cayenne
1 *bay leaf*
½ *teaspoon thyme*
2 *cups dry white wine*
4 *tablespoons butter*

Put mussels in a large kettle with the shallots or green onions, the sliced onion, parsley, pepper, cayenne, bay leaf, thyme, white wine, and butter. Cover and bring to a boil. Boil hard for 5 minutes, or until mussels have opened. Discard any mussels that do not open.

Strain liquid through a sieve lined with cheesecloth. Reserve mussels for another use or remove from shells and serve as garnish. Pour half the broth into freezer container to cool. When cool, label and freeze.

To finish half the soup (4 servings)

 2 cups heavy cream
 1 egg yolk

Return remaining broth to heat and bring to a boil. Stir in cream and remove from heat.

Combine egg yolk with a little of the hot soup, gradually stir into soup, and stir over low heat for 2 minutes, or until soup is slightly thickened. Do not boil. Serve hot or cold.

SPLIT PEA SOUP
(Makes 1 gallon)

 1 fresh pork hock (about
   2 pounds)
 4 quarts water
 2 pounds yellow or green
   split peas
 4 medium onions, chopped

 3 cups chopped celery
   with leaves
 2 tablespoons salt
 2 teaspoons freshly ground
   black pepper

Put pork hock and water into a large kettle. Bring water to a boil, skim surface, and simmer for 1¾ hours, or until meat is very tender. Remove meat and set aside.

To liquid remaining in kettle add split peas and simmer for 30 minutes, adding boiling water if mixture gets too thick and stirring frequently.

Add vegetables and seasoning and continue to cook for 30 minutes longer, stirring frequently and being careful that soup does not get too thick.

Dice meat from pork hock and add to soup a few minutes before it is finished cooking.

Cool.

Pour into pint or quart containers, leaving 1 inch head space. Seal and freeze.

To defrost and serve

Defrost soup over simmering water or over low heat, stirring frequently. One quart serves 6.

BLACK BEAN SOUP
(12 servings)

1 pound black beans	*1 tablespoon flour*
3 quarts cold water	*Rind and bone from a*
½ cup (1 stick) butter	*smoked ham*
2 stalks celery with leaves,	*1 bay leaf*
chopped	*2 teaspoons salt*
2 mediums onions,	*½ teaspoon freshly ground*
chopped	*black pepper*

Wash and pick over beans. Cover generously with water and soak overnight. Next day, drain. Add the 3 quarts cold water and bring to a boil. Cover and simmer for 1½ hours, or until beans are tender.

In heavy saucepan melt butter. Add celery and onions and cook over low heat for 20 minutes, or until vegetables are soft, but not browned.

Stir in flour and cook, stirring, for 1 minute.

Add beans and liquid, ham rind and bone, bay leaf, salt, and pepper.

Cover and simmer for 3 hours, adding more water if soup becomes too thick.

Remove from heat and purée through a sieve, or blend 2 cups at a time in an electric blender until smooth and strain.

Set aside half to cool for freezing. When cool, package and freeze.

To finish half the soup (6 servings)

¼ cup Port and Madeira
1 tablespoon vinegar or to
  taste
Chopped parsley

Sliced lemon
Chopped hard-cooked egg
  white

Return purée to heat. Stir in wine and vinegar and reheat.
Serve with chopped parsley, lemon slices, and chopped egg white.

KIDNEY BEAN AND LENTIL SOUP
(Makes 5 pints thick purée)

1 pound kidney beans
½ pound lentils
3 large stalks celery,
  chopped (1 cup with
  leaves)
½ cup chopped carrot
2 large onions, chopped
½ cup parsley clusters

2 cloves garlic, chopped
1 bay leaf
½ teaspoon thyme
1 teaspoon salt
½ teaspoon freshly ground
  black pepper
2 tablespoons butter
8 cups chicken stock

Soak beans and lentils overnight in water to cover by several
inches. Next day, drain and empty beans and lentils into large
soup kettle.

Add remaining ingredients. Bring to a boil, cover, and cook
over low heat for 1½ hours, or until beans are very tender.

Cool, then purée beans and liquid, 2 cups at a time, in an
electric blender for 20 seconds. Strain through sieve.

Pour into pint containers, leaving 1 inch head space, and freeze.

To defrost and finish 1 pint purée

Chicken stock
1 to 2 tablespoons vinegar
  or lemon juice to taste

1 tablespoon butter
Salt and freshly ground
  pepper

Defrost purée over simmering water or low heat, stirring frequently. Thin to desired consistency with chicken stock and stir in lemon juice or vinegar to taste. Stir in the butter and correct seasoning with salt and pepper. One pint serves 4.

Sour cream served on the side is a wonderful accompaniment to this soup. Also try it sometime with a last-minute addition of sliced green onions.

CHAPTER 3

Main Dishes

Before giving some favorite prepared fish, poultry, and meat dishes for the freezer, I must cite a few general rules applying to all these foods that should be kept in mind.

CREAMED DISHES AND SAUCES FOR CASSEROLES

To prevent the separation of sauces, use a combination of flour and cornstarch in the proportion of about one third cornstarch and two thirds flour. One teaspoon cornstarch is equivalent to 1 table-spoon flour. Mix it with a little cold water and stir into the cooked sauce. Cool and pack in freezer containers. Freeze immediately.

To defrost and serve creamed dishes

Defrost just enough to remove from container. Heat over simmering water for 25 to 30 minutes, stirring occasionally.

STEWS

Make as usual, but omit the potatoes. All vegetables may be omitted if desired. Cool quickly. Pack in freezer containers.

To defrost and serve stews

Defrost just enough to remove from container. Heat over low heat. Add vegetables in time to simmer until tender. Add additional liquid if necessary. Or defrost for about 8 hours in refrigerator, empty into casserole, add vegetables, and bake in a preheated 350° F. oven until vegetables are tender.

CASSEROLES

Line casserole with heavy-duty aluminum foil, leaving enough extending from top of dish to fold over top when food is frozen. Freeze.

When food is solidly frozen, remove from casserole and fold aluminum foil securely over top. Label and store. Include on label the size or make of casserole in which food was frozen.

To defrost and serve casseroles

Remove from freezer about 1 hour before time to bake. Remove foil wrapping and place in its original casserole. Bake in a preheated 350° F. oven for 1 to 1¼ hours. Or remove foil wrapping, place in original casserole, and defrost for about 8 hours in refrigerator. Heat until bubbling.

CROQUETTES

Make as usual up to frying. Freeze on baking sheet, then pack in box or bag and store.

To defrost and serve croquettes

Fry, without defrosting, in deep fat or cooking oil heated to 390° F. until golden on all sides.

MAIN-COURSE PIES

Pour filling into large or individual pie plates. Cover with top crust, but do not cut slits in top crust. Freeze on baking sheet, then wrap and store.

To defrost and serve main course pies

Defrost large pies for about 8 hours in refrigerator, then bake as usual. Bake small pies, without thawing, in preheated 425° F. oven for 30 minutes.

FISH AND SEA-FOOD DISHES

Your home freezer can put greater variety and better quality food on your table, and make the daily preparation of meals easier, if it is used wisely. There is little wisdom in storing fried, poached, or sautéed fish, for it takes only a matter of minutes to prepare and cook fresh fish in these ways. You may wish, however, to freeze certain ramekins or shells or larger containers of creamed fish or sea food to heat quickly over simmering water and serve with cooked rice, in patty shells or on toast. But it is in the province of fish sauces that the home freezer really shines. A few containers of fish velouté, sauce Nantua, sauce Americaine, and other typical fish sauces in your freezer enable you to produce many an elegant fish dish from the freezer in a matter of minutes. These sauces, and ways to use them to prepare truly gourmet fish dishes, are included in the chapter on sauces. So, if you want to get the most out of your freezer, make and store the sauces rather than the fish dishes themselves. Here are a few exceptions to this quite personal recommendation.

BAKED SEA FOOD IN SHELLS
(8 servings)

*1 cup cleaned shrimp, cut
into small pieces
1 cup flaked crab meat
1 cup bay scallops
4 tablespoons butter*

*Salt and pepper
3 cups freezer* CREAM
SAUCE
*Buttered crumbs
Grated Parmesan cheese*

Combine shrimp, crab meat, and scallops and sauté in butter for 5 minutes, stirring constantly.

Sprinkle fish with a little salt and pepper and stir in cream sauce.

Divide mixture among 8 individual shells or ramekins.

Sprinkle generously with buttered crumbs and cheese. To serve immediately, bake in a preheated 400° F. oven for 15 to 20 minutes. To freeze: freeze on baking sheet, then wrap each shell individually or pack in bag or box and store.

To defrost and serve

Unwrap shells, place on baking sheet, and bake in a preheated 400° F. oven for 25 to 30 minutes.

RAMEKINS OF SCALLOPS
IN VERMOUTH SAUCE
(8 servings)

*2 pounds scallops
1 tablespoon chopped
shallots or green onions
¼ teaspoon salt
⅛ teaspoon white pepper*

*¾ cup dry vermouth
1½ cups heavy cream
3 tablespoons flour
2 teaspoons cornstarch
4 tablespoons soft butter*

Wash scallops. If large, cut into quarters.

Put scallops into saucepan with shallots or green onions, salt, pepper, and vermouth.

Bring liquid to a boil, cover saucepan, and simmer over low heat for just 2 minutes. Do not overcook scallops, or they will be tough. Remove scallops with slotted spoon and divide into 8 au gratin dishes or scallop shells.

Cook liquid remaining in saucepan over high heat until reduced to ½ cup.

Add cream and continue to boil rapidly until cream is reduced and sauce is the consistency of a thin cream sauce. Combine flour, cornstarch, and butter. Stir into hot cream, bit by bit, and cook, stirring, until sauce is smooth and thickened. Cook over low heat for 5 minutes, stirring frequently. Divide sauce over scallops in dishes or shells. To serve immediately: bake in a preheated 450° F. oven for 6 to 8 minutes, or until sauce is lightly browned and bubbling. Sprinkle with chopped parsley. To freeze: freeze on baking sheet, then wrap each individually and store.

To defrost and serve

Unwrap shells, place on baking sheet. Bake in a preheated 400° F. oven for 25 to 30 minutes. Sprinkle with chopped parsley before serving.

SHRIMP IN SHERRY SAUCE
(6 servings)

½ cup butter
1 medium onion, minced
1 stalk celery, minced
1 carrot, finely chopped
¼ teaspoon thyme
2 pounds shrimp, shelled
   and deveined
¼ cup cognac

1½ cups heavy cream
⅓ cup sherry
1 cup freezer CREAM
   SAUCE
½ teaspoon salt
1 teaspoon lemon juice
¼ cup butter

In large skillet heat butter. Add vegetables and thyme and cook over moderate heat for about 10 minutes, or until vegetables are tender and lightly browned.

Add shrimp and cook for 10 minutes, turning shrimp frequently to cook on all sides.

Add cognac, ignite, and let flame burn out. Remove shrimp.

To vegetables in skillet add cream, sherry, and cream sauce. Simmer for 10 minutes, or until sauce is consistency of heavy cream. Add salt and lemon juice. Swirl in butter. To serve immediately, strain sauce into a saucepan, add shrimp, and heat to serving temperature.

To freeze: put shrimp into freezer container. Strain sauce over and cool quickly. Seal, label, and freeze.

To defrost and serve

Reheat over simmering water and serve with cooked rice.

SCALLOPS POULETTE
(6 servings)

6 tablespoons butter	½ pound mushrooms, finely chopped
2 teaspoons minced onion or shallots	4 tablespoons flour
2 pounds scallops (slice if large)	1 tablespoon cornstarch
1 cup dry white wine (Chablis)	2 tablespoons water
1 bay leaf	1 teaspoon salt
	¼ teaspoon white pepper

In saucepan melt 2 tablespoons of the butter and in it sauté onion or shallots for 3 minutes, or until transparent, but not browned. Add scallops, white wine, and bay leaf. Bring to a boil, cover, and simmer for 2 minutes only. Set aside.

In skillet melt remaining butter and in it cook mushrooms over low heat for about 6 minutes, or until tender. Stir in flour and cook, stirring, until sauce is smooth and thick. Stir in cornstarch mixed with water.

Stir in salt and pepper and cook over low heat for 10 minutes, stirring occasionally.

Stir in scallops.

Finish according to instructions and serve, or pour into freezer container and cool quickly. Seal, label, and freeze.

To finish

1 cup cream	*2 tablespoons minced*
3 egg yolks	*parsley*
2 teaspoons lemon juice	

Stir in cream lightly beaten with egg yolks. Add lemon juice and parsley and cook over low heat for 3 minutes, stirring constantly.

To defrost and finish

Reheat over simmering water for 30 minutes. Finish as above.

CODFISH CAKES
(Makes 16 cakes)

2 pounds salt cod	*Freshly ground black*
Water	*pepper to taste*
4 cups mashed potatoes	*1 cup bread crumbs*
4 eggs, lightly beaten	

Soak salt cod overnight in water to cover.

Next day, drain, cut into small pieces, and cover with fresh water. Bring to a boil. Taste for saltiness; if salty, drain and repeat until water tastes almost fresh.

Drain and mix fish with potatoes, eggs, and pepper to taste.

Form into 16 cakes and roll in crumbs.

Set aside as many cakes as needed for immediate service.

Arrange the rest on baking sheet and freeze. When frozen, wrap, label, and store.

To finish

Fat for deep frying

Fry the fresh cakes or the frozen, undefrosted, in deep fat heated to 380° F.

SALMON ARCHIDUC
(8 servings)

½ cup (1 stick) butter
½ cup minced onion
½ cup flour
3 cups hot milk
1 teaspoon salt

¼ teaspoon pepper
Dash of cayenne
2 (1-pound) cans salmon, flaked

In saucepan melt butter and in it cook onion over low heat until transparent.

Stir in flour and cook, stirring, for 2 minutes.

Add milk and stir vigorously over moderate heat until mixture is thick and smooth.

Stir in salt, pepper, and cayenne and cook over low heat for 10 minutes.

Add flaked salmon. Set aside half to cool for freezer. When cool, package and freeze.

To finish half the dish (4 servings)

½ cup heavy cream
2 tablespoons sherry
2 tablespoons cognac

1 tablespoon minced parsley

Return remaining salmon to heat and stir in cream, sherry, cognac, and parsley. Heat to serving temperature. Serve on toast or with rice.

To defrost and finish

Defrost over simmering water. Finish as above.

DEVILED CRAB
(12 servings)

4 tablespoons butter
1 tablespoon minced
onion
4 tablespoons flour
1 cup milk
1 cup cream
1 teaspoon dry mustard
Dash of cayenne

1 teaspoon Worcestershire
sauce
4 egg yolks
¼ cup sherry
Salt and freshly ground
pepper to taste
6 cups flaked crab meat
Buttered crumbs

In saucepan melt butter and in it cook onion for 5 minutes, or until tender. Stir in flour. Heat milk and cream to simmering and add all at once to butter-flour mixture. Stir vigorously over moderate heat until sauce is smooth and thick. Cook over low heat for 10 minutes, stirring occasionally. Stir in mustard, cayenne, and Worcestershire.

Beat eggs with a little of the hot sauce and stir into sauce. Cook for 3 minutes, stirring rapidly. Do not let sauce boil.

Remove from heat and stir in sherry, salt and pepper, and the crab meat.

Divide mixture into 12 individual crab shells or heatproof ramekins.

Sprinkle with buttered crumbs. Set aside as many as needed for immediate service. Freeze rest on baking sheet. When frozen, wrap, label, and store.

To finish

Bake in a preheated 400° F. oven for 10 minutes. If frozen, bake directly from freezer for 25 minutes.

SHRIMP AU GRATIN
(2 casseroles, each 4 servings)

2 cups water
1 small onion, sliced
1 clove garlic, sliced
1 stalk celery with leaves,
   chopped
1 bay leaf
¼ teaspoon peppercorns
4 sprigs parsley
3 pounds shrimp
½ cup butter

⅓ cup flour
2 cups light cream
1 tablespoon cornstarch
¼ cup sherry
1 cup shredded Swiss
   cheese
Salt and pepper to taste
½ cup grated Parmesan
   cheese

In saucepan bring water to a boil with onion, garlic, celery, bay leaf, peppercorns, and parsley. Cover and boil for 5 minutes. Add shrimp and simmer for 5 minutes. Drain, reserving broth. Shell and devein shrimp. Cut shrimp into bite-size pieces if large.

In saucepan melt butter and stir in flour.

Heat shrimp broth and cream to simmering point. Add to butter-flour mixture and cook over moderate heat, stirring rapidly, until sauce is smooth and thick. Stir in cornstarch mixed with sherry and cook, stirring, for 3 minutes longer. Add cheese and stir until cheese is melted. Season with salt and pepper and stir in shrimp.

Turn mixture into 2 shallow 6-cup baking dishes, and sprinkle with Parmesan cheese.

Freeze one dish for future use.

To finish

Bake in preheated 375° F. oven for 10 minutes, or until top is browned and sauce is bubbling. If frozen, bake directly from freezer in preheated 325° F. oven for 30 minutes.

FILLETS OF SOLE DUGLERE
(8 servings)

2 medium onions, finely
  chopped
4 large ripe tomatoes,
  peeled and diced
2 tablespoons chopped
  parsley
1 tablespoon butter
8 fillets of sole

1 teaspoon salt
¼ teaspoon white pepper
2 cups dry white wine
  (Chablis)
2 tablespoons flour
1 teaspoon cornstarch
2 tablespoons butter

Put onions, tomatoes, and parsley into a skillet rubbed with the
1 tablespoon butter.

Roll the fillets like tiny jelly rolls, secure with wooden pick, and
place on top of the vegetables. Sprinkle with salt and pepper. Add
white wine. Bring liquid to a simmer, cover skillet, and poach fillets
for 7 to 8 minutes. Remove fillets and keep 4 warm on serving dish
for immediate servings. Place remaining 4 fillets in freezer container
to cool.

Cook liquid and vegetables remaining in skillet over high heat
until liquid is reduced by half and the tomatoes are reduced to a
purée. Stir in flour and cornstarch mixed with the 2 tablespoons
butter and cook, stirring, until sauce is slightly thickened.

Pour half the sauce over fillets in freezer container. When cool,
seal, label, and freeze.

To serve half the dish (4 servings)

Pour remaining sauce over fillets on serving dish and serve very
hot.

To defrost and serve

Empty fillets and sauce into baking dish. Heat in a 350° F.
oven for 25 to 30 minutes, or until sauce is bubbling.

FILLETS OF SOLE NANTAISE
(8 servings)

2 *quarts mussels*
4 *shallots or green
  onions, minced*
1 *cup dry white wine
  (Chablis)*
2 *tablespoons butter*
8 *fillets of sole*

2 *pounds shrimp, shelled
  and deveined*
2 *cups heavy cream*
1 *tablespoon flour*
1 *teaspoon cornstarch*
3 *tablespoons butter*

Scrub mussels thoroughly. Put them in a heavy kettle with shallots
or green onions, white wine, and the 2 tablespoons butter. Cover
and cook over high heat until shells open.

Form fillets into tiny jelly rolls and secure with wooden picks.
Place in skillet and pour liquid from mussels over them. Bring
liquid to a boil, cover skillet, and poach the fish for 7 to 8 minutes.

Poach the shrimp in water to cover for 5 minutes. Drain. Place
half the fillets on a serving dish and keep warm. Place remaining
fillets in freezer container to cool.

To liquid remaining in skillet add cream and cook over high heat
until sauce is reduced to the consistency of a light sauce. Stir in flour
and cornstarch mixed with the 3 tablespoons butter. Cook, stirring,
for 3 minutes, but do not let the sauce boil.

To serve half the dish (4 servings)

Debeard mussels and arrange half of them around fillets on serving dish. Pour half the sauce over the fillets and garnish with half
the shrimp. Serve hot.

Remove remaining mussels from shells and add to fillets in freezer
container with remaining shrimp. Cover with remaining sauce. Cool,
label, and freeze.

To defrost and serve

Empty fish and sauce into a baking dish. Heat in a 350° F. oven for 30 minutes, or until sauce is very hot.

LOBSTER AMERICAINE
(8 servings)

*4 live lobsters, about 2
    pounds each
1 teaspoon salt
¼ teaspoon pepper
⅓ cup olive oil
4 tablespoons butter
¼ cup cognac
4 shallots, chopped
1 clove garlic, minced
1⅓ cups dry white wine
1 cup fish stock*

*6 whole canned tomatoes,
    chopped
¼ cup tomato purée
2 tablespoons chopped
    parsley
Pinch of cayenne
2 teaspoons chopped fresh
    tarragon, or ½ teaspoon
    dried tarragon
Dash of lemon juice*

Split lobsters down back. Remove and crush claws. Cut tail into sections. Reserve coral and tomalley and sprinkle lobster pieces with salt and pepper.

In large skillet heat oil and butter and in it sauté lobster pieces until shell turns red. Pour off excess butter and oil, sprinkle with cognac, and flame.

Add shallots, garlic, wine, fish stock, tomatoes, tomato purée, parsley, cayenne, and tarragon. Cover and simmer for 20 minutes. Remove lobster from sauce. Remove meat from tail sections and claws. Keep half hot for immediate service. Put rest into freezer container to cool.

Cook sauce over high heat until reduced by one third. Stir in tomalley and coral and correct seasoning with salt, pepper, and a dash of lemon juice. Strain half the sauce over lobster in freezer container. When cool, seal, label, and freeze. Strain remaining sauce over into saucepan.

To finish half the dish (4 servings)

4 tablespoons sweet butter
1 tablespoon minced parsley

Stir the sweet butter, bit by bit, into the hot sauce. Pour over lobster for immediate servings. Sprinkle with minced parsley.

To defrost and finish

Empty lobster and sauce into saucepan and heat over simmering water for 30 minutes. Stir in sweet butter as above. Sprinkle with chopped parsley.

LOBSTER NEWBURG
(8 servings)

*4 boiled lobsters, each
about 1½ pounds*
4 tablespoons sweet butter
½ teaspoon salt
¼ teaspoon pepper

Dash of cayenne
*1 cup sherry, Madeira, or
Marsala*
*2 cups fish velouté or
CREAM SAUCE*

Split lobsters and crack claws. Discard intestinal vein and small sac behind head. Reserve tomalley and coral and remove meat from shells and claws.

In skillet melt the butter. Add lobster meat and toss until heated through. Sprinkle with salt, pepper, and cayenne. Add sherry, Madeira, or Marsala and simmer until liquid is reduced by one third. Add fish velouté or cream sauce and simmer for 2 minutes. Add reserved coral and tomalley.

Pour half into freezer container to cool. When cool, seal, label, and freeze.

To finish half the dish (4 servings)

2 egg yolks
½ cup heavy cream

To remaining mixture stir in egg yolks mixed with cream and a little of the hot sauce. Heat to serving temperature. Serve in patty shells, on toast points, or with cooked rice.

To defrost and finish

Empty lobster and sauce into saucepan and cook over simmering water for 30 minutes. Finish and serve as above.

LOBSTER THERMIDOR
(8 servings)

*4 cooked lobsters, each
about 1½ pounds
1 pound mushrooms, sliced
or diced
1 tablespoon water
1 tablespoon lemon juice
1 tablespoon butter
4 tablespoons butter
4 shallots or green
onions, chopped*

*3 tablespoons flour
2 teaspoons dry mustard
2 cups hot milk
1 teaspoon chopped fresh
tarragon, or ¼ teaspoon
dried tarragon
Salt, pepper, and cayenne
to taste
1 cup hot cream*

Split lobsters and crack claws. Remove meat from claws and tail section and discard intestinal vein and small sac behind head.

Wash body shells and set aside. Reserve tomalley and coral.

Put mushrooms in saucepan with water, lemon juice, and the 1 tablespoon butter. Cover and cook over moderate heat for 6 minutes. Drain, reserving liquid.

Combine lobster meat and mushrooms.

In saucepan melt the 4 tablespoons butter and in it sauté shallots or green onions until tender.

Stir in flour mixed with mustard.

Stir in hot milk and the mushroom liquid. Add tarragon and cook over moderate heat, stirring briskly, until sauce is smooth and thickened. Add salt, pepper, and cayenne to taste. Stir in tomalley and coral.

Stir in hot cream and cook over low heat until sauce is reduced a little.

Strain sauce and mix with lobster and mushrooms.

Fill lobster shells with the mixture. Freeze half. Wrap, seal, label, and store in freezer.

To finish half the lobsters (4 servings)

Sprinkle each portion with 1 tablespoon grated Swiss cheese and bake in a 400° F. oven for 10 minutes.

To defrost and finish

Unwrap lobster halves and sprinkle with Swiss cheese as above. Bake in a 325° F. oven for 35 minutes, or until hot and browned.

POULTRY DISHES

Prepared chicken, duck, and turkey dishes, ready to reheat and serve with a minimum of last-minute additions, make the best use of the home freezer. Such dishes are many, so don't be afraid to experiment with your own family favorites, sauced poultry dishes, casseroles, and stews. There is no reason why most of these cannot be frozen.

Leftover roast poultry may also be frozen, but with the exception of small Rock Cornish game hens, any stuffing should be removed and frozen separately. It makes much more sense to take a few minutes to cut the meat off the bones, dice some to add to a cream sauce for chicken or turkey à la king, and slice the rest for packaged TV dinners, rather than take up freezer space with the carcass.

To defrost roast poultry for slicing cold, defrost, without unwrapping, at room temperature for 3 to 8 hours, depending on the size of the bird.

The storage time for stews, casseroles, and sauced poultry dishes is as long as 3 months, but sliced cooked poultry packaged plain or covered with gravy, fried chicken, chicken loaves and croquettes should be used within 4 weeks.

FRIED CHICKEN

Brown the pieces as usual and cook until almost tender. Cool. Freeze on baking sheets, then wrap or pack in freezer bag and store. To serve hot, place unthawed chicken pieces in a shallow baking pan and bake, uncovered, at 350° F. for 30 minutes.

STUFFED ROAST POULTRY

Stuff, truss, and roast the bird. As soon as it is cooked, discard trussings, carefully remove all the stuffing, and put it in a casserole or baking dish. This must be done in order to prevent the possible spoilage of the dressing deep in the center of the bird, where it would take hours to cool were it not removed. Cool the bird and stuffing partially, then chill in refrigerator for 2 to 3 hours.

Pour off half the drippings from the roasting pan into a small moistureproof, liquid-tight container to freeze as soon as cool, for later use in basting the bird when it is reheated. Use the rest of the drippings in the pan to make pan gravy. Cool gravy, package, label, and freeze.

Wrap the bird tightly in moisture-vaporproof paper and freeze. Wrap the dressing, baking dish and all, and freeze.

To reheat bird and stuffing

Allow 5 hours per pound defrosting time in the refrigerator to defrost the frozen bird completely. Return the defrosted cooked bird to the roasting pan, add drippings, and bake in a 325° F. oven for 1 hour, basting frequently with drippings in pan.

The stuffing needs no preliminary defrosting. Remove it from freezer, cover baking dish, and put in oven with the bird to defrost and heat.

Heat the gravy over simmering water, stirring occasionally.

CHICKEN A LA KING
(12 servings)

½ pound sliced mushrooms
6 tablespoons butter or
chicken fat
½ cup flour
3 cups hot chicken stock
2 cups light cream

1 tablespoon cornstarch
4 cups diced cooked
chicken
½ cup chopped pimiento
Salt and white pepper to
taste

Sauté mushrooms in butter or chicken fat for 3 minutes, or until tender.

Stir in flour. Add chicken stock and cook over moderate heat, stirring briskly, until sauce is smooth and thickened. Stir in 1½ cups of the cream and heat. Stir in cornstarch mixed with remaining cream, and cook, stirring, for 3 minutes longer. Add chicken, pimiento, and salt and pepper to taste.

Set aside half to cool. When cool, package, label, and freeze.

To finish half the dish (6 servings)

¼ cup sherry or Madeira

Stir in sherry or Madeira. Serve in patty shells, on toast, hot biscuits, squares of corn bread, or English muffins, or with cooked noodles or rice.

To defrost and finish

Turn from container into saucepan and cook over simmering water for about 1 hour, stirring occasionally. Finish and serve as above.

CHICKEN DIVAN
(2 casseroles, each 6 servings)

½ cup butter
½ cup flour
2 cups hot chicken broth
3 cups hot milk
1 cup heavy cream
1 tablespoon cornstarch
2 cups grated Cheddar
cheese

Salt and pepper to taste
2 bunches fresh broccoli,
cooked
8 cooked chicken breasts,
sliced, or ½ cooked
turkey breast, sliced

In large saucepan melt butter. Stir in flour.

Add chicken broth and milk and cook over moderate heat, stirring briskly, until sauce is smooth and thickened. Stir in ¾ cup of the cream and heat. Stir in cornstarch mixed with remaining ¼ cup cream. Cook, stirring, for 3 minutes. Add cheese and stir until cheese is melted. Stir in salt and pepper to taste.

Arrange broccoli heads in bottom of 2 shallow baking dishes. Cover broccoli with a layer of sliced chicken or turkey. Pour half the sauce over the sliced meat in each baking dish. Cool 1 dish, then wrap, label, and freeze.

To finish 1 casserole (6 servings)

¼ cup bread crumbs
¼ cup grated cheese
Paprika

Sprinkle with bread crumbs mixed with cheese. Sprinkle lightly with paprika. Bake in a 325° F. oven for 25 to 30 minutes.

To defrost and finish

Remove baking dish from freezer 1 hour before baking. Bake in a 300° F. oven for 20 minutes. Increase oven temperature to 350° F.

Sprinkle with bread crumbs and cheese. Dust lightly with paprika and bake for 25 to 30 minutes longer, or until sauce is bubbling.

It takes very little more time to make two casseroles as one. Order twice the amount of ingredients; make one casserole for dinner tonight; freeze the other for that "day off" next week.

POULET MARENGO
(6 servings)

½ cup flour	¼ cup butter
1 teaspoon salt	2 tablespoons cooking oil
½ teaspoon pepper	½ cup dry white wine
1 teaspoon dried tarragon	1 cup chicken stock
1 tender roasting chicken,	½ tablespoon cornstarch
cut into serving portions	2 tablespoons water

In paper bag combine flour, salt, pepper, and tarragon. Drop chicken parts into bag and shake gently until all pieces are coated.

In large skillet heat butter and oil and in it sauté pieces of chicken until golden brown on all sides. As pieces are browned, transfer to a 3-quart casserole.

Stir flour mixture remaining in bag into butter and oil remaining in skillet. Gradually stir in white wine and chicken stock and cook, stirring, until sauce is smooth and thickened. Stir in cornstarch mixed with water and cook, stirring, for 2 minutes longer.

Pour sauce over chicken. Finish casserole as follows or cool quickly and freeze.

To finish casserole

1 (1-pound) can tomatoes	8 mushrooms, sliced
2 cloves garlic, minced	¼ cup chopped parsley

Add tomatoes, garlic, mushrooms, and parsley. Cover and bake in a preheated 350° F. oven for 50 minutes, stirring once after half the cooking time is finished.

To defrost and finish

Remove casserole from freezer 1 hour before cooking. Cook in preheated 325° F. oven for 20 minutes. Add tomatoes, garlic, mushrooms, and parsley, as above. Increase heat to 350° F. Cover casserole and cook for 50 minutes, stirring once after half the cooking time is finished.

CHICKEN CACCIATORE
(6 servings)

½ cup flour	1 cup canned tomatoes
1 teaspoon salt	2 onions, sliced
½ teaspoon pepper	1 green pepper, sliced
1 tender roasting chicken,	1 clove garlic, minced
cut into serving portions	1 bay leaf, crumbled
¼ cup butter	½ cup chicken stock or
¼ cup cooking oil	white wine

Combine flour, salt, and pepper. Roll chicken parts in the seasoned flour until well coated on all sides.

In large skillet heat butter and oil and in it sauté chicken pieces until golden brown on all sides. Add tomatoes, onions, green pepper, garlic, bay leaf, and chicken stock or white wine. Cover and simmer for 30 minutes. Finish as follows or cool quickly and freeze in casserole dish.

To finish casserole

1 teaspoon lemon juice
¼ cup chopped parsley

Stir in lemon juice, sprinkle with parsley, and serve with cooked rice.

To defrost and finish

Remove casserole from freezer 1 hour before cooking. Cook in a preheated 325° F. oven for 20 minutes. Increase oven temperature to 350° F. Stir contents of casserole, cover, and cook for 40 minutes longer. Finish and serve as above.

CHICKEN PIES
(8 individual pies, 5⅜ × 1⅝ inches deep)

*1 (5-pound) ready-to-cook
chicken*
*3 stalks celery, coarsely
cut*
*2 medium onions, coarsely
cut*
3 sprays parsley
½ teaspoon peppercorns
1 bay leaf
2 teaspoons salt
2 quarts water
*1 pound carrots, peeled
and diced*
*2 pounds fresh peas,
shelled*

*1 pound tiny white onions,
peeled*
*½ pound medium
mushrooms, sliced*
2 tablespoons butter
Juice of ½ lemon
1 cup cream
¼ teaspoon nutmeg
½ teaspoon celery salt
½ cup all-purpose flour
1 tablespoon cornstarch
Salt and pepper to taste
*Flaky pastry for a 2-crust
pie*

In a 6-quart kettle put chicken, celery, onions, parsley, peppercorns, bay leaf, and salt. Add the 2 quarts water and bring to a boil. Cover and simmer for 2 hours, or until chicken is very tender. Let chicken cool in broth, then cut off all the meat and cut meat into bite-size pieces. Strain broth.

Cook carrots, peas, and onions in covered saucepan with 1 inch water for 15 minutes. Drain.

Sauté mushrooms in butter sprinkled with lemon juice, for 5 minutes, or until just tender.

Combine chicken and vegetables and divide evenly into 8 individual foil pans.

In saucepan combine 4 cups broth with cream, nutmeg, and celery salt. Bring to a boil.

Combine flour and cornstarch with 1 cup broth and stir into boiling broth. Cook over moderate heat for 3 minutes, stirring constantly. Correct seasoning with salt and pepper. Pour sauce over chicken and vegetables and let cool.

Roll out half the pastry at a time on lightly floured board and cut into 6-inch rounds. Transfer rounds over filling in each pan and press pastry edge to rim of pan to seal. Wrap, label, and freeze.

To defrost and finish

Unwrap pies and make gash in center of pastry for steam to escape. Bake in preheated 450° F. oven for 40 minutes, or until crust is golden brown and filling is bubbling.

CHICKEN WITH CREAM
OF CURRY SAUCE
(8 servings)

2 (3½-pound) chickens,
    cut into serving portions
2 carrots, chopped
1 medium onion, chopped
1 clove garlic, chopped
6 sprays parsley
1 stalk celery with leaves,
    chopped
1 bay leaf
½ teaspoon thyme
½ teaspoon peppercorns
1 tablespoon salt
2 cups dry white wine

6 cups water
6 tablespoons butter
1 large apple, peeled and
    minced
⅔ cup minced onion
2 tablespoons curry
    powder
4 tablespoons flour
1 tablespoon cornstarch
1 cup cream
Salt and pepper to taste
1 teaspoon lemon juice

Into a 6-quart casserole put chickens, carrots, chopped onion, garlic, parsley, celery, bay leaf, thyme, peppercorns, the tablespoon salt, wine, and water. Bring to a boil, cover, and cook over low heat for 50 minutes. Remove from heat, but keep chicken hot in the stock.

In saucepan melt butter. Add apple and minced onion and cook over moderate heat for 3 minutes, stirring occasionally. Stir in curry powder and cook, stirring, for 2 minutes longer.

Stir in flour.

Gradually stir in 4 cups of the chicken stock and cook, stirring, until sauce is smooth and slightly thickened. Cook over low heat for 25 minutes, stirring occasionally. Stir in cornstarch mixed with cream and cook, stirring, for 5 minutes longer. Correct seasoning with salt and pepper, and add lemon juice.

Put half the chicken and sauce in freezer container. Cool, then seal, label, and freeze.

Reheat remaining chicken in remaining broth.

Arrange chicken on serving platter and pour sauce over it. Serve with cooked rice or RICE PILAU.

To defrost and serve

Reheat over simmering water and serve as above.

NOTE: Strain remaining stock. Freeze in ice-cube trays. When frozen, remove cubes and store in freezer bags.

PAELLA VALENCIANA
(12 servings)

½ cup olive oil

2 frying chickens, cut into serving portions

1 pound diced lean pork

2 cloves garlic, minced

2 medium onions, finely chopped

4 teaspoons salt

½ teaspoon freshly ground black pepper

4 ripe tomatoes, peeled and chopped, or 2 (1-pound) cans whole tomatoes

4 cups rice

2 quarts water

2 sweet red peppers, chopped

2 (10-ounce) packages frozen peas

2 (10-ounce) packages frozen artichoke hearts

1 teaspoon saffron

2 pounds fresh lump crab meat, or 4 (7½-ounce) cans

In deep, heavy kettle heat olive oil and in it brown pieces of chicken and diced pork.

Add garlic and onions, mix well, and cook for 10 minutes, or until onions are transparent, stirring frequently.

Add salt, pepper, and tomatoes, cover, and cook over low heat for 10 minutes.

Add rice and water. Stir well. Add red peppers, peas, and artichokes, cover, and cook over low heat for 20 minutes.

Add saffron and turn rice from top to bottom of kettle to mix ingredients well.

Add crab meat, cover, and cook for 10 minutes longer.

Set aside half to cool for freezer. When cool, package, label, and freeze.

To finish half the paella (6 servings)

12 cherrystone clams	*12 asparagus tips*
12 mussels	*1 pimiento, cut into strips*

While paella is cooking, scrub clams and mussels well. Put into a heavy pot with ½ cup water. Cover and bring to a boil over high heat. Cook only until shells open.

Cook asparagus until tender in boiling, salted water. If canned asparagus is used, heat in its own juice.

Ladle paella into large serving dish and garnish with mussels and clams, still in their shells, asparagus, and strips of pimiento.

To defrost and finish

Remove from freezer and let defrost in refrigerator for 8 hours. Empty into casserole or paella pan. Cook in preheated 350° F. oven for 30 minutes, or until thoroughly hot, adding a little chicken broth if needed. Finish as above.

CHICKEN COPENHAGEN
(6 servings)

1 tender poaching chicken,
   cut into serving portions
2 teaspoons salt
¼ teaspoon peppercorns
1 small carrot, quartered
1 onion, coarsely chopped

1 bay leaf
5 sprays parsley
4 tablespoons butter
6 tablespoons flour
3 cups hot chicken broth

Poach chicken in water to cover with salt, peppercorns, carrot, onion, bay leaf, and parsley for 1¼ hours, or until tender.

In saucepan melt butter. Stir in flour. Add chicken broth and whisk vigorously over moderate heat until sauce is smooth and thickened. Cover and cook over low heat for 10 to 20 minutes, stirring occasionally. Cool both chicken parts and sauce for the freezer. When cool, package together, label, and freeze. Or finish and serve as follows:

To finish and serve

1 tablespoon drained horse-radish, or to taste
¾ cup freezer HOLLANDAISE

Add horse-radish to the hot sauce. Gradually stir in the hollandaise.

Arrange chicken on serving dish and pour sauce over it. Serve with cooked rice or RICE PILAU.

To defrost and finish

Remove chicken from freezer and empty into saucepan. Cook over simmering water for 1 hour, or until defrosted and chicken is hot. Arrange chicken on warm serving dish and finish sauce as above. Pour sauce over chicken and serve with rice.

POULET ROSETTE
(8 servings)

2 frying chickens, cut into parts
½ cup flour
2 teaspoons salt
¼ teaspoon pepper
½ cup (1 stick) butter
2 tablespoons minced onion or shallots
¼ cup bourbon or apple brandy
1 cup white wine
2 (10-ounce) packages frozen artichoke hearts
2 cups chicken stock
1 cup heavy cream
⅛ teaspoon nutmeg

Roll chicken parts in flour (reserve any remaining flour), and sprinkle with salt and pepper.

Heat butter in saucepan or stainless steel or aluminum fry pan (do not use iron) and in it sauté chicken parts until browned on all sides. Add onion or shallots and sauté for 2 minutes longer. Add bourbon or apple brandy, ignite the liquor, and let the flame burn out.

Add white wine and bring to a boil. Cover and simmer for 30 minutes. Add artichokes and chicken stock, cover, and simmer for 30 minutes longer.

Combine cream with reserved flour and gradually stir into hot liquid in pan. Stir in nutmeg and cook over low heat for 10 minutes. Set half the chicken, artichokes, and sauce aside to cool for the freezer. When cool, package, label, and freeze.

Arrange remaining chicken in serving dish and surround with artichokes.

Bring sauce to a boil and pour over chicken and artichokes. Serve with cooked, buttered noodles.

To defrost and serve

Empty frozen chicken into saucepan and heat over simmering water for 1 hour, stirring occasionally. Serve as above.

CURRY OF DUCKLING
(8 servings)

½ cup butter
2 (5-pound) ducklings,
  quartered
1 quart water
2 cloves garlic, minced
2 medium onions, chopped
1 (3-inch) piece fresh
  ginger root, or 6 slices
  preserved, chopped
  ginger root

2 tablespoons curry
  powder
½ cup flour
4 cups milk
1 tablespoon cornstarch
2 teaspoons salt
2 cups heavy cream
1 cup diced pineapple

In large skillet melt half the butter and in it brown pieces of duck lightly on all sides. Add water and bring to a boil. Cover and simmer for 1¼ hours, or until duckling is tender.

In large saucepan melt remaining butter. Add garlic, onions, and ginger and cook over low heat for 20 minutes, or until onions are tender and golden.

Stir in curry powder and cook, stirring, for 1 minute.

Stir in flour and cook, stirring, until all flour is absorbed by the butter.

Gradually stir in 3½ cups milk and cook, stirring, until sauce is thickened. Combine remaining milk and cornstarch and stir into sauce. Cook, stirring, for 3 minutes.

Stir in cream.

Drain duckling, remove meat from bones, and cut into bite-size pieces. Add duck and pineapple to curry sauce and cook over low heat for 10 minutes, without letting sauce boil.

Set aside half to cool. When cool, package, label, and freeze.

To finish half the curry (4 servings)

½ cantaloupe or papaya, sliced

Stir in cantaloupe or papaya and cook for 2 minutes longer. Serve with cooked rice, toasted coconut, and chutney.

To defrost and finish

Turn into saucepan and heat over simmering water, stirring occasionally.

Two minutes before serving, finish and serve as above.

CHICKEN BRAISED WITH MUSHROOMS
(8 servings)

½ cup (1 stick) butter
2 (2½-pound) frying
  chickens, quartered
2 teaspoons salt
½ teaspoon pepper
2 cups white wine
1 pound fresh button
  mushrooms

4 tablespoons soft butter
2 tablespoons flour
2 tablespoons cornstarch
2 cups heavy cream
¼ cup cognac

In large skillet melt butter and in it sauté chicken pieces until brown on both sides.

Sprinkle with salt and pepper. Add white wine and mushrooms. Cover and simmer for 45 minutes.

Remove chicken and mushrooms. Arrange half in freezer casserole to cool. To sauce remaining in pan stir in soft butter mixed to a paste with flour and cornstarch. Stir in cream and cognac. Cook, stirring, until sauce is smooth and thickened.

Pour half the sauce over chicken and mushrooms in freezer casserole. When cool, cover, label, and freeze.

Return remaining chicken and mushrooms to sauce and heat through. Serve with cooked rice or risotto.

To defrost and serve

Remove from freezer 1 hour before cooking. Bake in a preheated 350° F. oven for 1 hour, stirring occasionally. Serve as above.

CHICKEN IN RED WINE I
(8 servings)

8 strips bacon, diced
4 medium onions, chopped
2 large carrots, chopped
2 (3-pound) chickens,
   quartered
¼ cup cognac
½ cup flour
1 bottle (3 cups) red
   Burgundy wine

1 teaspoon salt
3 cups chicken stock
2 cloves garlic
6 sprays parsley
½ teaspoon thyme
½ teaspoon peppercorns
1 bay leaf
1 tablespoon cornstarch
2 tablespoons water

In heavy kettle cook bacon, onions, and carrots over moderate heat until bacon is crisp and vegetables are lightly browned.

Add chicken and brown well on both sides in bacon drippings in pan.

Add cognac, ignite, and let the flame die out.

Sprinkle with flour and stir to mix flour into vegetables and bacon drippings.

Add Burgundy, salt, and chicken stock. Add garlic, parsley, thyme, peppercorns, and bay leaf. Bring to a boil, cover, and cook over low heat for 1 hour. Stir in cornstarch mixed with water and cook, stirring, for 2 minutes longer.

Set half the chicken and sauce aside to cool. When cool, freeze in casserole.

Serve remaining half with boiled onions and sautéed mushrooms.

To defrost and serve

Remove casserole from freezer 1 hour before cooking. Cook in a preheated 350° F. oven for 1¼ hours, stirring occasionally. Serve as above.

CHICKEN IN RED WINE II
(8 servings)

½ cup butter
4 slices bacon, diced
4 broiler chickens, halved
24 small silverskin onions, peeled
2 cloves garlic, minced
8 medium mushrooms, sliced
¼ cup cognac

½ teaspoon thyme
1 bay leaf
2 teaspoons salt
½ teaspoon black pepper
3 cups red wine (Claret)
2 cups beef broth
1 tablespoon flour
1 tablespoon cornstarch
2 tablespoons butter

In heavy casserole heat the ½ cup butter and bacon. In it brown chickens on both sides.

Add onions, garlic, and mushrooms.

Add cognac, ignite, and let the flame burn out.

Add thyme, bay leaf, salt, pepper, wine, and 1 cup of the beef broth.

Bring to a boil, cover, and simmer for 15 minutes.

Stir in flour and cornstarch mixed to a paste with the 2 tablespoons butter. Add remaining cup beef broth, cover, and simmer for 30 minutes.

Set half the chicken and half the sauce aside to cool for freezer. When cool, freeze in casserole.

To finish half the dish (4 servings)

2 tablespoons chopped parsley
1 teaspoon minced fresh tarragon, or ¼ teaspoon dried tarragon

Two minutes before serving, stir in parsley and tarragon.

To defrost and finish

Remove casserole from freezer 1 hour before cooking. Cook in a preheated 350° F. oven for 1¼ hours, stirring occasionally. Finish as above.

CHICKEN BREASTS WITH ALMONDS
(8 servings)

8 breasts of chicken, boned	1 teaspoon tomato paste
6 tablespoons butter	2 tablespoons flour
2 tablespoons brandy	2 cups chicken stock
1 tablespoon minced shallots or green onions	½ tablespoon cornstarch
½ cup blanched almonds	¼ cup white wine
	Salt and pepper to taste
	¼ teaspoon dried tarragon

In skillet brown chicken breasts in half the butter on both sides. When brown, sprinkle with brandy. Ignite brandy and let flame die out. Transfer chicken to a heated platter.

To skillet add remaining butter and shallots. Cook for 30 seconds. Add half the almonds and cook until almonds begin to brown. Stir in tomato paste and flour.

Gradually add chicken stock and cook, stirring, until sauce is thickened.

Stir in cornstarch mixed with wine. Correct seasoning with salt and pepper.

Return chicken to skillet and add tarragon.

Cover and cook over low heat for 25 minutes.

Set half the chicken and half the sauce aside to cool for freezer. When cool, package, label, and freeze.

To finish half the dish (4 servings)

¼ cup slivered almonds
1 tablespoon butter

Sauté slivered almonds in the butter until golden.

Arrange chicken on serving dish, pour sauce over and sprinkle with the browned, slivered almonds.

70

To defrost and finish

Defrost in refrigerator for 8 hours, arrange in casserole, and cook in a preheated 350° F. oven for 35 minutes. Finish as above.

CHICKEN TETRAZZINI
(1 party casserole, 6 servings)

4 tablespoons butter
4 tablespoons flour
1 teaspoon salt
¼ teaspoon white pepper
⅛ teaspoon nutmeg
2 cups chicken broth
1 cup heavy cream
½ cup sherry

½ pound spaghetti, cooked
½ pound sliced, sautéed
fresh mushrooms
3 cups cooked, diced
chicken
½ cup toasted, slivered
almonds

In saucepan melt butter. Stir in flour, salt, pepper, and nutmeg. Heat chicken broth to simmering. Add to butter-flour mixture and cook over moderate heat, stirring briskly, until sauce is smooth and thickened. Stir in cream and sherry.

Combine sauce, spaghetti, mushrooms, chicken, and almonds. Pour into casserole. Freeze.

To defrost and finish

¼ cup grated Parmesan cheese
Paprika

Remove from freezer 1 hour before heating.
Sprinkle with cheese and paprika and bake in a preheated 375° F. oven for 1¼ hours.

GAME HENS VERONIQUE
(12 servings, ½ bird per serving)

6 Rock Cornish game hens
Salt and pepper
9 slices bacon, halved
½ cup cognac
2 cups heavy cream
3 tablespoons butter
6 green onions, finely
    sliced

2 (8¼-ounce) cans light
    seedless grapes, drained
1 cup Port wine
Salt to taste
Dash of cayenne
1 teaspoon lemon juice

Sprinkle game hens generously inside and out with salt and pepper.

Place in roasting pan and cover each with 3 half-slices bacon.

Roast in a preheated 350° F. oven for 60 minutes, basting occasionally with juices in pan.

Remove birds from oven and cut in half with poultry shears.

Arrange half the birds in a casserole to cool for the freezer.

Put roasting pan over direct heat. To liquid in pan add the cognac and cook until cognac is reduced by half. Add cream and boil rapidly until cream is reduced to the consistency of thin cream sauce.

In small saucepan heat the butter and in it sauté green onions for 2 minutes. Add grapes and Port wine. Heat and ignite wine. Stir until flame burns out.

Strain sauce from roasting pan into the wine and grape sauce.

Correct seasoning with salt, cayenne, and lemon juice.

Spoon half the sauce and grapes over hens in casserole.

When cool, freezer wrap, label, and freeze.

To serve half the dish (6 servings)

Arrange the halved hens on serving platter and pour sauce over them. Garnish with watercress.

72

To defrost and serve

Remove casserole from freezer about 1 hour before heating. Heat in a 350° F. oven, uncovered, for 15 minutes; cover and continue to cook for 30 minutes longer.

MEAT DISHES

Most cooked meats and meat dishes freeze well, but it is those long-cooking braised meats, stews, and goulashes which freeze best and keep their flavor and texture in the frozen state for as long as 6 months.

The economical homemaker will make two or three times the quantity of a stew or chili needed, and will freeze what isn't used that night for dinner for a meal a few weeks or even months later. She will have saved a substantial amount of gas or electricity in addition to being "one meal ahead"—family or party—for many of these dishes make delicious casseroles for buffet suppers.

Other dishes which freeze well for at least 3 months are veal birds, meat balls in gravy, Swiss steak, and braised chops.

All meat dishes should be cooled quickly before they are packaged and frozen.

Package in pint or quart freezer containers, whichever size is best suited to your family's needs. To defrost, remove as many packages as needed and turn into a casserole or baking dish. Heat in a 325° F. oven for 1 hour, or turn it into a saucepan, cover, and heat over low heat for 1 hour.

Stew may be frozen right in the casserole in which it was made. Once solidly frozen it may be removed, wrapped, and stored. To cook the stew, return it in its frozen state to its original container.

Good substitutes for casseroles are 8-inch layer-cake pans. They hold just a quart. Line with foil, allowing the foil to extend beyond the rim. Fill with stew, chili, meat balls and gravy, or veal birds and freeze. When frozen, remove from pan and wrap in the extending foil. To defrost, unwrap into an 8- or 9-inch skillet. Cover and heat slowly for about 25 minutes. Frozen in this way, meat dishes stack neatly and take a minimum of freezer space.

Leftover roast meats may be frozen in one large piece, in slices, or diced. But remove any bone; it's senseless to take up valuable freezer space with bone. Sliced or diced meat retains its flavor longer if covered with sauce, broth, or gravy. Wrap large pieces in sheet wrappings; use aluminum foil if the roast is to be reheated in the oven. Plan to use within a month for best eating enjoyment.

Defrost large chunks of meat for 5 hours per pound in refrigerator or 3 to 5 hours at room temperature to serve cold. To serve hot, bake, in the foil, in a 350° F. oven for about 1 hour.

Frozen baked ham requires 15 minutes per pound in a 350° F. oven to defrost and heat.

Defrost leftover frozen meat loaf for 6 hours in refrigerator or 2 to 3 hours at room temperature to serve cold. To serve hot, bake directly from freezer in foil in a 400° F. oven for 30 to 40 minutes.

BEEF IN RED WINE
(12 servings)

6 pounds top round, cubed	2 tablespoons chopped parsley
Flour	4 medium onions, chopped
4 tablespoons butter	2 bay leaves
½ cup olive oil	½ teaspoon thyme
Salt and pepper	1 bottle (3 cups) red Burgundy wine
½ cup cognac	4 cups water
½ pound bacon, diced	2 tablespoons flour
4 cloves garlic, chopped	
2 carrots, chopped	
2 leeks, chopped	

Roll meat in flour and brown a few cubes at a time in 2 tablespoons of the butter and the olive oil over high heat. Transfer meat to a large casserole as it is browned.

When all cubes are browned, sprinkle generously with salt and pepper, sprinkle with cognac, and flame.

In same pan in which meat was browned, sauté bacon until crisp. Add garlic, carrots, leeks, parsley, and onions and continue to cook until vegetables are lightly browned. Transfer to casserole. Add to casserole bay leaves, thyme, red wine, and water. Cover and cook in a 350° F. oven for 2 hours.

Stir in flour mixed to a smooth paste with the remaining 2 tablespoons butter, cover, and cook for 2 hours longer. The longer this dish cooks, the better it will be. If necessary add a little more water or wine to keep the meat covered with liquid at all times.

Serve with sautéed mushroom caps, tiny cooked onions browned in butter, and boiled potatoes.

To defrost and serve

Remove stew from freezer 1 hour before cooking. Empty into casserole, cover, and cook in a 350° F. oven for 1½ hours. Serve as above.

HUNGARIAN GOULASH
(12 servings)

1 cup bacon drippings
6 pounds top round, cut into 1½-inch cubes
4 pounds onions, peeled and sliced

2 (12-ounce) bottles beer or ale
2 cups tomato paste
2 bay leaves
Salt and pepper

In large heavy kettle heat bacon drippings. Add meat and sear over high heat until well browned on all sides.

Add onions, lower heat, and cook for 10 minutes.

Add ale, tomato paste, and bay leaves. Cover tightly and cook over low heat for 2½ hours, or until meat is tender.

Season to taste with salt and pepper.

Set half aside to cool for freezer. When cool, package, label, and freeze.

To finish half the dish (6 servings)

1 tablespoon paprika

Stir in paprika, being careful to keep paprika from burning onto sides of kettle.

Serve with cooked noodles tossed with bread crumbs browned in butter with 1 clove minced garlic.

To defrost and finish

Remove goulash from freezer 1 hour before cooking. Empty into kettle, cover, and cook over low heat for 30 minutes. Finish and serve as above.

NOTE: The finished goulash, with paprika added, may be frozen. In this case, defrost and heat over simmering water.

FLEMISH BEEF STEW
(12 servings)

½ cup butter, oil, or beef fat	*Flour*
	2 teaspoons salt
3 pounds onions, thinly sliced	*½ teaspoon pepper*
	½ teaspoon thyme
5 pounds round steak, cubed	*2 cloves garlic, minced*
	2 quarts beer

In heavy kettle heat butter, oil, or beef fat and in it sauté onions for 10 minutes, or until lightly browned. Remove onions and reserve.

Roll beef in flour until coated on all sides. Brown a few pieces at a time over high heat in drippings remaining in kettle.

Sprinkle with salt, pepper, and thyme. Add cooked onions, garlic, and beer. Cover and simmer for 1½ hours.

Set half aside to cool for freezer. When cool, package, label, and freeze.

To finish half the stew (6 servings)

2 tablespoons flour
2 tablespoons butter

Mix flour and butter to a smooth paste. Stir into hot gravy bit by bit. Cook, stirring, until sauce is slightly thickened, but do not boil. Serve with cooked potatoes.

To defrost and finish

Remove stew from freezer 1 hour before heating. Empty into heavy kettle and cook over low heat for 30 minutes, stirring occasionally. Finish and serve as above.

TEXAS CHILI CON CARNE
(12 servings)

3 pounds ground beef
4 medium onions, chopped
1 tablespoon salt
4 teaspoons turmeric
*2 tablespoons ground
coriander*
*4 tablespoons chili or
mole powder*

*2 teaspoons chopped hot
green pepper, fresh or
canned, or to taste*
*2 cups canned Italian
peeled tomatoes*

In large heavy kettle put beef, onions, salt, turmeric, coriander, chili or mole powder, and hot green pepper. Cook over moderate heat for 10 minutes, stirring constantly to break up meat and mix it with the seasonings.

Add tomatoes, bring to a boil, cover, and simmer over low heat for 1 hour. Set aside half to cool for freezer. When cool, package, label, and freeze.

To serve

Serve the chili hot with side dishes of grated Cheddar cheese, chopped onion, and shredded lettuce to be sprinkled on top of the chili. If desired, serve with tortillas fried in hot deep fat until golden brown and crisp.

To defrost and serve

Remove chili from freezer 1 hour before heating. Empty into saucepan and cook over low heat for 30 minutes, stirring occasionally. Serve as above.

CHILI CON CARNE II
(12 servings)

6 pounds cubed chuck
  of beef
¾ cup cooking oil
12 tablespoons chili or
  mole powder
6 tablespoons flour
2 teaspoons cumin seeds

2 teaspoons orégano,
  crumbled
2 teaspoons salt
6 cloves garlic, minced
4 (13½-ounce) cans
  beef broth

In heavy stew pot or kettle cook beef in the oil until meat loses color.

Stir in chili or mole powder mixed with flour.

Add remaining ingredients. Bring to a boil and cook over very low heat for 24 hours. Serve with cooked beans or rice or both.

To freeze

Cool. Package in freezer container, seal, label, and freeze.

To defrost and serve

Empty into saucepan and cook over low heat for at least 1 hour. Longer cooking will not hurt. Serve as above.

MEAT BALLS WITH CAPER SAUCE
(12 servings)

3 pounds raw ground veal
½ pound ground fat pork
4 tablespoons melted
    butter
4 slices bread
4 tablespoons grated
    onion
2 tablespoons butter
1 teaspoon grated lemon
    peel
6 eggs, lightly beaten
1 teaspoon freshly ground
    pepper

2 teaspoons salt
2 tablespoons lemon juice
2 teaspoons Worcestershire
    sauce
¼ cup minced parsley
3 (10½-ounce) cans
    beef consommé
3 cans water
½ cup soft butter
½ cup flour
1 tablespoon cornstarch
¼ cup chopped capers

In large mixing bowl combine veal, fat pork, and the 4 tablespoons melted butter.

Soak bread in water to soften, squeeze out excess water, and add bread to meat.

Sauté grated onion in the 2 tablespoons butter until golden. Add to meat.

Add lemon peel, eggs, pepper, salt, lemon juice, Worcestershire sauce, and minced parsley and mix well with hands. Shape into 24 large balls.

In large skillet heat beef consommé and water to boiling. Gently lower meat balls into liquid, cover, and simmer for 10 minutes. Turn balls with slotted spoon, cover, and simmer for 10 minutes longer. Cook only as many balls as the skillet will hold at one time. Remove balls as they are cooked to dish and, when all are cooked, strain stock into a saucepan.

Combine the ½ cup soft butter with flour and cornstarch.

Gradually stir into the hot stock and cook, stirring, until gravy is slightly thickened. Stir in capers.

Pack half the meat balls and half the sauce in freezer container. When cool, seal, label, and freeze.

To finish half the dish (6 servings)

> ½ *cup fresh bread crumbs*
> 1 *tablespoon butter*

Return meat balls to gravy to heat.

Brown bread crumbs in butter. Transfer meat balls and gravy to serving dish and sprinkle with the browned crumbs and the butter.

To defrost and finish

Remove meat balls from freezer 1 hour before heating.

Empty into skillet, cover, and cook over low heat for 30 minutes, stirring carefully once or twice. Finish as above.

STUFFED VEAL BIRDS
(12 servings)

4 *slices bread, crumbed*	1½ *teaspoons crumbled*
1 *large onion, minced*	*sage*
2 *teaspoons salt*	¼ *cup hot water*
½ *teaspoon pepper*	3 *pounds veal, cut into*
½ *cup melted butter*	12 *serving portions*
¼ *cup chopped parsley*	*and thinly pounded*
1 *cup minced celery*	*Flour*
	3 *tablespoons butter*

In mixing bowl combine bread, onion, salt, pepper, melted butter, parsley, celery, sage, and hot water.

Place a spoonful of stuffing on each slice meat, roll up like small jelly roll, and tie with string.

Roll the meat rolls in flour and brown in skillet in the 3 tablespoons butter. When well browned on all sides, transfer half the rolls to a baking sheet. Cool, then freeze until solid. Pack in freezer container, label, and freeze.

To finish half the birds (6 servings)

1 (10½-ounce) can beef consommé
1 can water
½ cup cream
1 tablespoon flour
1 tablespoon soft butter
2 tablespoons minced parsley

Transfer remaining birds to baking dish. Add consommé, water, and cream. Cover and bake in a 325° F. oven for 1½ hours. Just before serving, stir in flour blended to a paste with soft butter to thicken gravy slightly.

Sprinkle with parsley and serve.

To defrost and finish

Place birds directly from freezer into baking dish and finish as above, increasing baking time by 15 minutes.

CURRY OF LAMB
(12 servings)

4 medium onions, chopped
4 cloves garlic, minced
4 tablespoons chopped fresh or preserved ginger
2 sticks butter
4 tablespoons good curry powder
½ teaspoon red pepper flakes
½ teaspoon cumin
½ teaspoon coriander
1 tablespoon salt
1 teaspoon coarsely ground pepper
1 cup flour
6 cups hot chicken broth
2 quarts diced cooked lamb

Sauté onions, garlic, and ginger in butter for 10 minutes, or until onions are tender, but not browned. Add curry powder, pepper flakes, cumin, coriander, salt, and pepper and cook, stirring, for 2 minutes.

Stir in flour.

Gradually stir in the chicken broth and cook, stirring, until sauce is thickened. Add lamb and cook over low heat for 20 minutes, stirring occasionally. Set half aside to cool for the freezer. When cool, package, label, and freeze.

To finish half the curry (6 servings)

> *1 cup cream*
> *2 tablespoons curry paste or to taste*

Stir in cream and curry paste and heat. Serve with cooked rice.

To defrost and finish

Empty curry into saucepan and heat over simmering water for 30 minutes, stirring occasionally. Finish and serve as above.

Most Chinese dishes are quickly cooked and are much better when freshly made than when frozen. This one, however, may be made one day when you're in the mood for deep frying. It freezes better than most Chinese dishes.

SWEET AND SOUR PORK
(12 servings)

> *2 (13½-ounce) cans*   *Deep fat for frying*
> *pineapple chunks*   *2 green peppers, seeded*
> *2 eggs, beaten*   *and cut into strips*
> *1 teaspoon salt*   *1 cup vinegar*
> *1 cup flour*   *½ cup brown sugar*
> *3 pounds boned leg or*   *2 tablespoons molasses*
> *shoulder of pork, cut*   *2 tablespoons cornstarch*
> *into 1-inch cubes*

Drain and reserve syrup from cans of pineapple.

In mixing bowl combine eggs, 6 tablespoons of the reserved pineapple syrup, and salt. Stir in flour to make a thick batter.

Add pork cubes and toss until all are coated with batter. Fry cubes in deep fat heated to 365° F. for 6 to 7 minutes, or until well browned. Drain on absorbent paper.

In saucepan put all but ¼ cup of the remaining pineapple syrup. Add green peppers, vinegar, brown sugar, and molasses. Bring to a boil and simmer for 5 minutes.

Stir in cornstarch mixed with remaining pineapple syrup.

Add pork cubes and pineapple chunks and simmer for 15 minutes, or until pork is tender.

Set aside half to cool for freezer. When cool, package and freeze.

To finish half the dish (6 servings)

   1 tomato, peeled and diced
   2 green onions, sliced

Add tomato and green onions and cook for just 5 minutes longer. Serve with cooked rice.

To defrost and finish

Remove pork from freezer 1 hour before heating. Empty into saucepan and heat over simmering water for 30 minutes, stirring occasionally. Five minutes before serving, finish and serve as above. This dish should be defrosted and hot. Do not cook.

CECELIA'S SAUERBRATEN
(12 servings)

1 cup red wine vinegar
½ bottle red wine
12 peppercorns
1 teaspoon salt
1 bay leaf
6 cloves
2 cloves garlic, chopped
2 thin strips yellow rind
   of lemon

1 onion, halved
¼ teaspoon nutmeg
3 stalks celery, chopped
2 carrots, chopped
4 sprays parsley
6-pound rolled top round
   of beef
2 cups beef stock
3 tablespoons cornstarch

In earthenware or enamel container large enough to hold the roast, combine vinegar, red wine, peppercorns, salt, bay leaf, cloves, garlic, lemon rind, onion, nutmeg, celery, carrots, and parsley. Add beef, cover, and let marinate in refrigerator for at least 3 days, turning meat occasionally.

Remove meat from marinade; reserve marinade. Dry meat well with paper towels.

Bring marinade to a boil and simmer over low heat while meat is cooking.

Heat a heavy kettle or Dutch oven. Put meat in the pot, fat side down, and brown it well on all sides. This will take about 1 hour. When a rich brown all over, pour off excess fat from kettle.

Add half the beef stock to the meat. Cover tightly and cook over low heat for 3½ hours, basting occasionally with remaining cup of stock and with the hot marinade until all marinade has been added.

Remove meat to a hot platter.

Strain gravy, pressing vegetables through the sieve.

Remove fat from surface. Return gravy to heat and stir in cornstarch mixed with a little water.

Serve the sauce separately from the meat.

To freeze remaining meat and gravy

Slice remaining meat into serving pieces and arrange in a round shallow freezer container, or in a cake pan lined with foil. Cover with sauce and freeze. When frozen, wrap, label, and store.

To defrost and serve

Remove from freezer 1 hour before heating. Empty into large heavy skillet. Cover and defrost over low heat for about 30 minutes, or until hot. Do not let sauce boil.

Braised oxtails is another wonderful "bony" dish, well worthy of space in the freezer. If your butcher can get them for you, have him skin and section the tails. You'll need 1 oxtail for each 2 servings, so buy lots when you can get them. The raw tails keep well in the freezer, and they will be available to you when you want to take the time to braise them.

PEGGY'S BRAISED OXTAILS
(8 servings)

4 oxtails, skinned and cut
  into sections
4 tablespoons butter
4 tablespoons olive oil
4 stalks celery, chopped
1 tablespoon chopped
  parsley
1 clove garlic, minced
1 bay leaf, crumbled
2 carrots, chopped
2 tablespoons flour
2 cups beef stock or
  consommé

¼ cup brandy
1 pound ripe tomatoes,
  peeled, seeded, and
  chopped, or 1
  (1-pound) can whole
  tomatoes, drained and
  chopped
½ teaspoon pepper
Juice of ½ lemon
¼ teaspoon nutmeg
1 cup Madeira or
  Marsala

Soak oxtails in lukewarm water for 1 hour, changing water every 15 minutes. Drain and dry well.

In skillet heat butter and olive oil and in it sauté oxtails over moderate heat until well browned on all sides.

In bottom of a buttered casserole put the celery, parsley, garlic, and bay leaf. Place oxtails on this bed of vegetables.

In fat remaining in skillet cook the carrots until slightly browned. Stir in the flour and add carrots and liquid to casserole.

Add consommé, brandy, and tomatoes. Sprinkle with pepper, lemon juice, and nutmeg.

Cover casserole tightly and braise on top of stove or in a pre-heated 350° F. oven for 2½ to 3 hours.

Place oxtail sections in serving casserole or suitable freezer container.

Strain gravy, pressing as much of the cooked vegetables through the sieve as possible. Correct seasoning and stir in Madeira or Marsala.

To serve

Heat sauce to simmering and pour over oxtails. Sprinkle with chopped parsley and serve with cooked julienne carrots and boiled potatoes.

To freeze

Cool sauce and pour over oxtails. Seal, label, and freeze.

To defrost

Remove from freezer 1 hour before reheating. Empty into casserole and cook over low heat or in a 325° F. oven for about 1 hour. The longer this dish cooks the better it is. Serve as above.

BLANQUETTE DE VEAU
(12 servings)

4 to 5 pounds breast or shoulder of veal, cut into serving pieces	1 bay leaf
	¼ teaspoon thyme
	1 teaspoon salt
2 quarts water	½ teaspoon white pepper
24 small white onions, peeled	2 tablespoons butter
	1 tablespoon flour
3 medium carrots, cut into 1-inch pieces	1 tablespoon cornstarch
	1 cup sliced mushrooms
1 medium onion, stuck with 4 cloves	

Put veal into large heavy saucepan. Add water, bring to a boil, and skim well. Add small onions, carrots, the onion studded with cloves, bay leaf, thyme, salt, and pepper. Cover and simmer for 1½ hours, or until meat is tender.

Remove meat, small onions, and carrots. Strain the stock and reserve.

In another large saucepan melt butter. Stir in flour and cornstarch and cook, stirring, until smooth. Add reserved stock and the mushrooms and cook over low heat for 10 minutes, stirring occasionally. Return meat, onions, and carrots and cook for 5 minutes longer.

Set aside half the meat, onions, carrots, and sauce to cool for freezer. When cool, package and freeze.

To finish half the dish (6 servings)

¼ cup heavy cream   1 tablespoon minced
2 egg yolks   parsley
1 teaspoon lemon juice

Combine cream and egg yolks with about ½ cup of the hot sauce. Stir egg mixture into sauce in pan. Add lemon juice and cook over low heat for 3 minutes, stirring constantly. Do not let sauce boil.

Empty into heated serving dish and sprinkle with parsley.

To defrost and finish

Remove from freezer 1 hour before heating. Turn into kettle and defrost over low heat for about 30 minutes. When hot, finish and serve as above.

I never recommend filling up a freezer with bones! But this is such a good party buffet dish, that I want to include it.

OSSI BUCCHI MILANESE
(12 servings)

*4 meaty veal shanks with
marrow, each sawed
into 3 pieces, making
12 individual serving
pieces*
⅓ cup flour
2 teaspoons salt
*½ teaspoon freshly ground
pepper*
3 tablespoons olive oil
3 tablespoons butter

½ teaspoon crumbled sage
1 teaspoon rosemary
*1 medium onion, finely
chopped*
1 clove garlic, minced
2 small carrots, diced
1 cup diced celery
1½ cups dry white wine
1½ cups chicken stock
*2 tablespoons tomato
paste*

Roll meat in flour seasoned with salt and pepper.

In heavy kettle heat olive oil and butter and in it brown the veal pieces on all sides. When all are well browned, turn each on its side so the marrow in the bone does not fall out as the meat cooks.

Sprinkle meat with sage and rosemary. Add onion, garlic, carrots, and celery. Cover tightly and cook over moderate heat for 10 minutes.

Add wine, stock, and tomato paste. Cover and simmer for 1½ hours, or until meat is tender. Set aside half the meat pieces and sauce to cool for freezer. When cool, package and freeze.

To finish half the dish (6 servings)

*2 cloves garlic, minced
Grated rind of 1 lemon
2 tablespoons minced parsley*

One minute before serving, sprinkle meat with garlic, lemon rind, and parsley. Serve with cooked rice.

88

To defrost and finish

Defrost overnight in refrigerator. Heat to simmering and finish as above.

SWEETBREADS ROYALE
(2 casseroles, each 4 servings)

4 pair (3 pounds)
  sweetbreads
Juice of 1 lemon
6 tablespoons butter
6 shallots or green
  onions, minced
1 pound small mushrooms,
  sliced

½ teaspoon salt
⅛ teaspoon white pepper
2 tablespoons cognac
  (optional)
1 cup dry white wine
3 cups chicken broth
4 tablespoons flour
4 tablespoons butter

Soak sweetbreads in cold water for 30 minutes. Drain. Cover with fresh cold water and add lemon juice. Bring to a boil and simmer for 15 minutes. Drain. Remove tendons and cut sweetbreads into chunks.

In saucepan heat the 6 tablespoons butter. Add shallots or green onions and mushrooms and sauté for 5 minutes, stirring occasionally. Add sweetbreads, salt, pepper, cognac, white wine, and chicken broth. Bring to a boil and simmer for 30 minutes.

Combine flour and the 4 tablespoons butter to a smooth paste. Stir into sauce, bit by bit, and cook, stirring, until sauce is slightly thickened.

Pour half the sweetbreads and sauce into a freezer container to cool. When cool, seal, label, and freeze.

To finish 1 casserole

½ cup cream
2 egg yolks
Shredded Gruyère cheese

Combine cream and egg yolks. Gradually stir into sauce and cook, stirring, for 3 minutes, being careful that the sauce does not boil. Pour into 1½-quart casserole and sprinkle top generously with cheese. Place casserole in pan containing about 1 inch hot water and bake in preheated 350° F. oven for 20 minutes.

To defrost and finish

Remove from freezer and empty into saucepan. Cook over simmering water for 30 minutes, stirring occasionally. Finish as above.

CHAPTER 4

Vegetables

Most prepared vegetable dishes, sauced, stewed, or casseroles, freeze well, but it's those long-cooking vegetables—sweet potatoes, pumpkins, winter squash, whole beets—creamed vegetables such as onions and cauliflower au gratin, and the many varieties of dried legumes which are the best vegetable investment for the home freezer.

When baking a pot of beans or making a sweet potato casserole, prepare a double quantity and store half in your freezer. When baking white potatoes, use your oven heat to bake an ovenful, and take time to mash the pulp and stuff the shells for stuffed baked potatoes for the freezer. Flavor them with cheese or an herb—especially at those times of the year when chives, tarragon, and dill are fresh in garden or market.

When in the mood to prepare French fries, make lots of them, and pack them in family portions for your freezer. Why, you may well ask, should you freeze potatoes, for both baked stuffed and French fries are available in every frozen-food counter. Well, in the first place, the homemade potato products are much better than the commercially frozen ones and, in the second place, they are cheaper. Any homemaker on a tight food budget can save money at the expense of time, and only you can decide if your time is too valuable to spend in the kitchen.

COOKED POTATOES

Cooked potatoes, both white and sweet, freeze well.

Freshly mashed potatoes, whipped until light with milk or cream and butter, may be frozen in pint or quart containers ready to thaw and heat over boiling water, or they may be formed into potato croquettes or patties and packaged in layers with two sheets of freezer paper between layers for easy separation before being defrosted. They need no defrosting before heating, but may be browned slowly on both sides in butter in a skillet or in the oven, directly from the frozen state. Sweet potatoes may be treated in the same way.

BAKED POTATOES

Bake yams or sweet potatoes until fork tender. Halve and cool. Re-form each potato with two layers of freezer paper between the halves and wrap each re-formed potato individually.

Baked white potatoes may be prepared for the freezer as above for baked sweet potatoes. Or they may be stuffed: Cut the baked potatoes in half and scoop out the pulp. Mash and beat the pulp until fluffy with cream, butter, and seasonings. Refill halves, piling the mashed potato high in center. Freeze on baking sheets. When frozen, wrap each stuffed potato half in freezer paper and return to freezer.

To serve from freezer

Bake frozen white or sweet potatoes directly from freezer, in a preheated 400° F. oven for 20 to 30 minutes.

FRENCH FRIED POTATOES

French fried potatoes should not be stored for longer than 6 weeks.

Peel, cut, and scald potatoes in boiling water for 2 minutes. Drain and dry well on absorbent paper.

For the freezer, fry to a light brown. Drain and cool quickly. Freeze on baking sheets, then package and store.

To serve from freezer

Spread on baking sheet and bake in a 400° F. oven for 10 minutes. Sprinkle with salt and serve hot.

This sweet-potato casserole freezes well and makes an excellent buffet dish.

SHERRIED SWEET POTATOES
(6 to 8 servings)

3 pounds sweet potatoes	1/4 teaspoon cinnamon
1/2 cup butter	Milk
1/2 cup sherry	Salt and pepper to taste
1/4 teaspoon nutmeg	

Cook potatoes in their jackets until soft, peel, and put through ricer. Add butter, sherry, nutmeg, and cinnamon and beat until mixture is light and fluffy. Add a little milk if potatoes are dry and season with salt and pepper to taste.

Cool thoroughly and turn into a buttered baking dish. Cover, seal, label, and freeze.

Do not store longer than 1 month.

To defrost and serve

Remove baking dish from freezer and put into a cold oven. Heat oven to 325° F. and bake the casserole for 1 hour.

If frozen in a freezer-to-oven baking dish, the dish may be put directly from the freezer into the preheated oven.

Halfway through the baking, dot surface with butter and sprinkle with cinnamon.

PINEAPPLE YAM CASSEROLE
(2 casseroles, each 6 servings)

6 cups hot mashed sweet potatoes or yams	1 cup drained crushed pineapple
6 tablespoons butter	2 eggs, lightly beaten
2 teaspoons salt	1 cup chopped pecans
2 tablespoons brown sugar	

Beat potatoes with butter, salt, and brown sugar. Stir in pineapple, eggs, and nuts.

Divide mixture into 2 greased 1½-quart baking dishes. Cool 1 casserole and when cool, cover, seal, and freeze.

To finish 1 casserole

Bake in a preheated 350° F. for 45 minutes.

To finish frozen casserole

Remove from freezer and bake as above.

Baked beans are one of the most popular dishes served at any buffet supper. And baked beans will keep well in your freezer for as long as 1 year. Bake the beans New England style, or according to your favorite recipe, or try my favorite, seasoned with garlic and sage.

BAKED BEANS
(2 casseroles, each 6 servings)

2 pounds dry navy or pea beans	2 teaspoons salt or to taste
1 pound salt pork	½ teaspoon pepper
2 onions	2 teaspoons dry mustard
3 cloves garlic	½ teaspoon allspice
½ teaspoon crumbled sage	

Wash beans and soak overnight in plenty of water to cover. Drain, cover generously with fresh cold water, and add salt pork, onions, garlic, sage, salt, and pepper. Bring water slowly to a boil, cover, and simmer beans for 1½ hours, or until tender, adding more water if needed from time to time.

Remove and slice salt pork. Line bottom of two 2-quart casseroles or bean pots with half the slices. Fill pot with beans. Bury one of the onions in center of each pot and arrange remaining salt pork slices on top. Mix 1 teaspoon mustard with 1 cup of the bean water for each casserole and pour over beans. Sprinkle with allspice. Cover and bake in a preheated 325° F. oven for 3 to 4 hours, adding more bean water as needed. Uncover casseroles for the last hour of baking. Serve hot, or cool beans in the casseroles. Package and freeze.

To defrost and serve

Bake in covered casserole in 325° F. oven for 1½ hours.

These beans are traditionally served as an accompaniment to a roast leg of lamb. Just before serving, a few tablespoons of the pan juices from the roast meat are added to the beans.

LIMA BEANS A LA BRETONNE
(12 servings)

2 cups dried lima beans
2 onions, each stuck with
  1 clove
2 bay leaves

2 sprays parsley
2 teaspoons salt
¼ teaspoon pepper

Cover beans generously with cold water. Bring to a boil and simmer for 5 minutes. Remove from heat and let stand for 2 hours.

Return to heat and add remaining ingredients. Bring to a boil and simmer for 1½ to 2 hours, or until beans are tender, but not mushy. Set aside half the beans and liquid to cool. When cool, package, label, and freeze.

To finish half the beans (6 servings)

1 onion, chopped
1 clove garlic, minced
2 tablespoons butter
3 tomatoes, peeled,
  seeded, and chopped

2 tablespoons chopped
parsley
3 tablespoons roast lamb
juices or gravy

Sauté onion and garlic in butter until onion is transparent. Add tomatoes and simmer for 5 minutes. Add tomato mixture to the beans along with parsley and lamb juice or gravy. Simmer for 10 minutes longer.

To defrost and finish

Empty beans into saucepan and cook over low heat for 30 minutes. Finish as above.

SPANISH RICE
(8 servings)

6 tablespoons cooking oil
2 cups raw rice
2 medium onions,
  chopped
2 cloves garlic, minced
1 large green pepper,
  seeded and chopped

1 (1-pound) can Italian
plum tomatoes, drained
and mashed
3 cups chicken broth
1 (1-pound) can chick-
peas, drained

In large saucepan heat oil. Add rice and cook until rice is golden, stirring occasionally.

Add onions, garlic, and pepper and cook until onion is transparent.

Add remaining ingredients, cover tightly, and cook over low heat for 45 minutes. Do not stir.

Serve immediately, or cool for freezer. When cool, package in freezer containers, seal, label, and freeze.

To defrost

Turn into saucepan or casserole. Cover tightly and cook over low heat or in a 325° F. oven for 30 minutes, stirring occasionally.

RICE PILAU
(8 servings)

½ cup butter
1 large onion, minced
1 clove garlic, minced
2 cups rice

1 teaspoon salt
2 (13¾-ounce) cans
  chicken broth
Pinch of saffron (optional)

In saucepan melt butter and in it sauté onion and garlic until onion is transparent, but not browned.

Add rice and cook, stirring, until rice is golden. Add salt, broth, and saffron. Bring to a rapid boil. Reduce heat to very low, cover, and cook without stirring for 30 minutes.

Serve immediately, or cool for freezer. When cool, package in freezer containers, seal, label, and freeze.

To defrost

Turn into saucepan or casserole. Cover tightly and cook over low heat or in a 325° F. oven for 30 minutes. Stir once during the cooking.

SQUASH AND PUMPKIN

All varieties of winter squash and pumpkin may be cooked, puréed, and frozen for use as a vegetable, in pies, or in puddings. Baked acorn squash is an excellent and generally unavailable vegetable to store in the freezer and will keep well for 4 to 6 months. Bake the halved squash according to your favorite recipe, until barely tender. Cool, package each half individually in freezer paper, and freeze. Defrost in a preheated 325° F. oven in a baking dish containing 1 inch hot water for 30 minutes.

PEPPERS

When green peppers are at their peak in the stores or on the vine, stuff them according to recipe below or with a favorite combination of rice and sea food, or rice and meat. They can be kept frozen for as long as 4 months and make an economical and appetizing luncheon dish.

STUFFED GREEN PEPPERS
(Sufficient for 10 peppers)

2 onions, chopped
1 pound ground round or
  chuck of beef
4 fresh tomatoes, peeled
  and chopped
4 tablespoons butter

Salt and pepper to taste
2 cups fresh bread crumbs
10 peppers
⅔ cup dry, buttered
  bread crumbs

Sauté onions, ground steak, and tomatoes in butter until onions are soft and transparent. Season with salt and pepper and mix with the soft bread crumbs.

Remove stems, seeds, and membranes from the peppers and parboil in boiling salted water for 3 minutes.

Drain peppers and fill with the stuffing. Sprinkle stuffing with fine bread crumbs and freeze peppers on baking sheet.

When frozen, wrap each pepper in freezer paper and package 4 or 5, as desired, in 1 package. Overwrap and store.

98

To defrost and serve

Unwrap peppers and put, frozen, into a buttered baking dish. Dot each pepper with 1 teaspoon butter and bake in a preheated 350° F. oven for about 30 minutes.

RATATOUILLE
(12 servings)

1 cup olive oil
2 medium onions, finely
chopped
3 cloves garlic, minced
2 small eggplants, peeled
and diced
Flour
4 small zucchini, sliced
4 green peppers, seeded
and cut into strips

Salt and freshly ground
pepper to taste
2 tablespoons chopped
fresh basil, or 1
teaspoon dried basil
8 ripe tomatoes, peeled,
seeded, and chopped

In skillet heat half the olive oil and in it sauté onions and garlic until onions are golden. Do not brown.

Dredge eggplants with flour.

In separate skillet heat remaining oil and in it cook eggplants for about 10 minutes, or until lightly browned.

Combine eggplants, onions, and garlic in large saucepan.

Add remaining ingredients, bring to a boil, and simmer for about 30 minutes, or until mixture is thick and well blended. Pack half into freezer container to cool. When cool, seal, label, and freeze.

To serve half the dish (6 servings)

Serve hot as a vegetable or cold as an appetizer. If cold, flavor with a little lemon juice or serve with a wedge of lemon on each serving.

To defrost and serve

Empty into saucepan and defrost over low heat for 30 minutes. Serve as above.

DEEP-FRIED ONION RINGS
(6 servings)

6 large Bermuda onions
1 egg, beaten
½ cup milk
1 cup presifted flour
½ teaspoon salt
¼ teaspoon pepper

1 teaspoon sugar
1 tablespoon melted
    shortening
Shortening for deep-
    frying

Slice onions ¼ inch thick and separate into rings.

Combine egg, milk, flour, salt, pepper, and sugar. Stir in melted shortening.

In skillet heat shortening to a depth of 1 inch to 365° F.

Dip a few onion rings at a time into batter and fry in hot shortening for 2 to 3 minutes, or until lightly browned. Drain on absorbent paper.

To freeze

Freeze on baking sheets and when frozen, package in family-size portions, label, and return to freezer.

To defrost and serve

Spread onion rings on baking sheet and bake in preheated 400° F. oven for 10 minutes.

CORN CASSEROLE
(1 casserole, 6 servings)

4 tablespoons soft butter	½ tablespoon cornstarch
2 tablespoons sugar	4 eggs, beaten
1 teaspoon salt	1¾ cups milk
1 tablespoon flour	2 cups fresh corn kernels

Combine butter, sugar, salt, flour, and cornstarch. Stir in eggs, milk, and corn.

Pour into buttered 1½-quart casserole and bake in a preheated 325° F. oven for 45 minutes, or until lightly browned on top, stirring once during baking time. Serve hot or freeze.

To freeze

Cool casserole, cover, and freeze.

To serve

Remove casserole from freezer and reheat in a preheated 325° F. oven for 30 minutes.

SPINACH AU GRATIN
(2 casseroles, each 4 servings)

2 pounds spinach, washed and shredded	2 cups shredded cheese
3 cups CREAM SAUCE	8 slices bacon, crisply cooked

Steam spinach in water clinging to leaves for 10 minutes, or until tender. Drain.

Combine cream sauce and cheese and stir over low heat until cheese is melted. Combine spinach and sauce.

Divide vegetable mixture into two 1-quart casserole dishes and crumble 4 slices bacon on top of each. Cool 1 casserole, then cover and freeze.

To finish 1 casserole

Bake in preheated 350° F. oven for 20 minutes.

To finish frozen casserole

Remove from freezer and bake in preheated 350° F. oven for 30 minutes.

EGGPLANT SICILIENNE
(2 casseroles, each 6 servings)

2 *(1-pound, 4-ounce)*
  cans tomatoes
2 *medium onions, sliced*
2 *large cloves garlic,*
  minced
2 *teaspoons salt*
1 *teaspoon orégano*
½ *teaspoon thyme*
½ *teaspoon basil*

½ *teaspoon pepper*
4 *stalks celery, sliced*
4 *carrots, thinly sliced*
2 *medium eggplants,*
  pared and cut into
  1-inch cubes
1 *cup soft bread crumbs*
1 *cup shredded Cheddar*
  cheese

Empty tomatoes into a large saucepan and break up large tomatoes into smaller pieces. Add onions, garlic, salt, spices, celery, and carrots and bring to a boil. Add eggplants, mix well, cover, and cook over low heat for 30 minutes.

Divide mixture into two 6-cup casserole dishes and sprinkle with bread crumbs mixed with cheese. Finish and serve, or cool, cover, and freeze.

To finish 1 casserole

Bake in a preheated 375° F. oven for 20 minutes, or until topping is browned and mixture is bubbling.

To defrost and serve frozen casserole

Put casserole directly from freezer into a cold oven. Set oven for 375° F. and bake for 20 minutes. Remove cover and bake for 20 minutes longer.

BROCCOLI AND ONION CASSEROLE
(2 casseroles, each 6 servings)

2 bunches (4 pounds) broccoli
1 pound small silverskin onions
4 cups CREAM SAUCE
¼ cup sherry
1 cup shredded cheese
1 teaspoon dry tarragon
1 teaspoon celery salt

Discard tough outer leaves and lower stalks from broccoli. Wash well and slash stems. Cook, covered, in a small amount of salted water for 20 minutes, or until just tender. Drain.

Cook onions in salted water for 10 to 15 minutes, or until just tender.

Drain.

Divide cooked vegetables into 2 buttered 2-quart baking dishes.

Combine cream sauce, sherry, cheese, tarragon, and celery salt and stir over low heat until cheese is melted. Pour half the sauce over vegetables in each casserole. Cool 1 casserole, and when cool, cover and freeze.

To finish 1 casserole

4 tablespoons fine bread crumbs
1 tablespoon butter

Sprinkle top of vegetables with bread crumbs and dot with butter. Bake in preheated 350° F. oven for 30 minutes.

To finish frozen casserole

Remove casserole from freezer and bake in preheated 350° F. oven for 20 minutes. Sprinkle with bread crumbs and dot with butter. Continue to bake for 20 to 25 minutes longer.

CHAPTER 5

Sauces and How to Use Them

One of the most important categories of prepared foods in the freezer, if not *the* most important for the gourmet cook, is ready-made sauces. Sauces are the basis of many dishes, from the simple creamed chicken à la king or a dish of pasta with spaghetti sauce to the extravagantly rich and deliciously sauced fish, meat, and poultry dishes so esteemed in French cuisine. Often a dish that seems complicated and time-consuming to make is really the essence of simplicity. If you take time to analyze it, you'll find that most of the preparation time is spent making the sauce, and it is this sauce or, perhaps, a combination of sauces which makes the dish seem involved.

With a constant supply of basic sauces in your freezer you can prepare many great dishes in 30 minutes or less. It's well worth devoting a morning to sauce-making to keep your freezer well stocked. In addition to the fundamental white sauce, or béchamel, you should have a supply of both chicken and fish velouté, brown sauce, or Espagnole, tomato or spaghetti meat sauce, hollandaise sauce, and others in your freezer. You should freeze most of the sauces in 1 cup or pint containers, but it's also convenient to freeze some of each sauce in ice-cube trays. When frozen, remove the frozen cubes and pack them in polyethylene bags. These cubes are handy when a recipe calls for just a tablespoon or 2 of a basic sauce. All you have to do is take one or more of the frozen cubes from the bag, put them in a measuring cup, and set the cup into a saucepan or skillet of simmering water. In 10 minutes, the sauce will be ready to use. Ice-cube trays differ in the quantity of sauce they hold, but the average frozen cube is equivalent to 2 to 3 tablespoons defrosted sauce.

In this chapter I am giving not only recipes for the basic sauces, but a few recipes to show you how to use them in making classic dishes. But before the sauces, I'd like to tell you about two other great aids to expert cooking. One is CLARIFIED BUTTER. This is the most perfect fat there is for sautéeing fish and chicken. The food doesn't stick to the pan, for clarified butter doesn't burn as easily as regular butter. In addition it imparts a butter flavor to the food. A pound of clarified butter will last a long time in your freezer.

CLARIFIED BUTTER

Melt 1 pound butter over low heat. Skim foam from surface and pour the clear oil carefully off the milky sediment which settles to the bottom of the saucepan. Pour into pint freezer container or bowl. Cool, cover, and freeze.

The second important aid to expert cooking is a ROUX. This is a mixture of butter and flour used to thicken sauces and gravies. Rather than simmer meat, fish, or poultry in a thickened sauce which is apt to stick to the pan, the meat simmers in milk, stock, or wine and the liquid is thickened a few minutes before serving. By stirring in the roux bit by bit, you can arrive at the perfect consistency of sauce desired. Keep a container or crock of roux in your freezer at all times. It can be stirred into the liquid without defrosting.

ROUX

Let 1 cup butter soften at room temperature. Gradually stir and beat in 2 cups flour. This is an equal amount of butter and flour by weight. Spoon roux into freezer container, cover, and store in the freezer. When a recipe instruction reads, "Stir in 1 tablespoon butter mixed to a smooth paste with 2 tablespoons flour," stir in, bit by bit, a good rounded tablespoon of the frozen roux.

For our sauces we begin with the most basic and valuable sauce of them all—the basic white sauce. This can be made thin, medium, or thick in consistency, but for the freezer, it is best to use a thick white sauce, for it can always be thinned with milk or other liquid.

THICK BASIC WHITE SAUCE (*Béchamel*)
(Makes 1 quart)

½ cup (1 stick) butter　　*¼ teaspoon white pepper*
¾ cup flour　　　　　　　*4 cups milk*
2 teaspoons salt

In saucepan melt butter over moderate heat without letting it brown. Stir in flour until it is well blended with the melted butter. Add salt and pepper. Meanwhile bring milk almost but not quite to a boil. Remove butter-flour mixture from heat, add milk all at once, and stir vigorously with a wooden spoon or, preferably, with a wire whisk. Return saucepan to heat and continue to stir until thick and smooth. It will thicken almost immediately. Turn heat to low and cook for 10 minutes, stirring occasionally. Cool quickly. Package, label, and freeze.

Thin White Sauce
Thin THICK WHITE SAUCE with an equal amount of hot milk.

Medium White Sauce
Thin THICK WHITE SAUCE with half the amount of hot milk.

Cream Sauce
Stir into 1 cup hot THICK WHITE SAUCE ½ cup heavy cream.

Mornay Sauce
Stir into 1½ cups hot CREAM SAUCE 2 tablespoons each grated Swiss and Parmesan cheese. Cook, stirring, until cheese is melted.

Sauce Royale
Stir into 1½ cups hot CREAM SAUCE 1 egg yolk beaten with ¼ cup of the hot sauce.

Sherry Cream Sauce
Stir into 1½ cups hot CREAM SAUCE 2 tablespoons sherry.

Newburg Sauce
Stir into 1 cup THICK WHITE SAUCE ½ teaspoon paprika, dash of cayenne, 2 egg yolks lightly beaten with ¼ cup warm cream, and 2 tablespoons sherry.

Mushroom Sauce
Sauté ¾ pound of mushrooms, thinly sliced, 1 small onion, chopped, and ½ clove garlic minced in 2 tablespoons butter for 5 minutes. Add to 1½ cups CREAM SAUCE or SHERRY CREAM SAUCE and cook over low heat for 15 minutes, stirring frequently.

Sauce Velouté (Chicken, Beef, or Fish)
Make THICK WHITE SAUCE, but substitute chicken, beef, or fish stock for the milk.

Mustard Sauce
Mix 1 tablespoon dry mustard with the flour in making THICK WHITE SAUCE or VELOUTÉ.

CAULIFLOWER MORNAY AU GRATIN
(6 servings)

3 cups cauliflower flowerets	*¼ cup toasted bread*
1½ cups hot MORNAY	*crumbs*
SAUCE	*1 tablespoon butter*

Cook cauliflower in salted water until barely tender. Drain and empty into 1-quart casserole. Cover with Mornay sauce. Sprinkle with bread crumbs and dot with butter. Bake in a preheated 350° F. oven for 20 minutes.

CRAB MEAT LOUIS
(4 servings)

4 green onions, sliced
½ cup minced green
pepper
2 tablespoons butter
1½ cups CREAM SAUCE
1 teaspoon dry mustard
Few drops Tabasco
1 cup shredded Cheddar
cheese

1 tablespoon chopped
parsley
2 (7½-ounce) cans
Alaska King crab meat
½ cup toasted bread
crumbs
4 slices Cheddar cheese

Sauté onion and green pepper in butter until vegetables are tender, but not browned. Add cream sauce and cook over low heat until sauce is hot. Stir in mustard, Tabasco, shredded cheese, parsley, and crab meat. Turn mixture into a 1-quart casserole dish. Sprinkle with bread crumbs and top with the sliced cheese. Bake in a preheated 350° F. oven for 15 minutes, or until sauce is bubbling and cheese on top is melted.

EGGS FLORENTINE
(6 servings)

1½ cups cooked, chopped
spinach, or 2 (10-ounce)
packages frozen chopped
spinach, cooked
1 tablespoon butter
1 teaspoon lemon juice
¼ teaspoon salt

⅛ teaspoon pepper
Dash of nutmeg
1½ cups hot MORNAY
SAUCE
6 poached eggs
2 tablespoons grated
Parmesan cheese

Drain spinach well and stir in butter, lemon juice, salt, pepper, and nutmeg. Make a layer of spinach in bottom of a shallow baking dish and cover with half the sauce. Place poached eggs on top and cover with remaining sauce. Sprinkle with grated Parmesan and bake in a preheated 350° F. oven for 15 minutes.

CHIPPED BEEF ROYALE
(4 servings)

Shred 8 ounces chipped beef into a saucepan. Cover with boiling water, let stand for 2 minutes, then drain thoroughly.

In saucepan sauté 1 small onion, minced, in 1 tablespoon butter for 3 minutes, or until onion is transparent. Add 1½ cups SAUCE ROYALE and cook until sauce is hot. Cook over low heat for 10 minutes, stirring occasionally. Serve on buttered toast.

CHICKEN A LA KING
(4 servings)

Sauté 1 small onion, minced, and 1 cup sliced mushrooms in 2 tablespoons butter for 5 minutes. Add 1½ cups SHERRY CREAM SAUCE and cook until sauce is hot. Add 1½ cups diced cooked chicken and cook over low heat for 10 minutes, stirring occasionally. Serve on buttered toast or in patty shells.

LOBSTER NEWBURG

Heat 1½ cups NEWBURG SAUCE. Stir in 1 tablespoon brandy and 2 cups diced cooked lobster. Cook until lobster is heated and serve immediately on buttered toast or in patty shells.

SPAGHETTI MEAT SAUCE
(Makes 6 pints)

2 pounds ground beef
½ pound ground veal
½ teaspoon sage
1 teaspoon orégano
2 tablespoons salt
1 teaspoon freshly ground
pepper
2 large onions, minced
1 pound mushrooms,
chopped

3 cloves garlic, minced
2 quarts canned tomatoes
with liquid
1 (1-pound) can tomato
purée
1 (6-ounce) can tomato
paste

Sauté meat in heavy-bottomed kettle or Dutch oven for 30 minutes, stirring occasionally. Sprinkle with sage, orégano, salt, pepper, onions, mushrooms, and garlic and continue to cook for 30 minutes longer, stirring occasionally.

Add remaining ingredients. Stir to mix. Reduce heat to low and cook for 1½ hours, or until desired sauce consistency. Cool. Pour into pint containers, leaving 1 inch head space. Seal and freeze.

To defrost and serve

Heat over simmering water for 30 minutes, stirring occasionally. Correct seasoning and serve over cooked spaghetti, noodles, or macaroni. Serve grated Parmesan cheese on the side.

BROWN SAUCE (*Espagnole*)
(Makes 2 quarts)

½ cup (*1 stick*) butter
1 cup flour
2 quarts beef or brown
stock
2 tablespoons diced salt
pork
2 carrots, chopped
2 medium onions, chopped
2 leeks (*white part only*),
chopped

2 cloves garlic, chopped
2 cups dry white wine
4 tablespoons tomato purée
1 teaspoon thyme
1 large bay leaf
Salt and pepper to taste
½ cup sherry or Madeira

In heavy saucepan or Dutch oven melt butter. Add flour and cook, stirring, until mixture is dark brown in color.

Stir in stock and bring to a boil. Simmer over low heat for 30 minutes. Meanwhile, in skillet sauté salt pork until pork is crisp and fat is rendered. Add pork bits to sauce. To fat remaining in skillet add carrots, onions, leeks, and garlic and cook until vegetables are well browned, stirring occasionally. Add vegetables to sauce. Add wine, tomato purée, thyme, and bay leaf. Bring to a boil and simmer for 30 minutes, stirring occasionally. Remove from heat.

Skim off fat that rises to surface of sauce. Correct seasoning with salt and pepper and strain through sieve, pressing through as much of the vegetables as possible (or purée in electric blender). Stir in sherry or Madeira. Cool sauce. Pour into pint containers, leaving ½ inch head space. Seal, label, and freeze.

To defrost

Heat over simmering water for 30 minutes.

MARCHAND DE VIN SAUCE
(Makes 1½ cups)

4 tablespoons butter
2 tablespoons finely
  chopped green onions
½ cup dry red wine
1 cup freezer BROWN
  SAUCE

1 tablespoon cognac
1 teaspoon lemon juice
Salt and freshly ground
  pepper to taste

In saucepan melt half the butter and in it sauté onions for 2 minutes, or until transparent. Add wine and cook until wine is reduced to half. Add brown sauce and simmer for 15 minutes. Remove from heat. Add cognac, lemon juice, salt and pepper to taste, and remaining butter. Swirl pan until butter melts. Serve with broiled steak, fillets of beef, or lamb chops.

COQ AU VIN
(4 servings)

1 (2½-pound) chicken,
  cut into portions
1 teaspoon salt
Freshly ground black
  pepper
¼ pound salt pork, diced
1 tablespoon finely
  chopped green onions
  or shallots

1 clove garlic, minced
1 cup sliced mushrooms
8 small white onions
1 cup dry red wine
1½ cups freezer BROWN
  SAUCE
1 bay leaf
¼ teaspoon thyme

Sprinkle chicken with salt and pepper.

In heavy saucepan heat salt pork until browned and crisp. Remove pork to absorbent paper to drain. To fat remaining in saucepan brown chicken portions on all sides. Drain off all but 2 tablespoons fat from pan. Add onions or shallots, garlic, mushrooms, small onions, and reserved salt pork. Cook over moderate heat for 2 minutes, stirring.

Add wine, brown sauce, bay leaf, and thyme. Cover and cook over low heat for 30 minutes, or until chicken is tender. Serve with boiled small potatoes.

CHICKEN BORDELAISE
(4 servings)

1 (2½-pound) chicken, quartered	¾ cup sliced mushrooms
1 teaspoon salt	¾ cup red wine
Freshly ground black pepper	1½ cups freezer BROWN SAUCE
3 tablespoons butter	1 tablespoon lemon juice
2 tablespoons finely chopped green onions	2 tablespoons minced parsley
	Salt and pepper to taste

Sprinkle chicken with salt and pepper.

In skillet melt butter and in it brown chicken on both sides. Remove chicken and set aside. To butter remaining in skillet add onions and mushrooms and cook for 5 minutes, stirring frequently. Return chicken to skillet. Add red wine and bring to a boil. Simmer until red wine is reduced to half. Add brown sauce and bring to a boil. Cover and simmer for 20 minutes, or until chicken is tender. Stir in lemon juice and parsley and correct seasoning with salt and pepper.

Next to butter as a staple for gourmet cooking, hollandaise sauce is next on my list. It can transform an ordinary dish into the sublime in seconds. Many dishes in French cuisine are finished by stirring egg yolks into the sauce, swirling in a chunk of butter, and adding a good dash of lemon juice. You can accomplish this same finishing touch by stirring in ½ cup hollandaise sauce from your freezer. It keeps well for months and can be added to a sauce while still frozen, bit by bit, in the same way as you add a frozen roux. It's not a difficult sauce to make if you know how, and if you have an electric blender it's a cinch. Here are both methods.

HOLLANDAISE SAUCE (*Regular Method*)
(Makes 1¼ cups)

4 egg yolks	⅛ teaspoon salt
2 tablespoons cream	Pinch of cayenne
1 tablespoon lemon juice	1 cup (2 sticks) butter

Into a small bowl put egg yolks, cream, lemon juice, salt, and cayenne. Set bowl into a skillet of hot, but not boiling, water and beat well over low heat until sauce begins to thicken. Beat in butter bit by bit and continue to beat until sauce is thick. Cool. Freeze in container, leaving ½ inch head space.

To Serve

Stir into a sauce, bit by bit, without defrosting; or for eggs Benedict, defrost over hot, but not boiling, water, stirring frequently.

HOLLANDAISE SAUCE (*Blender Method*)

Into container of an electric blender put egg yolks, cream, lemon juice, salt, and cayenne.

Heat butter until very hot, but do not let it brown.

Turn blender on low speed. Remove cover and pour in hot butter in a heavy stream. Empty into freezer container, leaving ½ inch head space, cool, seal, and freeze.

FILLETS OF SOLE IN WHITE WINE SAUCE
(4 servings)

4 fillets of sole	1 cup hot THICK WHITE
½ cup water	SAUCE
1 cup dry white wine	½ cup freezer HOLLANDAISE
½ teaspoon salt	SAUCE
⅛ teaspoon white pepper	½ cup whipped cream

Arrange fillets in a buttered skillet. Add water, wine, salt, and pepper. Bring to a boil, cover, and simmer fillets over very low heat for 8 minutes.

Transfer fillets to a heatproof serving platter.

Cook liquid in which fish were poached over high heat until reduced to ½ cup. Stir this liquid into the white sauce. Fold in hollandaise sauce and whipped cream. Spoon sauce over fillets and brown under broiler heat for 1 minute.

BAY SCALLOPS NANTUA
(6 servings)

2 tablespoons butter
1 tablespoon finely
  chopped green onions
¼ teaspoon salt
Pinch of cayenne
2 pounds bay scallops, or
  sea scallops, quartered

2 cups hot THICK WHITE
  SAUCE
½ cup heavy cream
1 tablespoon cognac
½ cup freezer HOLLANDAISE
  SAUCE

In large skillet heat butter. Add green onions, salt, and cayenne and cook, stirring, for 2 minutes, or until onions are tender. Add scallops and toss in the butter until coated on all sides. Add thick white sauce, heavy cream, and cognac. Bring to a simmer and cook over low heat for 2 minutes. Remove from heat and gradually stir in hollandaise sauce. Turn into heatproof serving dish and brown under broiler heat for 2 minutes.

If desired, garnish with poached shrimp and steamed mussels.

FILLETS OF SOLE ROYALE
(4 Servings)

4 fillets of sole
1 cup white wine
½ teaspoon salt
⅛ teaspoon pepper
4 medium mushrooms,
 trimmed
8 shrimp, peeled and
 deveined

1 cup SAUCE ROYALE
½ cup freezer HOLLANDAISE
SAUCE
1 tablespoon chopped
 parsley

Arrange fillets in a buttered skillet. Add wine, salt, pepper, mushrooms, and shrimp. Bring liquid to a boil, cover, and cook over low heat for 10 minutes.

Remove fillets to serving dish and garnish with the mushrooms and shrimp. Keep warm.

Cook liquid remaining in skillet over high heat until reduced to ½ cup. Gradually whisk in the sauce royale. Stir in hollandaise sauce bit by bit.

Pour sauce over fish and sprinkle with chopped parsley.

WHITE WINE SAUCE
(Makes 1 quart)

½ stick butter
½ cup flour
1 cup white wine
1 cup chicken stock or
 fish stock

2 cups cream
Salt and pepper to taste

In saucepan melt butter. Stir in flour and cook over moderate heat for 3 minutes, without letting the mixture brown, stirring occasionally.

Gradually stir in white wine, chicken or fish stock, and cream. Cook, stirring, until sauce is smooth and thickened. Season to taste with salt and pepper and cook over low heat for 10 minutes, stirring frequently. Cool. Pour into pint containers, leaving ½ inch head space, seal, label, and freeze.

To defrost

Thaw over simmering water for 30 minutes, stirring occasionally.

To use

Stir ½ cup freezer HOLLANDAISE SAUCE into 1 cup hot wine sauce. Use the chicken white wine sauce for poached chicken. Use the fish white wine sauce for poached fillets, shrimp, or scallops.

CHAPTER 6

Baked Products

One of the most popular and rewarding uses of the home freezer is the storing of a wide variety of home-baked products. Certainly everyone will want to keep on hand a couple of loaves of good bakery variety breads, a loaf of sandwich bread and, perhaps, some hamburger and hot dog rolls. But to be able to go to the freezer and take out a home-baked loaf, a batch of cinnamon buns, or a Swedish tea ring, a roll of cooky dough ready to slice and serve hot and freshly baked, an apple pie ready to pop into the oven, gives one a satisfaction that no bakery products can supply.

It's really worth the trouble and time to have an old-fashioned baking day once a week to keep your freezer well stocked for family enjoyment and for special occasions.

YEAST BREAD AND ROLLS

Yeast bread and rolls, baked before freezing, will remain fresh in your freezer for as long as 6 months.

Cool breads to room temperature after baking, then wrap and seal in freezer paper. Frozen loaves may be sliced while still frozen, or the amout needed for a meal can be cut from the loaf and the rest returned to the freezer.

Cool baked rolls to room temperature and package in amounts sufficient for a meal. A variety of shapes and flavors—cloverleaf, Parker House, orange, cinnamon, and so on—frozen together in one package make an attractive variety.

Always make bread dough in 4-loaf quantity; shape part into loaves and part into rolls. A good batch of sweet yeast dough can be shaped into a wide selection of breakfast breads, tea rolls, buns, and coffee rings.

Baked breads and rolls defrost quickly at room temperature because of their low moisture content. A 1-pound loaf of bread defrosts in about 1 hour, while buns and rolls need only half an hour. The best way to serve them, however, is hot. Heat bread and rolls in a preheated 350° F. oven for 10 to 20 minutes, depending on the size.

Sliced frozen bread may be toasted without defrosting.

PARTIALLY BAKED YEAST BREADS

Yeast bread and rolls that are baked just long enough to destroy the action of the yeast and set the dough may be stored in the freezer for 3 months. Bake in a preheated 275° F. oven for 20 minutes. Cool the partially baked breads, wrap or package, seal, and freeze. Bake directly from freezer in a preheated 450° F. oven for 10 minutes, or until golden brown. They will taste exactly like freshly baked bread.

UNBAKED YEAST BREADS

Unbaked bread and rolls are less satisfactory for freezing than the partially or fully baked product and should not be stored longer than 2 weeks. Make the dough, let it rise until double in bulk, and punch down. Shape dough into loaves, rolls, or coffee rings. Brush surface with olive oil or melted sweet butter to prevent dough from drying out, and freeze. When frozen, remove and package. Wrap loaves and coffee rings in moisture-vaporproof paper and seal. Package frozen rolls close together in shallow freezer containers with freezer paper between.

The activity of the yeast is slowly destroyed in frozen unbaked breads, so the sooner they are used the lighter they will be. To bake, unwrap the frozen breads and let rise, covered lightly, in a warm place for 2 to 3 hours, or until double in bulk. Bake in usual way.

BASIC YEAST BREAD
(Makes 4 loaves, 4 dozen rolls, or 4 coffee rings)

1 yeast cake or package	*4 tablespoons sugar*
active dry yeast	*4 teaspoons salt*
2 cups lukewarm water	*4 tablespoons shortening*
2 cups milk	*About 12 cups flour*

Soften yeast in ½ cup of the lukewarm water.

Scald milk and pour into mixing bowl. Add sugar, salt, and shortening and stir until shortening is melted. Stir in remaining water and cool to lukewarm.

Stir in 2 cups of the flour. Add softened yeast. Beat in about 4 cups flour to make a batter that is smooth and elastic.

Work in remaining flour to make a dough that is light but does not stick to the hands.

Turn dough out on lightly floured board, let rest for 10 minutes, then knead until dough is smooth and satiny. Shape into a ball and put into greased bowl. Brush surface with cooking oil, cover, and let rise for about 2 hours, or until dough is double in bulk.

Punch dough down and divide into 4 equal portions. Shape each portion into a smooth ball and let rest for 10 minutes. Then shape each portion into a loaf or into rolls.

Loaves: Put loaves into greased bread pans (3½ ×7½ ×2¾ inches), cover, and let rise for about 1½ hours, or until double in bulk. Bake in a preheated 400° F. oven for 50 minutes. Remove from pans to cake rack to cool. When cool, wrap, label, and freeze.

PAN ROLLS

Place small balls of dough almost touching in a greased square pan. Cover and let rise until double in bulk. Bake in preheated 425° F. oven for 15 minutes, or until lightly browned.

DINNER ROLLS

Form dough into cylindrical shapes with tapered ends. Place 1 inch apart on lightly greased baking sheet and let rise until double in bulk. Bake in preheated 425° F. oven for 15 minutes, or until lightly browned.

PARKER HOUSE ROLLS

Roll dough out ¼ inch thick on lightly floured board and cut into rounds with a biscuit cutter. Brush each round with melted shortening. Make a crease with back of knife across each round, just off center. Fold smaller half over larger half and pinch ends together. Arrange close together in greased shallow pan or on baking sheet. Brush with melted shortening and let rise for about 1 hour, or until double in bulk. Bake in preheated 400° F. oven for about 15 minutes.

CRESCENTS

Roll dough out into a circle ¼ inch thick on lightly floured board. Cut dough into 12 pie-shaped wedges. Brush surface of dough with melted butter and roll up, beginning at wide end and rolling to the pointed end. Place crescents on baking sheet and brush with melted butter. Let rise for about 1 hour, or until double in bulk. Bake in preheated 425° F. oven for about 15 minutes, or until browned.

FRENCH BREAD
(Makes 4 loaves)

4 cups lukewarm water	1 tablespoon melted
2 cakes yeast or envelopes	shortening
active dry yeast	About 12 cups flour
1 tablespoon salt	1 egg white
	1 tablespoon cold water

Measure water into mixing bowl. Sprinkle or crumble in yeast and stir until yeast is dissolved.

Add salt and shortening. Gradually stir in enough flour to make a sticky dough. Put dough into a greased bowl, turn dough to grease all surfaces, cover, and let rise in warm place for about 2 hours, or until double in bulk.

Punch dough down. Turn out on lightly floured board and divide into 4 equal portions. Roll each portion into an oblong about 15×10 inches. Roll lengthwise tightly and pinch edges together. Roll ends gently back and forth on board to taper them.

Place loaves on greased baking sheets. Cover and let rise in warm place for about 1 hour, or until double in bulk.

With sharp knife, make 4 diagonal cuts on top of each loaf.

Bake in preheated 425° F. oven for 25 minutes. Remove from oven and brush loaves with egg white mixed with water. Return to oven and bake for 5 minutes longer, or until golden brown.

Sesame braids

Divide dough into 4 equal portions. Cut each portion into 3 pieces. Roll each piece into a strip about 15 inches long. Place 3 strips on greased baking sheet and braid, fastening strips securely at both ends. Repeat with remaining portions of dough. Cover and let rise in a warm place for about 1 hour, or until double in bulk.

Combine 1 egg yolk and 1 tablespoon water. Brush top and sides of braids with egg mixture and sprinkle with sesame seeds. Bake in preheated 400° F. oven for 30 to 35 minutes, or until golden brown.

WHOLE-WHEAT BREAD
(Makes four 1-pound loaves)

2 cakes yeast or packages active dry yeast

2 cups lukewarm water

4 cups presifted all-purpose flour

2 cups milk

3 tablespoons shortening

¼ cup molasses

2 tablespoons sugar

1 tablespoon salt

About 8 cups sifted whole-wheat flour

Melted shortening

Soften yeast in lukewarm water. Beat in all-purpose flour to make a thick batter. Cover and let stand in a warm place overnight. Next day, scald milk with shortening, molasses, sugar, and salt. Cool to lukewarm.

Stir down yeast sponge and stir in milk mixture. Beat and work in enough whole-wheat flour to make a stiff dough. Turn dough out on lightly floured board and knead until smooth. Divide into 4 equal portions. Cover with a towel and let rest for 10 minutes. Then shape into loaves and put into greased 1-pound loaf pans. Brush tops with melted shortening, cover, and let rise for about 1½ hours, or until double in bulk.

Bake in preheated 400° F. oven for 45 to 50 minutes, or until well browned.

OATMEAL BREAD
(Makes 6 loaves)

2 cups quick-cooking oatmeal	4 cups boiling water
½ cup dark molasses	2 cakes yeast or envelopes active dry yeast
½ cup shortening	½ cup warm water
1½ tablespoons salt	About 16 cups presifted all-purpose flour
½ cup sugar	

Measure oatmeal, molasses, shortening, salt, and sugar into large mixing bowl. Stir in boiling water and cool to lukewarm.

Soften yeast in the ½ cup warm water. Add yeast to cooled oatmeal mixture and beat in about 2 cups flour. Work in enough additional flour to make a firm dough that does not stick to hands. Turn out on floured board and knead until dough is smooth and elastic. Cover dough and let rise in warm place for about 2 hours, or until double in bulk. Punch down, knead, and again let rise for about 1½ hours, or until double.

Divide dough into 6 portions, shape each into a loaf, and place three loaves side by side in a 9×13×2-inch baking pan. Let rise for about 1 hour, or until double in bulk.

Bake in preheated 400° F. oven for 40 to 50 minutes.

BASIC SWEET DOUGH
(Makes 3 dozen sweet rolls or 3 coffeecakes)

2 cakes yeast or packages
    active dry yeast
¼ cup lukewarm water
1 cup milk
½ cup sugar
1 teaspoon salt

½ cup shortening (part
    butter)
About 6 cups presifted
    all-purpose flour
2 eggs, beaten

Soften yeast in lukewarm water.

Scald milk, add sugar, salt, and shortening and cool to lukewarm. Beat in part of the flour to make a thick batter. Add softened yeast and eggs and beat thoroughly. Add enough additional flour to make a dough which is soft but does not stick to hands. Turn out on lightly floured board and knead until smooth and satiny. Place in greased bowl, grease surface, cover, and let rise in a warm place for 1½ hours, or until double in bulk.

Punch down and let rest for 10 minutes. Then shape into rolls, tea rings, or coffeecakes. Let rise for about 1 hour, or until double in bulk.

Bake in a 350° F. oven for 30 minutes for coffeecakes; 20 to 25 minutes for rolls.

CINNAMON ROLLS
(Makes 1 dozen)

⅓ portion BASIC SWEET
    DOUGH
½ cup brown sugar
¼ cup (½ stick) butter

1 cup light corn syrup
½ cup sugar
2 teaspoons cinnamon

When basic sweet dough is light, punch down and let rest for 10 minutes.

In an 8-inch square baking pan combine brown sugar, butter, and syrup. Heat, stirring, until brown sugar is melted. Remove from heat and mix part of the syrup with sugar and cinnamon to make a paste.

Roll dough out thinly into a rectangle on floured board and spread with the sugar paste. Roll up lengthwise like a jelly roll and cut into slices about ½ inch thick. Arrange slices in baking pan on top of remaining syrup and let rise in warm place for about 30 minutes.

Bake in preheated 375° F. oven for 25 to 30 minutes. Immediately turn rolls out onto plate to cool.

SWEDISH TEA RING

⅓ portion BASIC SWEET
  DOUGH
¼ cup melted butter
½ cup brown sugar

1 teaspoon cinnamon
½ cup raisins or chopped
  nuts

When basic sweet dough is light, punch down and let rest for 10 minutes. Roll out into a rectangle on a lightly floured board and brush with half the melted butter. Sprinkle with brown sugar, cinnamon, and raisins or nuts.

Roll up lengthwise like a jelly roll, sealing edge. Place on greased baking sheet and form into a ring. Moisten ends of ring and pinch together.

With kitchen scissors, make deep diagonal cuts in the ring at intervals of about 1 inch. Turn each slice partly on its side. Brush with remaining butter, cover, and let rise for about 1 hour, or until double in bulk.

Bake in preheated 350° F. oven for 30 minutes. Remove from oven and, while warm, frost with confectioners' sugar icing.

This is a tea bread that is worth freezer space at all times. It's equally good for breakfast, served warm with honey or jam. It's also delicious toasted.

SALLY LUNN EGG BREAD
(Makes 4 loaves)

2 cups milk
1 cup (2 sticks) butter
¼ cup sugar
1 tablespoon salt
2 yeast cakes or envelopes
active dry yeast

1 cup lukewarm water
About 12 cups presifted
all-purpose flour
4 eggs, lightly beaten

Scald milk. Add butter, sugar, and salt and stir until butter is melted. Cool to lukewarm.

Soften yeast in the lukewarm water. When milk mixture is cooled, stir in softened yeast and beat in about 4 cups flour. Stir in eggs and gradually beat in about 6 cups flour. Beat until batter is smooth and elastic. Work in enough additional flour to make a dough which is soft but does not stick to hands. Cover and let rise for 1½ hours, or until double in bulk.

Punch dough down and turn out on lightly floured board.

Knead until dough is smooth and elastic. Cut into 4 equal portions. Form each portion into a loaf and put in greased baking pans (4½ × 8½ × 2½ inches). Cover and let rise for about 1 hour, or until dough is nicely rounded over tops of pans.

Bake in preheated 425° F. oven for 30 minutes, or until lightly browned. Turn loaves out onto cake racks to cool.

QUICK BREADS

Quick baking-powder breads, biscuits, muffins, pancakes, and waffles all freeze well, and may be stored in the freezer for as long as 3 months. So, when making a batch of baking-powder biscuits, muffins, pancakes, or waffles, make twice as many as you need and freeze those that are left over. When making a nut or fruit bread or a spicy coffeecake, it's just as easy to make and bake two as one. Eat one and store the other in the freezer. You're one up for a rainy day.

The breads may be served at room temperature, sliced and toasted, or served hot. They defrost in about 1 hour at room temperature; leave them in the freezer wrap until ready to slice and serve.

To serve hot, heat in a preheated 350° F. oven for 15 to 20 minutes.

Baking-powder biscuits, corn bread, and muffins do not need to be defrosted and are infinitely superior in all ways if served hot. Heat them directly from the freezer in a preheated 350° F. oven for 10 to 15 minutes.

Frozen waffles and regular pancakes may be defrosted and heated in a toaster.

Thin pancakes or crêpes defrost at room temperature in about 30 minutes, and are ready to be made into dozens of wonderfully good quick entrees and desserts.

RICH BAKING-POWDER BISCUITS
(Makes 2 dozen 2½-inch biscuits)

4 cups presifted flour　　　*2 teaspoons salt*
5 teaspoons double-acting　*1 cup shortening*
*　baking powder*　　　　　*1⅓ cups milk*

In mixing bowl combine flour, baking powder, and salt. With pastry blender or 2 knives cut in shortening until it is broken into fine particles. Add milk and stir gently with a fork until dough holds together.

Gather dough into a ball, turn out on lightly floured board, and knead gently with floured fingers about 10 kneading strokes. Roll out dough ½ inch thick and cut into biscuits with floured biscuit cutter.

Arrange biscuits on baking sheet about 1 inch apart.

Bake in preheated 425° F. oven for 12 to 15 minutes.

BUTTER BISCUITS
(Makes 1 dozen)

⅓ cup butter
½ RICH BAKING-POWDER BISCUIT dough
1 tablespoon sugar

Melt butter in an 8-inch square cake pan.

Roll out biscuit dough ½ inch thick and cut into strips about 4 inches long and 1½ inches wide.

Dip 1 strip at a time in the melted butter, turning to coat both sides, and arrange strips close together in same pan in which butter was melted. Sprinkle with sugar.

Bake in preheated 425° F. oven for 12 to 15 minutes.

Cool and freeze in the pan. When frozen, remove from pan, package, and return to freezer. Reheat in same pan in which biscuits were baked in a preheated 350° F. oven for 10 minutes.

CINNAMON APPLE BISCUITS
(Makes 1 dozen)

½ RICH BAKING-POWDER BISCUIT *dough*
2 tablespoons soft butter

2 *apples, peeled, cored, and finely chopped*
¼ *cup brown sugar*
1 *teaspoon cinnamon*

Roll dough out into a rectangle ¼ inch thick on lightly floured board.

Spread surface of dough with butter and sprinkle with apples, brown sugar, and cinnamon.

Roll up like a jelly roll and slice 1 inch thick. Arrange slices, cutside down, in greased muffin cups.

Bake in preheated 425° F. oven for 12 to 15 minutes.

Cool and freeze. When frozen, package and return to freezer. Reheat in muffin cups in 350° F. oven for 10 minutes.

HONEY BISCUITS
(Makes 1 dozen)

½ *cup honey*
¼ *cup butter*
½ RICH BAKING-POWDER BISCUIT *dough*

2 *tablespoons melted butter*
½ *cup brown sugar*
½ *teaspoon cinnamon*
½ *cup chopped nut meats*

Cream together the honey and the ¼ cup butter.

Spread mixture in bottom of an 8-inch square baking pan.

Roll out dough into a rectangle ¼ inch thick on lightly floured board. Spread surface with the 2 tablespoons melted butter, and sprinkle with sugar, cinnamon, and nuts. Roll up lengthwise like a jelly roll and cut into slices 1 inch thick. Arrange slices in the prepared pan and bake in a preheated 425° F. oven for 15 minutes. Immediately turn out onto plate to cool. When cool, wrap and freeze.

To defrost and serve

Return biscuits, honey-side down, to same 8-inch square pan. Reheat in preheated 350° F. oven for 10 to 15 minutes.

BANANA NUT BREAD
(Makes 2 loaves, each 8×4 inches)

1 cup butter	*2 teaspoons baking soda*
2 cups sugar	*6 small ripe bananas (2*
4 eggs	*cups) mashed*
4 cups presifted flour	*2 cups chopped pecans*
2 teaspoons salt	

In mixing bowl cream butter and sugar. Beat in eggs. Combine dry ingredients and stir into butter mixture alternately with bananas. Stir in pecans.

Turn batter into greased loaf pans and bake in preheated 350° F. oven for 40 to 50 minutes, or until loaves test done.

STEAMED BOSTON BROWN BREAD
(Makes two 1-pound loaves)

1 cup corn meal	*1 tablespoon water*
1 cup presifted all-purpose	*¾ cup molasses*
flour	*2 cups buttermilk*
1 cup whole-wheat flour	*1 cup raisins*
1 teaspoon salt	*2 tablespoons all-purpose*
1⅓ teaspoons baking soda	*flour*

In mixing bowl combine corn meal, the 1 cup all-purpose flour, whole-wheat flour, and salt.

Dissolve soda in water and stir in molasses. Stir molasses mixture into buttermilk. Gradually stir liquid into dry ingredients.

Mix raisins and the 2 tablespoons flour and stir into batter.

Divide batter into 2 greased 1-quart molds with tight covers.

Place molds on rack in kettle. Add boiling water to halfway up around sides of molds. Cover and steam for 3 hours, adding more water to the kettle as needed.

Unmold loaves and bake in a preheated 325° F. oven for 10 minutes.

Cool, wrap, and freeze.

PINEAPPLE NUT BREAD
(Makes four 1-pound loaves)

6 cups all-purpose flour
1 teaspoon baking soda
8 teaspoons double-acting
   baking powder
2 teaspoons salt
3 cups coarsely chopped
   nuts

¾ cup butter
3 cups light brown sugar
4 eggs
4 cups crushed pineapple
   with juice

Combine flour, soda, baking powder, and salt. Stir in nuts.

In large mixing bowl cream butter until light and fluffy. Beat in sugar a little at a time. Beat in eggs, one at a time, beating well after each addition.

Stir in flour-nut mixture alternately with the pineapple.

Divide into 4 greased 1-pound loaf pans and bake in preheated 350° F. oven for 50 to 60 minutes, or until bread tests done.

Cool for 5 minutes, then turn out on cake rack to cool.

Wrap and freeze.

WAFFLES

Keep a supply of baked waffles in your freezer. Make and bake them according to your favorite recipe. Cool thoroughly. Package in family-size portions with a double thickness of waxed paper between each. Freeze.

To defrost and serve

Reheat in toaster or bake on rack in a preheated 450° F. oven for 3 to 5 minutes.

PANCAKES

Pancakes in your freezer can also be a useful item. When baking a batch, always make extra to have on hand when time is short. Cool and package as for waffles.

To defrost and serve

Unwrap, rewrap in aluminum foil, and bake in preheated 450° F. oven for 15 to 20 minutes.

CREPES

Very thin pancakes and pancake skins are fun to make, but they do take time. They freeze well and can be used in so many ways, not only for desserts, but for appetizers and for luncheon dishes. You should have a stack of both crêpes with and without sugar, as well as the skins for egg rolls and blintzes. Package in stacks of 6 or a dozen with a double thickness of waxed paper between. Wrap in freezer paper, label, and freeze.

To defrost

Remove from freezer about 30 minutes before using.

PANCAKE SKINS FOR EGG ROLLS
AND BLINTZES
(Makes 36 rolls)

2 cups flour	4 eggs, beaten
2 cups water	1 teaspoon salt

Combine flour, water, eggs, and salt to make a thin batter. Pour batter into a large measuring cup or jug and stir occasionally. Heat a small frying pan about 6 inches in diameter and brush lightly with butter. Pour into it about 2 tablespoons batter and tip pan over the cup or jug, rotating it so that the bottom will be covered with a thin layer of batter and any excess batter will drain back into remaining batter.

Hold pan over moderate heat for about 30 seconds, or until the skin is dry. Bake on one side only. Shake out onto a damp towel and repeat, first heating the pan again thoroughly.

When all batter has been used, roll skins in a damp towel until ready to fill and cook, or freeze.

To freeze

Stack the cool skins with a square of waxed paper between each skin. Wrap in freezer paper, label, and freeze.

To defrost

Remove from freezer about 30 minutes before using.

RICH EGG CREPES
(Makes 32)

6 large eggs	1/4 teaspoon salt
1 1/2 cups presifted flour	2 cups milk
1 tablespoon sugar	

In mixing bowl beat eggs. Beat in flour, sugar, and salt. Gradually beat in milk and continue to beat for about 3 minutes. The batter should be smooth and thin. Pour into a 1-quart pitcher and let stand for 30 minutes before baking.

BASIC RECIPE FOR CREPES (*with sugar*)
(Makes 24)

1⅛ cups presifted flour	1½ cups milk
4 tablespoons sugar	1 tablespoon melted butter
Pinch of salt	1 tablespoon brandy or
3 eggs	cognac (*optional*)

In mixing bowl combine flour, sugar, and salt.
Beat eggs and gradually beat in milk.
Stir the egg-milk mixture into the dry ingredients and continue to stir until batter is smooth. Batter should be just thick enough to coat a spoon.
Stir in melted butter and brandy or cognac and let batter stand for 1 to 2 hours before using it. This improves the texture of the cakes.

LEMON CREPES WITH SUGAR
(Makes 12)

3 eggs	Grated rind of 1 lemon
½ cup presifted flour	1½ cups light cream
1 tablespoon sugar	6 tablespoons melted
¼ teaspoon salt	butter

Beat together eggs, flour, sugar, salt, and lemon rind. Gradually stir in light cream and butter. Let batter rest for at least 30 minutes before using.

CREPES WITHOUT SUGAR

Use any of the recipes above. Simply omit the sugar.

To cook crêpes

Heat a small frying pan from 5 to 6 inches in diameter until very hot. The crêpes must cook quickly or they will be tough. Put ½ teaspoon butter in the pan and swirl pan to coat bottom and sides with butter.

As soon as the butter stops foaming and begins to turn golden brown, pour in about 2 tablespoons crêpe batter, and again tilt pan in a circular motion to spread batter evenly and thinly over bottom of pan. This must be done quickly before the batter has a chance to set. Cook crêpe for about 1 minute, or until set and brown on one side; turn and brown other side.

Turn crêpe out onto absorbent paper.

Serve warm with a dessert sauce, honey, jam, or preserves or, as the Swedes do, simply sprinkle with confectioners' sugar and a wedge of lemon. Or cool and freeze.

CAKES

Cakes, baked and frosted or not as preferred, freeze well and remain fresh in the freezer for as long as 3 months. The texture of angel food remains the same, but the texture of buttercakes becomes slightly finer and firmer during frozen storage. Fruitcakes actually improve with freezing as the flavor of the fruits and spices becomes blended. They remain moist and do not crumble when sliced after they are defrosted. Filled cakes are not recommended for the freezer, as the filling soaks into the cake and may cause sogginess. Better to freeze the layers and put them together with filling and frost them after they are defrosted.

Cakes may be frozen whole, in meal-size wedges, or in individual slices (good for the lunch box). Also the entire cake can be sliced before it is frozen so that any number of slices desired may be removed without defrosting the entire cake.

Bake cakes as usual. Cool quickly and freeze before packaging.

FROSTED CAKES

Uncooked butter frostings made with confectioners' sugar are the best to use on cakes destined for the freezer. Boiled frostings crumble when cut after as short a time as 2 to 3 weeks' storage, and egg-white icings become frothy. Cool the cake thoroughly before icing or decorating. Place on a sturdy cardboard base and put in the freezer until the icing is solid. Remove and overwrap cardboard base and cake in moisture-vaporproof paper, or use a plastic cake box designed especially for the freezer, and return to the freezer.

Unwrap frozen frosted cakes immediately after removing from freezer to prevent the frosting from sticking to the wrappings. If frozen in plastic cake box, leave covered. Let stand at room temperature for 50 to 60 minutes before serving.

UNFROSTED CAKES

Cool cakes before wrapping or packaging. Since cakes do not freeze solidly, some outer protection is needed to prevent them from being crushed during storage. Plastic containers are best, but heavy cardboard cartons may be used. Wrap layers of cake separately, then wrap two or three together depending on their ultimate use. Fruitcakes do not need support. They may be wrapped in transparent film and overwrapped with freezer paper or aluminum foil. Cake layers will defrost at room temperature in 30 minutes. Keep uniced cakes in their original wrappings to prevent moisture from condensing on the surface. Frozen cake layers may be unwrapped and filled and frosted without defrosting.

Unfrosted angel food, spongecakes, and butter cakes keep well for 6 to 8 months. Fruitcakes will keep a year or longer.

CAKE BATTERS

While cake batters may be frozen, it is much better to freeze the baked cake. In an emergency, however, pour the batter into the pan in which it is to be baked. Freeze batter in the pan, then package pan and batter in moisture-vaporproof paper.

Defrost batter for a large cake for about 1 hour at room temperature, then bake as usual. Batter frozen in 8-inch layer-cake pans may be baked without defrosting. Bake at 375° F. for 35 to 40 minutes, or until layers test done. Do not store batters for longer than 2 months, but the sooner used the better.

CUPCAKES

Cupcakes are a good item to keep in the freezer for lunch box, teas, or a quick dessert. They may be frozen plain or frosted. Try scooping out the centers, filling with a scoop of ice cream, and sprinkling with chopped nuts before freezing.

Cupcake batter may be frozen in paper baking cups in pans. When frozen, remove from the pan and package. Return to the pans when ready to bake, without defrosting. Bake in a preheated 375° F. oven for 15 minutes; reduce oven temperature to 350° F. and continue to bake for 15 minutes longer. Do not store longer than 6 weeks.

JELLY ROLLS

These may be filled with butter frosting, sugared fruits and berries, jams or marmalades or jellies, or with softened ice cream. Freeze before wrapping for frozen storage.

PETITS FOURS

These may be made weeks ahead of a party and frozen. Freeze on baking sheets, then package in layers with a double thickness of waxed paper between the layers. Return to freezer.

FILLINGS AND FROSTINGS

If you are going to store cake layers in your freezer, then you will also want a supply of fillings and frostings, for these frequently take as long to make as to prepare a cake batter for the oven. Pastry creams, cornstarch egg custard, and fruit-flavored cornstarch fillings all freeze well. Cool them quickly over ice water or in the refrigerator, then package, label, and freeze. To defrost, remove from freezer and store in refrigerator overnight. They should be kept cold at all times.

The best icings are the butter-base type. Cream cheese, fudge, or penuche type also freeze well either in containers or on the cakes themselves.

VANILLA BUTTER ICING
(Fills and frosts two 9-inch layers)

½ cup soft butter
3½ cups confectioners'
   sugar (*sift if lumpy*)

Dash of salt
¼ cup light cream
2 teaspoons vanilla

Cream butter with 1 cup of the sugar. Stir in salt. Stir in remaining sugar alternately with the cream and vanilla.

Chocolate Butter Icing
   Add 3 squares unsweetened chocolate, melted, to the butter.

Lemon Butter Icing
   Subsitute lemon juice for the cream and omit vanilla. Tint icing a pale yellow if desired.

Orange Butter Icing
   Substitute orange juice for the cream and omit vanilla. Add a little grated orange rind and tint pale orange if desired.

DATE CREAM FROSTING
(Fills and frosts two 8-inch layers)

*1 (3-ounce) package soft
  cream cheese
1 tablespoon milk
2½ cups confectioners'
  sugar (sift if lumpy)*

*1 teaspoon vanilla
½ cup cut dates
¼ cup chopped nut meats*

Combine cheese and milk. Gradually stir in sugar, beating well after each addition. Stir in remaining ingredients.

ORANGE EGG FROSTING
(Frosts one 10-inch angel cake or spongecake)

*1 egg yolk
1 tablespoon soft butter
1½ cups confectioners'
  sugar (sift if lumpy)*

*2 tablespoons orange juice
1 tablespoon grated orange
  rind*

Beat egg yolk well with butter. Gradually beat in sugar alternately with orange juice and grated orange rind.

FRENCH COFFEE ICING
(Fills and frosts two 9-inch layers)

*2 tablespoons instant
  coffee
4 tablespoons boiling water
1 cup soft butter*

*¼ teaspoon salt
2½ cups confectioners'
  sugar (sift if lumpy)
1 tablespoon rum*

Dissolve coffee in boiling water.

Combine butter and salt. Beat in confectioners' sugar alternately with coffee. Stir in rum and let stand for 10 minutes. Beat again thoroughly.

FRENCH CHOCOLATE BUTTER CREAM
(Makes enough to fill and frost two 8-inch layers
or 12 cupcakes)

1 (6-ounce) package
semisweet chocolate
pieces
⅓ cup water

4 egg yolks
1 teaspoon vanilla
½ cup (1 stick) soft
butter

In small saucepan combine chocolate and water. Stir over low heat until chocolate is melted and mixture is smooth and hot. In mixing bowl of an electric beater beat egg yolks until thick and pale in color. Gradually beat in hot chocolate mixture. Add vanilla. With beater at high speed, add butter, bit by bit, beating until frosting is smooth and thick. In warm weather it may be necessary to chill the frosting before using it. Use immediately or pour into pint container and freeze.

To defrost

Remove from freezer and let defrost at room temperature for 2 hours.

CHOCOLATE FILLING

Cream together ¼ cup butter and 1 cup confectioners' sugar. Stir in 2 ounces unsweetened chocolate, melted, and ½ teaspoon vanilla.

THICK PASTRY CREAM
FOR CAKE FILLINGS OR FRUIT TARTS
(Makes 5 cups cream)

1 quart milk
8 egg yolks
¾ cup sugar

¾ cup flour
1 tablespoon cornstarch
1 tablespoon vanilla

Heat milk to scalding.
In saucepan combine egg yolks, sugar, flour, and cornstarch.

Gradually stir in the hot milk and cook, stirring rapidly, for about 3 minutes, or until cream is smooth and thick. Remove from heat and stir in vanilla. Cool thoroughly and quickly.

Strain into cup or pint containers and freeze.

To defrost

Empty cream into saucepan and heat over hot, not boiling, water, stirring occasionally.

FRUIT TART

Bake an 8-inch pie shell. Defrost 1 pint THICK PASTRY CREAM and empty into pie shell. Top with whole strawberries, raspberries, peaches, blueberries, or dark sweet cherries, pitted and halved. Sprinkle generously with confectioners' sugar and chill until serving time.

For a thin pastry cream

Make as above, but reduce flour to ⅔ cup.

It's very difficult to know where to begin or stop in giving cake recipes, for all freeze well. There just aren't any "don'ts" when it comes to cakes. Your favorite recipes for buttercakes, angel, sponge, and chiffons, graham-cracker tortes, cheesecakes, upside-down cakes, pound cakes, and fruitcakes are all suitable for freezer storage. Herewith are a few deluxe specialties that are, perhaps, new to you, and are not found in the average cookbook.

CHEESECAKE
(Makes one 8-inch cake)

1½ tablespoons butter
½ cup graham-cracker
    crumbs
4 (3-ounce) packages
    soft cream cheese
¾ cup sugar

4 eggs, separated
2 tablespoons flour
½ teaspoon salt
2 teaspoons vanilla
2 cups scalded cream

Spread the butter thickly over the sides of an 8-inch spring-form pan. Turn pan on its side and sprinkle with cracker crumbs. Keep turning pan and sprinkling with crumbs until sides are coated. Turn pan upright and sprinkle remaining crumbs on bottom. Freeze for 30 minutes.

In mixing bowl (use an electric beater if available) beat together cream cheese, sugar, egg yolks, flour, salt, and vanilla. When mixture is smooth, gradually beat in the hot cream.

Beat egg whites until stiff but not dry. Add to cheese mixture and fold in lightly but thoroughly. Pour mixture into prepared pan and set pan in a shallow pan containing 1 inch warm water. Bake in preheated 300° F. oven for 1½ hours. Cool, chill for 6 hours in refrigerator, then turn out of pan and freeze before wrapping.

To defrost

Remove from freezer about 2 hours before serving and let defrost in wrappings.

CHERRY CHEESECAKE
(Makes two 8-inch cheesecakes)

3 cups crushed
graham-cracker crumbs
2 cups sugar
½ cup (1 stick) butter,
melted
1 (8-ounce) container
cottage cheese
1 (8-ounce) package
cream cheese

2 eggs
2 teaspoons vanilla
2 (1-pound 3-ounce)
cans sour pitted cherries
2 tablespoons cornstarch
Few drops red food
coloring
6 tablespoons sugar

Combine graham-cracker crumbs, ½ cup of the sugar, and the melted butter. Line two 8-inch spring-form pans with the crumb mixture and set aside.

In mixing bowl beat remaining 1½ cups sugar with cottage cheese, cream cheese, eggs, and vanilla, until mixture is very smooth. Use an electric beater if possible and beat for about 10 minutes.

Divide cheese mixture into the 2 prepared pans and bake in a preheated 350° F. oven for 25 to 30 minutes. Remove from oven and cool.

Drain cherry juice into a saucepan and stir in cornstarch, food coloring and the 6 tablespoons sugar. Bring to a boil, stirring.

Top cheesecakes with the drained cherries and cover with the cherry glaze. Chill and serve, or freeze.

To defrost

Defrost at room temperature for 2 to 3 hours.

PINEAPPLE TORTE
(Makes two 8-inch layer cakes)

8 eggs, separated	2 teaspoons baking
2 cups sugar	powder
18 zwieback, finely	2 cups crushed pineapple,
ground	drained
2 cups ground nuts	1 quart heavy cream

Grease and flour four 8-inch layer-cake pans.

In mixing bowl beat egg yolks and sugar until mixture is pale and very thick. Use an electric beater if possible.

Combine crumbs, nuts, and baking powder and stir into egg-yolk mixture.

Beat egg whites until very stiff and fold into egg-yolk mixture. Fold in crushed pineapple.

Divide batter into prepared pans and bake in a preheated 350° F. oven for 25 minutes, or until layers test done. Turn out on cake racks to cool. When cool, whip cream until stiff. Put layers together and frost top and sides with the whipped cream. Chill until ready to serve, or chill, then freeze.

To defrost

Defrost in refrigerator for 4 to 6 hours.

GENOISE
(Makes one 8-inch layer cake)

½ cup (*1 stick*) *sweet*
  butter
¾ *cup sugar*

6 *large eggs*
1½ *cups sifted cake flour*
1 *teaspoon vanilla*

Melt butter and set aside to cool.

In mixing bowl of an electric beater combine sugar and eggs. Beat at top speed for 5 to 8 minutes, or until the mixture is as thick as a cake batter and holds soft peaks when the beater is withdrawn.

Fold in half the flour, then the melted butter, being careful not to include the milky sediment in bottom of pan.

Fold in remaining flour.

It is very difficult to get the flour mixed into the egg-sugar mixture without releasing the air beaten into the eggs. The best way to do it is with the hand, turning the batter over and over from bottom of mixing bowl to top. When thoroughly mixed, fold in vanilla.

Divide batter into 2 greased and floured 8-inch cake pans and bake in preheated 325° F. oven for 35 to 40 minutes, or until layers test done.

Run spatula around cake to loosen from pan, and turn out on cake rack to cool. Cool thoroughly and put the layers together with filling and frost top, or freeze the layers.

To defrost layers

Let defrost at room temperature in wrapping paper for 30 minutes.

NUT TORTE

2 cups heavy cream
½ cup sugar
2½ cups ground nuts
1 teaspoon vanilla

2 (8-inch) layers
Génoise, freshly baked
or defrosted

Whip cream until stiff. Fold in sugar, 2 cups of the nuts, and vanilla. Put Génoise layers together and frost top and sides with the nut-cream. Sprinkle with remaining ½ cup nuts.

BITTER CHOCOLATE CAKE
(Makes one 9-inch layer cake)

5 ounces unsweetened
  chocolate, chopped
1 cup milk
1 cup granulated sugar
3 eggs, separated
½ cup butter

1 cup light brown sugar,
  firmly packed
2 cups sifted cake flour
1 teaspoon baking soda
½ teaspoon salt
¼ cup coffee
1 teaspoon vanilla

In saucepan combine chocolate and ½ cup of the milk. Stir over low heat until chocolate is melted and mixture is smooth. Stir in the granulated sugar and 1 egg yolk and cook, stirring, for 3 minutes. Cool.

Cream together butter and brown sugar until mixture is light and fluffy. Beat in remaining egg yolks, one at a time, beating well after each addition. Stir in chocolate mixture.

Sift together cake flour, soda, and salt.

Combine remaining milk, coffee, and vanilla.

Add dry ingredients to chocolate mixture alternately with liquid, mixing well after each addition.

Beat egg whites until stiff but not dry and fold into cake batter. Divide batter into 2 greased 9-inch layer-cake pans and bake in a preheated 375° F. oven for 25 to 30 minutes, or until layers test done.

Turn cakes out onto racks to cool, then put together and frost with FRENCH COFFEE ICING. Freeze entire cake or part of it. When frozen, wrap, label, and return to freezer.

To defrost

Remove from freezer and unwrap. Defrost at room temperature for 1 hour.

ORANGE CAKE
(Makes one 9-inch tube cake)

1 cup butter	*1 teaspoon baking soda*
1 cup sugar	*1¼ cups sour cream*
3 eggs, separated	*Grated rind of 1 orange*
2 cups presifted	*1 cup chopped walnuts*
all-purpose flour	*½ cup sugar*
1 teaspoon baking powder	*1 cup orange juice*

Cream together butter and sugar until mixture is fluffy. Add egg yolks, one at a time, beating well after each addition.

Combine flour, baking powder, and soda. Stir dry ingredients into butter mixture alternately with the sour cream. Stir in orange rind and walnuts.

Beat egg whites until stiff, but not dry, and fold into batter. Turn batter into a greased 9-inch tube pan and bake in a preheated 350° F. oven for 50 to 55 minutes, or until cake tests done. Remove from oven.

Combine the ½ cup sugar and orange juice. Pour over hot cake while it is still in the pan. Let cake cool before removing from pan.

Freeze, then wrap, label, and store.

To defrost

Remove from freezer and defrost, in wrappings, for 1 hour at room temperature.

WALNUT TORTE
(Makes one 3-layer cake)

6 eggs
¾ cup sugar
1⅓ cups cake flour
¾ cup strawberry jam
½ cup Grand Marnier or
    other liqueur

3 cups heavy cream
½ cup sugar
½ cup chopped walnuts
2 tablespoons Grand
    Marnier
Whole walnuts

Beat eggs and ¾ cup sugar with electric beater for 5 to 8 minutes, or until very thick and pale in color and it takes some time to level out when beater is withdrawn. Sift flour into egg mixture and fold in gently with palm of hand. Divide batter into three 8-inch layer-cake pans lined with waxed paper. Bake in a preheated 350° F. oven for 20 to 25 minutes, or until cake layers test done. Cool for 5 minutes, then turn out on cake rack to cool. Spread tops of all three layers thinly with strawberry jam and sprinkle with the ½ cup Grand Marnier.

Whip cream until stiff. Beat in the ½ cup sugar and fold in nuts and the 2 tablespoons Grand Marnier. Put cake layers together and frost top and sides with the whipped cream. Garnish with whole walnuts. Freeze, then wrap, label, and store.

To defrost

Remove from freezer, unwrap, and defrost in refrigerator for about 3 hours before serving.

JELLY ROLL
(Makes one 18-inch roll)

5 large eggs, separated
4 tablespoons sugar
3 tablespoons presifted
    all-purpose flour

1 teaspoon vanilla
Jam or jelly

Oil a large baking sheet (18×12 inches), line it with waxed paper, and oil again.

Beat egg yolks and sugar until mixture is thick and pale in color. Fold in flour and vanilla.

Beat egg whites until stiff, but not dry, and fold into egg-yolk mixture.

Spread batter evenly on baking sheet. Bake in preheated 350° F. oven for 12 to 15 minutes. Do not overbake. Loosen paper from sheet, sprinkle top with a little granulated sugar, and turn out, sugar side down, onto a strip of waxed paper. Carefully remove paper from bottom of cake and spread a flavorful jam or jelly lightly over bottom. Roll lengthwise into a long, thin roll. To serve, sprinkle generously with confectioners' sugar. Or cool completely and freeze. When frozen, wrap, label, and return to freezer.

To defrost and serve

Remove from freezer and defrost in wrapping paper at room temperature for 1 hour. Sprinkle generously with confectioners' sugar as above.

COOKIES

Baked cookies may be frozen, but there is little logic in filling valuable freezer space with them. Most baked cookies stay fresh in cooky jars for many days, longer at least than they can be preserved from a hungry household. I've never known cookies to go stale in my house! Freezing the cooky dough is the answer for a constant supply of freshly baked cookies. The unbaked dough keeps well for 6 months. When you have time, double or triple a favorite cooky recipe. Bake a batch and fill the cooky jar and freeze the rest of the dough. Often the oven is hot from a casserole, roast, cake, or pie. Pop a tray of cookies into the oven when the other food comes out.

BAKED COOKIES

Baked cookies will keep in the freezer for 8 months. Bake as usual, cool quickly, and freeze before packaging. Pack in cartons,

148

separating layers with a double thickness of freezer paper, over-wrap, label, and freeze. To serve, defrost cookies at room temperature for 10 to 15 minutes.

ROLLED COOKY DOUGH

Roll out dough and cut into various shapes. Stack the cutouts in cartons with a double thickness of freezer paper between layers. Overwrap, label, and freeze. Bake without defrosting. Will keep for 6 months.

UNROLLED COOKY DOUGH

Form the dough into long rolls or rectangular bricks, wrap in freezer paper, and freeze. Remove a roll and defrost just long enough to be able to cut into thin slices. Arrange slices on greased baking sheet and bake. Will keep well for at least 6 months.

DROP COOKY DOUGH

Drop the dough on a baking sheet by the spoonful, about ¼ inch apart, in exactly the same manner as if you were going to bake the cookies. Freeze until frozen. Remove the frozen drops of dough from freezer and pack in layers in cartons with a double thickness of freezer paper between layers. To bake, place the frozen drops on greased baking sheet and bake without defrosting. Will keep for 6 months.

BASIC DROP COOKIES
(Makes 8 dozen 2-inch drops)

1 cup butter
1½ cups sugar
2 eggs
4 cups presifted
  all-purpose flour

½ teaspoon salt
1 teaspoon cream of tartar
1 teaspoon baking soda
1 cup milk
1 teaspoon vanilla

In mixing bowl cream butter and sugar until mixture is light and fluffy. Add eggs, one at a time, beating well after each addition.

Combine flour, salt, cream of tartar, and baking soda. Add dry ingredients to butter mixture alternately with the milk and vanilla.

Drop batter from teaspoon onto greased baking sheet. Freeze or bake in preheated 375° F. oven for 10 to 12 minutes.

Spice Drops
Add to dry ingredients 1 teaspoon cinnamon, 1 teaspoon nutmeg, and 1 teaspoon ginger.

Nut Drops
Add to butter-egg mixture 2 cups chopped nuts.

Fruit Drops
Add to butter-egg mixture 2 cups cut dates and 1 cup seedless raisins.

Chocolate Drops
Stir 1 (6-ounce) package semisweet chocolate pieces into butter-egg mixture.

CHOCOLATE NUT DROPS
(Makes 6 dozen 2-inch drops)

2 (6-ounce) packages semisweet chocolate pieces	2 cups presifted all-purpose flour
1 cup butter	1 teaspoon baking soda
1 cup sugar	1 teaspoon salt
1 egg	½ cup milk
	1 cup chopped nuts

Melt half the chocolate pieces. Cream butter and sugar until mixture is light and fluffy. Beat in egg and melted chocolate. Combine flour, soda, and salt and stir into butter-egg mixture alternately with the milk. Stir in nuts and remaining chocolate pieces. Drop batter from a teaspoon onto greased baking sheet and freeze, or bake in a preheated 350° F. oven for 12 to 15 minutes.

PEANUT BUTTER COOKIES
(Makes 4 dozen 1½-inch cookies)

½ cup butter
½ cup brown sugar,
  firmly packed
½ cup sugar
1 egg

½ cup peanut butter
1¼ cups presifted
  all-purpose flour
½ teaspoon baking soda

Cream butter and sugars until mixture is fluffy. Beat in egg and peanut butter. Combine flour and soda and stir into peanut butter mixture. Form dough into small balls and arrange on ungreased baking sheet. Flatten with a fork dipped in flour. Freeze, or bake in a preheated 375° F. oven for 10 to 12 minutes.

ALMOND BALLS
(Makes 5 dozen 2-inch balls)

1 cup butter
1½ cups confectioners'
  sugar
1 egg
1 teaspoon vanilla
½ teaspoon almond extract
2½ cups presifted
  all-purpose flour

1 teaspoon salt
1 teaspoon baking soda
1 teaspoon cream of
  tartar
5 dozen blanched almonds

Cream butter and sugar together until mixture is light and fluffy. Beat in egg, vanilla, and almond extract. Combine dry ingredients and stir into butter-egg mixture. Chill for at least 1 hour. Form dough into small balls with floured fingers and arrange on greased baking sheet. Into the center of each ball press a blanched almond. Freeze, or bake in a preheated 375° F. oven for 12 to 15 minutes.

Coconut Balls
  Instead of pressing an almond into center of each ball, roll it in moist shredded coconut before freezing or baking.

Cherry Nut Balls

Stir into butter-egg mixture 1 cup finely chopped walnuts or pecans. Form into balls as above and press a candied cherry into center of each instead of a blanched almond.

CHOCOLATE VANILLA PINWHEELS
(Makes 3 dozen 2-inch cookies)

½ cup butter
½ cup sugar
1 egg yolk
1¾ cups presifted
   all-purpose flour

½ teaspoon salt
3 tablespoons light cream
1 teaspoon vanilla
1 square unsweetened
   chocolate, melted

Cream butter and sugar until mixture is light. Beat in egg yolk. Combine dry ingredients and stir into egg mixture alternately with the cream and vanilla.

Divide dough in half and into one half work in the melted chocolate. On lightly floured board roll out chocolate dough thinly into a rectangle. Roll out vanilla dough to same size and thickness and place on top of the chocolate dough. Trim edges and roll lengthwise like a jelly roll. Wrap in freezer paper and chill for several hours. Freeze, or slice crosswise ¼ inch thick and place cut-side down on greased baking sheet. Bake in preheated 350° F. oven for 8 to 10 minutes.

LEMON PECAN TEA WAFERS
(Makes 5 dozen 2-inch wafers)

½ cup butter
1 cup sugar
1 egg
1 tablespoon lemon juice
1 tablespoon grated lemon
   rind

2 cups presifted
   all-purpose flour
1 teaspoon baking powder
¼ teaspoon salt
1 cup chopped pecans

Cream butter and sugar until mixture is light and fluffy. Beat in egg, lemon juice, and rind. Combine dry ingredients and stir into egg mixture. Stir in nuts. Shape dough into rolls, wrap in freezer paper, and chill. Freeze, or slice crosswise thinly, place on greased baking sheet, and bake in a 350° F. oven for 12 to 15 minutes.

PIES

Pies, baked or unbaked, pie shells, baked or unbaked, and rolled and cut pastry may be frozen for future use and, when you make a pie, it is almost as easy to make several. Bake and eat one and freeze the rest. Then you will always have a pie ready to pop into the oven for either baking or heating, but more important, you'll have strawberry rhubarb pie in late summer and fresh peach pie in November because you have preserved the garden-fresh fruit between crusts.

In general, pies that are frozen unbaked have flakier, more tender crusts and fresher flavor than those baked before freezing, and the very best are double-crust such as fruit, berry, or mince. But baked pie shells filled with chiffon mixtures, creams, lemon and pumpkin custards are also delicious. Meringue toppings toughen and separate during frozen storage, so save the topping to put on and brown in the oven before serving.

UNBAKED PIES

Make pies in the usual way in metal, glass, or special metal-rimmed paper baking plates. Don't cut vents in the top crust. They may be packaged and frozen in the pie plate or may be frozen first, removed from the pie plate, and then wrapped. Package in freezer paper and protect them from damage by inserting them in a carton or plastic pie container. Unbaked frozen pies need no defrosting. Cut vents in top crust and bake in a preheated 425° F. oven for 45 to 50 minutes, or until the crust is golden. Don't store longer than 3 months.

BAKED PIES

Make and bake pies according to your favorite recipes. Let them cool completely, then package them in the pie plate in

freezer paper and freeze. Defrost for 45 minutes at room temperature, or defrost in a slow 250° to 300° F. oven for 30 minutes and
serve warm. Baked pies will keep for 5 to 6 months.

FILLED PIE SHELLS

Baked pie shells filled with chiffon or cream mixtures should be
frozen before they are wrapped. To protect from damage, insert
the wrapped pie in a sturdy box or plastic container. Defrost at
room temperature for 45 minutes. They may be garnished with
whipped cream before they are frozen, but this addition is best
added just before serving. For a meringue topping, defrost the pie,
then cover with meringue and bake until the meringue is browned.
These pies will keep well in your freezer for 6 months.

PIE FILLINGS WITHOUT CRUST

Often when fresh fruits are in season you wish you had time to
make a batch of pies for the freezer. Perhaps you have enough time
to make the filling, even if you don't have those extra minutes to
make the crust and put the filling between the rolled dough. Here is
the answer.

Make the filling according to your favorite recipe. Line a 9-inch
pie plate with heavy-duty aluminum foil, letting it extend about 6
inches above the rim of the plate. Fill foil-lined pan with the pie
mixture, cover loosely with overhanging foil, and freeze until filling
is firm. When frozen, remove from pie plate and double-fold the
edges of the foil to make an airtight package. Label and return to
the freezer. Frozen in this manner, the filling will keep for as long
as 6 months.

To bake a pie

Line a 9-inch pie plate with pastry. Remove filling from freezer,
unwrap, and place in lined pie plate. Dot with butter, sprinkle with
spices if desired, and cover with the top crust. Slash top crust to allow steam to escape and bake in a preheated 425° F. oven for 45
to 50 minutes, or until golden brown. Serve hot or warm.

RICH PASTRY
(Makes six 2-crust pies or 12 pie shells)

12 cups (3 pounds)
presifted all-purpose
flour
2 tablespoons salt

6 cups (3 pounds)
shortening
2¼ to 2½ cups water

In large mixing bowl combine flour and salt. Cut in shortening with pastry blender until mixture resembles meal. Sprinkle water over flour mixture, ½ cup at a time, and mix with a fork until flour is moistened. With hands gather dough into a ball and divide into 12 portions.

2-Crust Pie

Roll out 1 portion of dough into a circle ⅛ inch thick and about 1½ inches in diameter larger than pie plate. Plates may be either 8 or 9 inches in diameter. Fit circle of pastry into plate and trim overhanging edge.

Put in desired filling.

Roll out another portion of dough ⅛ inch thick. To bake immediately, fold dough in half and cut several slits for steam to escape. Omit this step if pie is for the freezer. Transfer pastry to filled pie plate and trim edge, leaving ½ inch overhanging. Fold edge of top pastry under edge of lower pastry. Flute edge. Bake according to directions for pie recipe, or freeze. When frozen, remove pie from plate and wrap. Label and return to freezer.

To freeze baked pie: let cool completely, then freeze as above.

1-Crust Pie

Roll out 1 portion of the dough into a circle ⅛ inch thick and about 2 inches larger in diameter than pie plate. Fit dough loosely into pie plate and trim edge, leaving ½ inch overhanging. Fold overhanging edge back and under. Build up a fluted edge. Fill and bake according to recipe. Cool thoroughly before freezing. When frozen, wrap and store. To serve, defrost at room temperature for 45 minutes.

Pie Shells
Make as above, but do not fill. Prick bottom and sides of pastry with fork tines and freeze. Or bake in a preheated 425° F. oven for 12 to 15 minutes, or until golden brown. Cool, wrap, and freeze.

SWEET PASTRY FOR FRUIT PIES, TARTS, OR LATTICE-TOPPED PIES
(Makes two 2-crust pies, 4 open tarts, or pie shells, or 3 lattice-topped pies)

4 cups presifted all-purpose flour	1 pound butter, sliced
1 teaspoon salt	4 egg yolks
½ cup sugar	3 to 4 tablespoons water

In mixing bowl combine flour, salt, and sugar. Make a well in center and in the well put the butter, egg yolks, and water. Work center ingredients to a smooth paste, then knead in the flour. Divide into 2 or 3 portions. Form each portion into a ball, wrap in waxed paper, and chill for 30 minutes for easier rolling.

2-EGG MERINGUE

2 egg whites
¼ teaspoon cream of tartar
4 tablespoons sugar

Beat egg whites until frothy. Add cream of tartar and continue to beat until egg whites are stiff enough to hold a peak. Gradually beat in the sugar and continue to beat until meringue is stiff and glossy.

3-EGG MERINGUE

Make as above, using 3 egg whites and 6 tablespoons sugar. Do not increase amount of cream of tartar.

4-EGG MERINGUE

Make as above, using 4 egg whites and ½ cup sugar. Do not increase amount of cream of tartar.

CURRANT TART
(Makes one 9- or 10-inch tart)

Pastry for a double-crust
  pie
1 cup currants
6 tablespoons sugar

½ cup broken walnuts
4 tablespoons butter
Juice of 1 lemon
Grated rind of ½ lemon

Make pastry and divide in half.

Roll out half the pastry on lightly floured board and cut into a round 9 or 10 inches in diameter. Transfer to baking sheet. Sprinkle pastry with currants, keeping them ½ inch away from outer edge. Sprinkle with sugar and nuts. Dot with butter. Sprinkle with lemon juice and grated rind.

Roll out second half of pastry and cut into a round about 1 inch larger in diameter than the bottom round. Place over first round. Tuck overhanging edge under bottom pastry and flute edge. Freeze on baking sheet. When frozen, remove from baking sheet, wrap, label, and return to freezer.

To bake fresh or frozen

Cut slashes in top crust to allow steam to escape. Place on baking sheet and bake in a preheated 425° F. oven for 35 minutes if fresh; 45 minutes if frozen.

Fruit and berry pies are my favorite. I enjoy them at any time of the day, even for breakfast. Freshly baked cherry, blueberry, rhubarb, or apple pie for breakfast is nothing new—it's an old New England custom. Try it sometime and see what a refreshing change it is from bacon and eggs! Here are two of my favorite apple pies, but both are a little rich for breakfast.

APPLE APRICOT TART
(Makes one 8-inch tart)

*Pastry for a lattice-topped
  pie*
*3 large cooking apples,
  peeled, cored, and
  thinly sliced*
1 tablespoon lemon juice

¼ teaspoon nutmeg
*½ cup broken walnuts,
  pecans, or pistachios*
12 ounces apricot jam
1½ tablespoons butter

Line an 8-inch pie plate with pastry. Cover neatly with apple slices beginning in center and overlapping in circles to the edge. Sprinkle apples with lemon juice, nutmeg, and nuts. Spread with apricot jam and dot with butter.

Cover filling with a lattice topping.

Freeze, then wrap and return to freezer.

To bake fresh or frozen

Bake in a preheated 425° F. oven for 40 minutes if fresh; 45 to 50 if frozen.

TART TATIN
(Makes one 9-inch tart)

This tart must be made and frozen in a glass pie dish.

½ cup (1 stick) butter
*1 cup brown sugar, firmly
  packed*
*4 large apples, peeled
  and thinly sliced*

Nutmeg
Pastry for a 1-crust pie

Spread pie plate with half the butter and sprinkle with half the sugar. Cover the sugar with even layers of the apple slices. Sprinkle with remaining sugar, dot with butter, and sprinkle with nutmeg.

Cover fruit with a round of pastry. The edge may be fluted, but do not press it against the rim of the plate.

Bake the tart in a 425° F. oven for 40 minutes, or until crust is browned, fruit is tender, and the butter and sugar have begun to caramelize. Finish and serve, or cool quickly and freeze, then wrap and return to freezer.

To finish and serve immediately

Remove from oven and place directly over medium heat. Watch carefully until brown sugar and butter mixture is caramelized, being careful that it does not burn. Cover tart with serving plate and reverse the plate so the tart will slip out, crust side down. Sprinkle with shaved almonds and serve with lightly whipped cream or with sour cream.

To defrost and serve

Unwrap frozen tart and reheat in a 350° F. oven for 20 minutes. Finish and serve as above.

PUMPKIN PIE
(Makes two 9-inch pies)

Pastry for two 1-crust
    pies
3 cups canned pumpkin
1½ cups sugar
1 teaspoon salt
1 teaspoon ginger
½ teaspoon nutmeg
6 eggs, beaten
2½ cups milk
1½ cups heavy cream

Line pie plates with pastry and flute edges.

Combine pumpkin, sugar, salt, and spices. Add eggs, milk, and cream and blend thoroughly. Divide filling into the two prepared plates and bake in a preheated 425° F. oven for 15 minutes. Reduce oven temperature to 350° F. and continue to bake for 30 minutes longer, or until filling is set.

Serve warm with whipped cream, sprinkled with a little ginger, or cool thoroughly and freeze.

To defrost

Defrost at room temperature for 1½ hours, or warm in a 350° F. oven for 20 minutes.

Rum-Nut Pumpkin Pie
Substitute ½ cup dark rum for ½ cup of the milk. Sprinkle pastry in each plate with ½ cup chopped walnuts or pecans before adding filling.

PECAN PIE
(Makes two 9-inch pies)

Pastry for two 1-crust pies *¼ cup flour*
2 cups pecan halves *4 cups dark corn syrup*
6 eggs *2 teaspoons vanilla*
2 tablespoons sugar *½ teaspoon salt*

Line pie plates with pastry and flute edges. Sprinkle pastry in each plate with half the pecans.

Beat eggs until light. Add sugar and flour and beat well. Stir in corn syrup, vanilla, and salt. Divide filling into the two prepared pans. Bake in a preheated 350° F. oven for 45 to 50 minutes, or until filling is set.

Serve warm with whipped cream, or cool thoroughly and freeze.

To defrost

Defrost at room temperature for 1½ hours, or heat in a 350° F. oven for 20 minutes.

BUTTERSCOTCH CREAM PIE
(Makes two 9-inch pies)

4 tablespoons flour
4 tablespoons cornstarch
1 teaspoon salt
1½ cups brown sugar,
   firmly packed
4 cups milk

6 egg yolks
2 teaspoons vanilla
2 tablespoons butter
2 baked pie shells, freshly
   baked or defrosted

In saucepan combine flour, cornstarch, salt, and sugar. Stir in milk and bring to a boil over moderate heat, stirring constantly. Beat egg yolks with a little of the hot mixture and stir into remaining mixture. Cook, stirring, over low heat for 3 minutes. Remove from heat and stir in vanilla and butter. Cool slightly before dividing into the baked pie shells.

Serve cold, or chill and then freeze.

To defrost and serve

Defrost at room temperature for 2 hours, or in refrigerator for 6 to 8 hours. Serve cold with whipped cream or meringue topping.

LEMON MERINGUE PIE
(Makes two 9-inch pies)

2 cups sugar
½ teaspoon salt
½ cup presifted
   all-purpose flour
6 tablespoons cornstarch
4 cups water
6 eggs, separated

½ cup lemon juice
Grated rind of 2 lemons
2 tablespoons butter
2 baked pie shells,
   freshly baked or
   defrosted

In saucepan combine sugar, salt, flour, and cornstarch. Gradually stir in water. Bring to a boil over moderate heat, stirring constantly, and cook, stirring, until mixture is thickened. Beat egg yolks with a little of the hot mixture and stir into remaining mixture. Stir over low heat for 2 minutes. Remove from heat and stir in lemon juice, rind, and butter. Cool slightly before dividing into prepared pie shells.

Top with a 3-egg white meringue and brown in oven, cool, and serve, or cool thoroughly and freeze. Freeze remaining egg whites also.

To defrost and finish

Defrost egg whites at room temperature for 2 hours. Then top the frozen pie with a 3-egg white meringue and brown in a 350° F. oven for 20 minutes. Cool and serve.

HEAVENLY PIE
(Makes two 8-inch pies)

6 oranges	2 cups heavy cream
2 tablespoons sugar	1 cup flaked coconut
2 envelopes plain gelatin	½ cup chopped
¼ cup water	maraschino cherries
½ cup sugar	2 baked pie shells, freshly
Juice of 1 lemon	baked or defrosted
4 eggs, separated	

Grate the rind of 3 oranges and set aside. Peel all oranges, removing all the thick white inner rind, and cut orange sections free from membranes. Put sections into a sieve over a bowl, sprinkle with the 2 tablespoons sugar, and let drain. Soften the gelatin in the water.

In saucepan combine the ½ cup sugar, lemon juice, 1 cup drained orange juice, and egg yolks. Stir over simmering water until custard coats the spoon. Add softened gelatin and stir until gelatin is thoroughly dissolved. Cool.

Beat egg whites until stiff. Beat the cream. Fold egg whites, cream, orange sections, coconut, and cherries into the custard.

Divide filling into the baked pie shells. Chill and serve, or freeze.

To defrost

Let pie defrost at room temperature for 2 hours, or in refrigerator for 6 to 8 hours.

RUM CREAM PIE
(Makes one 9-inch pie)

6 egg yolks
⅞ cup sugar
1 envelope plain gelatin
½ cup cold water
2 cups heavy cream,
  whipped

½ cup Jamaica rum
1 baked pie shell, freshly
  baked or defrosted
Shaved bittersweet
  chocolate

In bowl of electric beater beat egg yolks and sugar until mixture is thick and pale in color.

Soak gelatin in the cold water for 5 minutes, then stir over boiling water until gelatin is thoroughly dissolved. Stir gelatin into egg-yolk mixture. Cool.

Fold whipped cream and rum into egg-yolk mixture and turn into baked pie shell. Chill until set, then sprinkle top generously with shaved chocolate. Serve, or wrap and freeze.

To defrost

Remove from freezer and defrost in refrigerator for 6 to 8 hours.

LIME CHIFFON PIE
(Makes one 9-inch pie)

1 envelope plain gelatin
¾ cup sugar
½ teaspoon salt
4 eggs, separated
½ cup lime juice

1 teaspoon grated lime
rind
1 baked pie shell,
freshly baked or
defrosted

Combine gelatin, ¼ cup of the sugar, and salt. Beat in egg yolks and lime juice. Cook over low heat, stirring constantly, until custard coats the spoon. Stir in lime rind and cool. When mixture begins to thicken, beat egg whites until stiff, gradually beat in remaining ½ cup sugar, and beat until meringue is thick and glossy. Fold into custard mixture. Turn into prepared pie shell and chill until set. Serve or freeze. Wrap and store.

To defrost and serve

Defrost, unwrapped, at room temperature for 2 to 3 hours or in refrigerator for 6 hours. Serve topped with whipped cream if desired.

CREAM PUFFS, ECLAIRS, AND PETITS CHOUX
(Makes 8 to 10 puffs, 12 éclairs, or 32 petits choux)

1 cup hot water	*1 cup presifted*
¼ cup butter	*all-purpose flour*
Pinch of salt	*4 large eggs*

In saucepan pour hot water over butter and stir until butter is melted. Add salt and bring mixture to a rapid boil. Add flour all at once, raise saucepan over heat, and stir vigorously with a wooden spoon until mixture comes away cleanly from sides of pan and forms a ball in the center.

Remove from heat and add eggs, one at a time, beating vigorously with a wooden spoon or a rotary electric beater after each addition until batter is smooth and glossy. The batter must be thick enough to hold its shape and, if the eggs are very large, it may not be necessary to add quite all the last egg. On the other hand, if the eggs are small, it may be necessary to add an additional yolk or white.

CREAM PUFFS

Drop cream-puff paste from tablespoon onto a greased baking sheet, keeping the mounds 2 inches apart. Bake in a preheated

425° F. oven for 15 minutes. Lower temperature to 350° F. and continue to bake for 30 to 40 minutes, or until browned and dry. If you can see any little beads of moisture on them, cook a little longer, or the puffs will collapse when taken from the oven.

ECLAIRS

Shape the paste on a greased baking sheet with a pastry bag fitted with a ½-inch flat tube, making strips 1×4 inches. Bake as for cream puffs.

PETITS CHOUX

With a pastry bag fitted with a small plain tube, shape paste into small mounds on a greased baking sheet (or drop paste from tip of a teaspoon). Bake in preheated 425° F. oven for 15 minutes, or until puffed to twice their size. Reduce oven temperature to 350° F. and continue to bake for 15 to 20 minutes longer, or until dry and browned.

Cool puffs thoroughly, then freeze until firm. Remove from freezer and package in cartons, seal, label, and freeze.

Or fill the puffs with ice cream or sweetened and flavored whipped cream and freeze until firm. Remove from freezer, wrap each individually, and store in freezer.

To defrost and serve

If unfilled, heat in a 325° F. oven for 10 minutes. Cool and fill. If filled and frozen, remove from freezer about 15 minutes before serving. Serve with a hot chocolate or a flavored fruit sauce.

NOTE: The petits choux may also be filled with a savory mixture and served as an hors d'oeuvre.

CHAPTER 7

Desserts and Dessert Sauces

In addition to the all-American favorites, pies and cakes, most desserts and dessert sauces freeze well. Fruit compotes, made of fruits and berries in season, fresh or cooked, remain in good condition for many months, and can be defrosted at room temperature in about 2 hours. Keep them in the closed containers in which they were frozen while they defrost.

Favorite baked puddings also freeze well and may be stored in the freezer for as long as 6 months. They should be served hot or warm the way you would serve them if freshly baked: remove from freezer and heat in a 350° F. oven for 20 to 30 minutes. Cold fruit soufflés, mousses, parfaits, sherbets, and, of course, ice cream are excellent to have available in the freezer for family and company dinners. Cold creamy or chiffon desserts are ready to serve if left standing at room temperature for 30 minutes or in the refrigerator for 3 hours, for they should be served cold—almost frozen. Parfaits, sherbets, and ice-cream desserts are served directly from the freezer.

About the only "don't" in the dessert field is—don't freeze egg custards. Egg creams and sauces are fine if they contain a stabilizer like cornstarch or gelatin, but just plain custard will separate at zero temperature.

As with all categories of food: if an example of a specific type of dessert is not among the recipes in this book, and when in doubt, my advice is, try it—you have little to lose.

If you and your family love a variety of desserts and you would like to increase your repertoire, there are hundreds of delicious desserts in my last cookbook, also published by Doubleday, *The Complete Book of Desserts*.

BLINTZES
(Makes 12)

1 cup cottage cheese
1 tablespoon sugar
1 egg, or 2 egg yolks
¼ cup shredded blanched
* almonds*

1 teaspoon vanilla
12 PANCAKE SKINS, fresh
* or defrosted*

Combine cottage cheese and sugar. Beat in egg or egg yolks, almonds, and vanilla. Chill.

Place a spoonful of filling in center of each pancake skin. Fold sides over and roll up. Seal edge with a little beaten egg or some remaining batter.

To freeze

Pack in layers in freezer container with a double thickness of waxed paper between the layers. Seal, label, and freeze.

To serve fresh

Melt a little butter in a skillet and in it sauté the blintzes until golden brown, turning to brown all sides. Serve with sour cream and a little jelly or jam.

To defrost and serve

Heat ¼ cup butter in a skillet. Place blintzes in it and cook over low heat until browned on all sides and hot. Serve as above.

STRAWBERRY CREPES AU LIQUEURS
(6 servings)

½ cup (1 stick) butter
2 tablespoons sugar
3 tablespoons curaçao or
Grand Marnier
1 pint strawberries, hulled
and sliced

¼ cup cognac
¼ cup maraschino or
kirsch
1 quart vanilla ice cream
12 crêpes, freshly made or
defrosted

In skillet or chafing dish melt butter. Add sugar and curaçao or Grand Marnier and heat to simmering. Add strawberries and heat, but do not cook. Add cognac and maraschino or kirsch. Light the liqueurs and ladle sauce over berries until flame burns out.

Put a scoop of ice cream on cold serving plate. Dip a crêpe into sauce, turning to coat both sides. Arrange crêpe over ice cream and top with strawberries and more sauce. Serve, if desired, with whipped cream.

HAZELNUT CREPES WITH FRUIT SAUCE
(6 servings)

1 (10-ounce) package
frozen strawberries,
defrosted
1 (10-ounce) package
frozen raspberries,
defrosted
1 teaspoon cornstarch
1 tablespoon water
1 cup heavy cream,
whipped

¼ cup chopped hazelnuts
(walnuts or pecans
may also be used)
1 tablespoon sugar
12 crêpes, defrosted
2 cups fresh strawberries
or raspberries
2 ounces each brandy
and kirsch (optional)

Put strawberries and raspberries through food mill, or purée in an electric blender and strain into a saucepan. Heat to simmering and stir in cornstarch mixed with water. Cook, stirring, until mixture is clear. Keep hot.

Combine whipped cream, nuts, and sugar.

Put 1 tablespoon of the whipped-cream filling on each crêpe, roll up, and arrange on serving dishes, 2 per serving.

Bring fruit sauce to table in chafing dish or electric skillet. Add the fresh strawberries or raspberries and heat sauce to simmering. Add brandy and kirsch, ignite, and stir until flame burns out. Serve the hot fruit sauce over the cold crêpes.

LEMON CREAM
(6 servings)

½ cup sugar
2 tablespoons cornstarch
¼ teaspoon salt
1 cup water
⅓ cup lemon juice

2 egg yolks, lightly beaten
1 teaspoon grated lemon rind
1 cup heavy cream, whipped

In saucepan combine sugar, cornstarch, and salt. Gradually stir in water. Bring to a boil over moderate heat, stirring constantly, until mixture is thickened.

Stir in lemon juice. Combine egg yolks with a little of the hot mixture. Stir into remaining hot mixture and cook over low heat for 2 minutes, stirring constantly. Remove from heat and stir in lemon rind. Cool. Fold in whipped cream. Serve in sherbet glasses topped with a dab of whipped cream and a fresh strawberry, or freeze in one large dish or individual serving dishes.

To defrost and serve

Remove from freezer and defrost in refrigerator for 2 to 3 hours. Serve as above.

ZUPPA INGLESE

1 *quart diced fresh fruit*
and berries
¼ *cup sugar*
4 *tablespoons light rum or*
Madeira
1 *(8-inch) layer Génoise*
or spongecake, freshly
made or defrosted

1 *quart* THIN PASTRY
CREAM, *freshly made or*
thawed
FOUR EGG MERINGUE

Combine fruit, sugar, and half the rum or Madeira. Chill until ready to use.

Split layer cake in half to make 2 thin layers. Place 1 layer in a large serving bowl and cover with fruit and juice. Place second layer of cake on top of fruit and sprinkle with remaining rum or Madeira. Pour the pastry cream over cake and top with the meringue. Set bowl into a pan containing cracked ice and bake the dessert in a preheated 425° F. oven for 5 to 6 minutes.

CHARLOTTE RUSSE
(6 servings)

1 *envelope plain gelatin*
¼ *cup cold water*
½ *cup hot milk*
⅓ *cup confectioners'*
sugar

2 *teaspoons vanilla*
2 *cups heavy cream,*
whipped
6 *ladyfingers, separated*

In small bowl soften gelatin in water, then add hot milk and stir until gelatin is thoroughly dissolved. Stir in sugar and vanilla. Set bowl in a pan of ice water and stir constantly until mixture begins to thicken. Fold in whipped cream.

Oil a 6-cup mold lightly and line it with ladyfingers. Pour the cream into the mold and chill for 2 hours. When ready to serve, unmold and garnish with whipped cream. Or unmold onto baking sheet and freeze. When frozen, wrap and return to freezer.

170

To defrost and serve

Remove from freezer, unwrap, and defrost in refrigerator for 3 hours before serving. Garnish as above.

MOUSSE AU CHOCOLAT
(8 servings)

1 (6-ounce) package
semisweet chocolate
pieces

5 tablespoons strong coffee
4 eggs, separated
2 tablespoons dark rum

In small saucepan combine chocolate and coffee. Stir over low heat until chocolate is melted and mixture is smooth and hot. Remove from heat and beat in egg yolks. Cool. Stir in rum.

Beat egg whites until stiff and fold into chocolate mixture. Spoon into serving dish or individual dishes and chill for 1 hour before serving, or freeze in serving dish.

To defrost and serve

Remove from freezer and defrost in refrigerator for 2 to 3 hours before serving.

PAVE AU CHOCOLAT
(8 servings)

2 tablespoons cognac
½ cup cold water
2 (5-ounce) packages
ladyfingers

FRENCH CHOCOLATE BUTTER
CREAM, *freshly made or*
defrosted

Line bottom of a small spring-form pan with waxed paper. Combine cognac and water. Dip ladyfingers into the liquid, one at a time, and arrange a layer of the moistened ladyfingers in bottom of pan. Spread with half the cream. Arrange another layer of ladyfingers on the cream and top with remaining cream. Cover with remaining ladyfingers and chill for 2 hours. To serve: run knife around sides of pan and invert on serving plate. Discard waxed paper and decorate with rosettes of whipped cream. Or unmold, leave waxed paper on top, and freeze. When frozen, wrap and return to freezer.

To defrost and serve

Remove from freezer, unwrap, and defrost in refrigerator for 3 hours. Serve as above.

FRUIT AND ICE CREAM IN CHOCOLATE CUPS
(12 servings)

12 CHOCOLATE CUPS
2 cups sliced strawberries or orange sections mixed with diced melon
¼ cup sugar
2 tablespoons raspberry syrup or Grand Marnier

2 tablespoons water
12 rounds spongecake (2 inches in diameter)
1 pint ice cream
Whipped cream
12 whole strawberries

Make chocolate cups.
Combine fruit and sugar.
Combine syrup or Grand Marnier and water.
Dip a round of spongecake into the liquid and put into bottom of a chocolate cup. Cover cake with a spoonful of fruit mixture and top with a large spoonful ice cream. Top with whipped cream. Keep cold in freezer until ready to serve. To serve: garnish each portion with a strawberry. Frozen cups must be individually wrapped if they are going to be stored in freezer for any length of time.

Chocolate cups (*Colettes*)

Melt 12 squares semisweet chocolate and ¼ cup butter over low heat, stirring until mixture is smooth. Using a flexible steel spatula, swirl chocolate mixture around bottom and sides of 12 (5-ounce) paper baking cups, covering the entire inner surface with a thin layer. Place cups in muffin pans and chill. Peel off paper and store in refrigerator or freezer until ready to fill.

LEMON FOAM
(12 servings)

¾ cup crushed chocolate
  cookies
¾ cup chopped nut meats
6 eggs, separated
1 cup sugar

⅓ cup lemon juice
Grated rind of 1 lemon
1 cup heavy cream,
  whipped

Combine cooky crumbs and nuts. Sprinkle 1 tablespoon of the mixture into the bottom of 12 (5-ounce) paper baking cups. Reserve the rest of the mixture.

Beat eggs whites until they stand in soft peaks. Gradually beat in sugar and continue to beat until meringue is stiff and glossy.

Beat egg yolks until thick and pale in color. Beat in lemon juice and grated rind. Fold egg-yolk mixture and whipped cream into egg-white mixture. Spoon into prepared baking cups and top each cup with another tablespoon of the cooky-nut mixture. Wrap, label, and freeze.

To defrost

Defrost in refrigerator for 30 minutes.

Frozen whipped cream is handy to have in the freezer. If frozen in mounds it may be stored in polyethylene bags.

FROZEN WHIPPED CREAM

Whip 2 cups heavy cream until stiff. Beat in ¼ cup confectioners' sugar. Drop by mounds onto baking sheet covered with waxed paper and freeze for about 2 hours, or until firm. Transfer quickly to plastic bag, label, and return to freezer.

To serve

Remove as many mounds of whipped cream as needed and place immediately on the dessert. It will be defrosted in 10 minutes.

Whether you make your own ice cream or buy commercial brands, you'll want to keep a good supply of ice cream of many flavors in your freezer for quick, easy, and luscious desserts for family or for guests. Homemade ice creams are, of course, hard to beat whether you use an old-fashioned hand-turned freezer or one of the newer varieties which churns electrically in your freezer. Here is a very rich, creamy favorite of mine which is frozen in an ice-cube tray.

FRENCH CHOCOLATE ICE CREAM
(Makes 1 quart)

¼ cup sugar
⅓ cup water
1 (6-ounce) package
*   semisweet chocolate*
*   pieces*

3 egg yolks
1½ cups heavy cream,
*   whipped*

In small saucepan combine sugar and water. Bring to a boil and boil rapidly for 3 minutes. Add chocolate and cook, stirring, over low heat until chocolate is melted and mixture is hot.

In bowl of an electric mixer beat egg yolks until fluffy. Gradually beat in the chocolate syrup and beat until mixture is thick and cool. Fold into the whipped cream. Spoon into refrigerator tray, cover with waxed paper, and freeze for 2 to 3 hours. When frozen, wrap tray in freezer paper or aluminum foil.

BISCUIT TORTONI
(Makes 16 servings)

⅔ cup sugar
¼ cup water
¼ cup sherry
6 egg yolks

2 cups heavy cream,
  whipped
⅔ cup ground toasted
  almonds

In small saucepan combine sugar and water. Bring to a boil and boil rapidly for 3 minutes.

In bowl of an electric mixer beat sherry and egg yolks until mixture is thick and well blended. Gradually beat in the hot syrup. Cool.

Fold egg-yolk mixture into whipped cream.

Arrange 16 individual 5-ounce paper soufflé cups on a baking sheet. Spoon dessert into the cups and sprinkle with the ground nuts. Freeze. They will be ready to serve in 2 to 3 hours, or will keep well in freezer for 2 months. When frozen, wrap each in freezer paper and return to freezer.

To serve

Unwrap and serve without defrosting.

COFFEE PARFAIT
(6 servings)

¾ cup sugar
2 tablespoons instant
  coffee
⅓ cup water
2 squares unsweetened
  chocolate, grated

4 egg yolks
2 cups heavy cream
2 teaspoons vanilla

In saucepan combine sugar, coffee, and water. Bring to a boil and boil rapidly until syrup spins a thread (230° F.). Remove from heat and stir in chocolate.

In bowl of electric beater beat egg yolks until thick and pale in color. Gradually beat in the hot syrup. Chill for 30 minutes.

Whip cream until stiff and stir in vanilla. Fold whipped cream into chocolate mixture.

Spoon into 6 parfait glasses. Cover top of each glass with foil and freeze until firm.

To serve

Serve directly from freezer. Garnish top of each serving with a dab of whipped cream, or sprinkle with grated chocolate.

BAKED ALASKA
(6 servings)

1 loaf cake (7½ × 3½ × 2 inches)—buttercake, angel, sponge, or pound

1 quart ice cream—vanilla, chocolate, or other flavor

Cut a slice ¾ inch thick from bottom of cake and place on large square of heavy-duty aluminum foil. Cover cake with scoops of ice cream.

Slice remaining cake into 3 thin layers. Put 1 layer on top of the ice cream. Cut a second slice in half, lengthwise, and press one half against each lengthwise side of the ice cream. Cut the third layer in half crosswise and press against ends of loaf, completely covering the ice cream with cake. Trim pieces of cake to fit if necessary.

Wrap in the foil and freeze.

To finish baked Alaska

4 egg whites
Pinch of salt
1 teaspoon lemon juice

1 cup confectioners'
sugar (sift if lumpy)

Beat egg whites and salt until frothy. Add lemon juice and beat until egg whites stand in soft peaks. Gradually beat in sugar and continue to beat until meringue is thick and glossy.

Remove baked Alaska from freezer and cover top and sides with a 1-inch-thick layer of the meringue. Swirl remaining meringue on top or decorate with rosettes and scrolls by pressing meringue through fluted pastry tube. Bake in preheated 450° F. oven for 6 to 8 minutes, or until meringue is lightly browned.

And here are some quick ice-cream desserts:

BERRY SPECIAL

Put a scoop of vanilla ice cream in serving dish. Cover with THIN PASTRY CREAM, freshly made or defrosted, and sprinkle with sliced strawberries, raspberries, or blueberries. Sliced banana is also good. Or, if berries are out of season, sprinkle with shaved chocolate.

PEACH MELBA

Put a scoop of vanilla ice cream in serving dish. Top with half a cooked or canned peach and RASPBERRY SAUCE.

FRUITED ICE-CREAM CUP

Into a large brandy snifter put ½ cup mixed fruits, sweetened to taste (peaches, melon, oranges, banana, strawberries, raspberries). If desired, add a spoonful of favorite liqueur. Top fruit mixture with a scoop of vanilla ice cream. Cover with about 3 tablespoons RASPBERRY SAUCE, top with a dollop of whipped cream, and garnish with a large fresh strawberry.

MARRON GLACE

Into large brandy snifter put a spoonful of chestnut cream flavored with vanilla (this is available in cans). Top with a scoop of vanilla ice cream. Cover ice cream with CHOCOLATE RUM SAUCE and garnish with a glacéed chestnut.

ICE-CREAM CAKE ROLL

Spread a large sheet of yellow or chocolate sponge cake (or see recipe for JELLY ROLL) with soft ice cream and roll up lengthwise like a jelly roll. Frost with butter cream icing and freeze. Wrap and store. May be stored for 2 months. Serve directly from freezer.

STRAWBERRY ICE-CREAM ROLL

Spread a large sheet of yellow sponge cake or JELLY ROLL cake with 1 quart vanilla ice cream mixed with 1½ cups sliced fresh strawberries. Roll up lengthwise and frost with whipped cream flavored to taste with sugar and vanilla. Freeze. When firm, wrap and store. May be stored for 2 months. Serve directly from freezer.

ICE-CREAM RIBBON CAKE

Bake angel food in a loaf pan 10×5×3 inches. When cool, cut lengthwise into 3 layers. Spread a layer of ice cream 1 inch thick between first and second layers of cake and ice cream or sherbet of another flavor and color between second and top layer of cake. Frost top and sides with whipped cream flavored with sugar and vanilla to taste and sprinkle with shredded coconut. Freeze until firm. Wrap and store. May be stored for 1 month. Serve directly from freezer.

ICE-CREAM BOMBE
(10 to 12 servings)

1 pint soft ice cream
1½ pints fruit-flavored sherbet

Use any pleasing combinations of ice cream and sherbet such as chocolate ice cream and lemon sherbet, strawberry ice cream and orange sherbet, vanilla ice cream and raspberry sherbet.

Chill a decorative 5-cup mold or ice cream bombe mold.

With back of a spoon or rubber scraper, press a layer of ice cream evenly over the inside of the mold, making a shell. Freeze for about 1 hour, or until ice cream is very firm. Remove from freezer and pack center of mold with the sherbet. Cover with mold cover or with aluminum foil and return to freezer.

To serve

Wipe outside of mold with a hot wet cloth. Turn bombe out onto chilled serving plate. Serve at once with fruit or dessert sauce. Garnish, if desired, with whipped-cream rosettes.

ICE-CREAM PIE

Roll chocolate or vanilla wafers into fine crumbs and combine 2 cups crumbs with ¼ cup sugar and ½ cup soft butter. Press mixture over bottom and sides of a buttered 9-inch pie plate. Fill shell with 1 quart vanilla ice cream. Arrange sliced and sugared fresh fruit, or partially defrosted frozen fruit, on the ice cream. Freeze until solid, then wrap. May be stored for 2 months. Serve directly from freezer.

ICE-CREAM SANDWICHES

Cut a brick of ice cream into thin slices and put 2 slices together with a layer of crushed fruit or berries between. Freeze until firm, then wrap individually and store. Will keep for 2 months. Serve directly from freezer.

Plus some specials for children:

ICE-CREAM FLOWERPOTS

Fill flat-bottomed cones with ice cream. Sprinkle each with grated chocolate or chocolate cooky crumbs and freeze. When ready to serve, insert into top of each cone a few wooden picks each stuck with a gumdrop.

ICE-CREAM ANGELS

Pack ice cream into cone-shaped paper cups and freeze. When ready to serve, peel off paper cups and place on cold serving plate, pointed end up. Place a large marshmallow on the end for the head and add foil halo and wings.

MICKEY MOUSE ICE CREAM

Put a large chocolate cooky on a serving plate and top with a scoop of ice cream. The ice cream should be smaller in diameter than the cooky, so that the edge of the cooky forms a collar. Insert thin chocolate mints into the ice cream for ears, and make a face with chocolate bits or gumdrops.

ICE-CREAM CLOWNS

Pack ice cream into cone-shaped paper cups and freeze. Place a large sugar cooky on a serving plate. On top of the cooky put a scoop of ice cream. Peal paper off the cone-shaped ice cream and place on top of scoop of ice cream for a pointed hat. Make face with gumdrops or chocolate bits.

EASTER-EGG NESTS

Cut center out of chocolate cupcakes to form nests. Brush edges of nests with syrup and sprinkle with shredded coconut. Fill nests with tiny balls of different flavored and colored ice cream, using a melon-ball scoop to make the balls. Freeze on baking sheets, then wrap individually and return to freezer. Serve directly from freezer. May be stored for 1 month.

COCONUT BALLS

Shape ice cream into balls with an ice-cream scoop. Roll each ball in shredded coconut and freeze on baking sheet. Wrap each ball individually and store in freezer. Serve directly from freezer with CHOCOLATE, BUTTERSCOTCH or fruit sauce. May be stored for 2 months. One quart ice cream will make 8 balls.

SNOWMEN

With a large ice-cream scoop form a large ball of ice cream. Make a smaller ball with a smaller scoop and place on top of large ball. With a toothpick dipped in melted chocolate draw eyes, nose, and mouth on the flat side of a marshmallow. Fasten marshmallow on top of small ball of ice cream with a wooden pick and balance a red or green maraschino cherry on the marshmallow. Stick currants down front for buttons. Freeze on baking sheet, then wrap each snowman individually and store in freezer. May be stored for 1 month. One quart ice cream makes 4 snowmen.

DESSERT SAUCES

The following sauces are very quick and easy to make to serve with puddings, over slices of cake, or with ice cream. Freeze any remaining sauce in plastic freezer containers. Defrost at room temperature for 2 hours, or heat over simmering water for 20 minutes, stirring occasionally.

Butterscotch sauce (Makes 2 cups)

In saucepan combine 2 cups brown sugar, firmly packed, ½ cup cream, ¼ cup light corn syrup, 6 tablespoons butter. Bring to a boil and boil rapidly for 3 minutes. Serve hot or cold.

Uncooked butterscotch sauce (Makes 1½ cups)

Beat with electric mixer or blend in electric blender until smooth, 1 cup evaporated milk, ¾ cup brown sugar, ½ cup white sugar, 2 tablespoons soft butter, 1 tablespoon corn syrup, dash of salt, and 1 teaspoon vanilla.

Thick chocolate sauce (Makes 1¾ cups)

In saucepan combine 4 squares unsweetened chocolate, chopped, 1 cup sugar, ⅔ cup milk, cream, or coffee, 1 teaspoon vanilla, and dash of salt. Cook over low heat, stirring, until chocolate and sugar are melted and mixture is smooth.

Chocolate rum sauce (Makes 1 cup)

In saucepan combine 1 (6-ounce) package semisweet chocolate pieces, ⅓ cup milk or water. Cook over low heat, stirring, until chocolate is melted and mixture is smooth. Remove from heat and stir in 2 tablespoons dark rum.

Raspberry sauce (Makes about 1 cup)

Defrost 1 (10-ounce) package frozen raspberries. Mash and press through food mill or strainer, or purée in electric blender and strain to remove seeds. Any favorite liqueur, rum, or spirits such as kirsch or *eau-de-vie de framboise* may be added.

Lemon sauce (Makes 1½ cups)

In saucepan combine ½ cup sugar, 1 tablespoon cornstarch, and pinch of salt. Stir in 1 cup water and juice of 1 lemon. Bring to a boil and cook, stirring, until sauce is clear and thickened. Remove from heat and stir in 1 teaspoon grated lemon rind and 1 tablespoon soft butter.

Orange sauce (Makes 1 cup)

In saucepan combine ½ cup sugar, 2 tablespoons cornstarch, and ¼ teaspoon salt. Stir in 1 cup orange juice. Bring to a boil and cook, stirring, until sauce is clear and thickened. Remove from heat and stir in grated rind of ½ orange. Add a dash of curaçao or Grand Marnier or Triple Sec if desired.

Strawberry cream sauce (Makes 1½ cups)

Defrost 1 (10-ounce) package frozen sliced strawberries. Purée with food mill or in an electric blender. Stir in 2 teaspoons cornstarch, bring to a boil, and cook for 10 minutes, or until sauce is thick. Remove from heat, cool, and stir in ½ cup heavy cream. Cream may be whipped if desired.

Freezer jams are not true jams, but make excellent dessert toppings and sauces for ice cream.

GINGER PEACH JAM
(Makes 4 pints)

*3 pounds (or 4 cups)
  fresh peaches, chopped
¼ cup chopped crystallized
  ginger*

*5 cups sugar
2 (1¾-ounce) packages
  powdered pectin
1 cup cold water*

In large mixing bowl combine peaches and ginger. Gradually stir in sugar.

In small saucepan combine pectin and water. Bring to a boil, stirring constantly, and boil rapidly for 1 minute.

Pour pectin over fruit mixture and stir for 5 minutes.

Ladle into pint containers, leaving ½ inch head space. Cover and let stand at room temperature for 24 hours. Label and freeze. Will keep for 6 months.

To defrost

Remove from freezer and let stand at room temperature for 1 hour.

STRAWBERRY PINEAPPLE JAM
(Makes 4 pints)

2½ cups crushed fresh strawberries (2 pints whole berries)
2½ cups chopped fresh pineapple

7½ cups sugar
2 (1¾-ounce) packages powdered pectin
1 cup cold water

In large bowl combine strawberries and pineapple. Gradually stir in sugar.

In small saucepan combine pectin and water. Bring to a boil, stirring constantly, and boil rapidly for 1 minute.

Pour pectin over fruit and stir for 5 minutes. Ladle into containers, leaving ½ inch head space in a pint container. Cover and let stand at room temperature for 24 hours to set. Label and freeze. Will keep for 6 months.

To defrost

Remove from freezer and let stand at room temperature for 1 hour.

CHAPTER 8

Leftovers, the Lunch Box, and Frozen-Food Menus

As much as you may relish a turkey, a ham, or a roast of beef, no one wants to eat the leftovers from a roast several more times that same week. With a freezer you don't have to. The freezer is the solution to mealtime monotony, for leftovers of all kinds may be frozen and served a week or two or a month later, when they seem to be an entirely new meal and not a duplicate of yesterday's dinner.

Slice leftover roasts and wrap the slices compactly in moisture-vaporproof paper, or better still if you have the time, make leftover meat and poultry into ready-to-serve creamed dishes, casseroles, croquettes.

Plastic refrigerator dishes are ideal for storing leftover soups, stews, and gravies. They can be used over and over again. Their tight-fitting lids fit securely in place. Be sure to leave ½ inch head space.

But rather than freeze sliced meat separately from gravy or sauce, it's better to package the sliced meat with a coating of gravy, for the meat remains more moist. If you wish you can make up plate dinners in individual partitioned aluminum plates for the freezer. When you are cooking a roast and know there will be some left over, cook an extra quantity of potatoes and vegetables and make a good quantity of gravy.

Slice the meat into the largest partition of the plate and cover with gravy. Fill other partitions with potatoes or rice and vegetables. Place freezer foil over the dish and crimp edges. Label contents and date. Plan to use within 2 months, but the sooner used the better.

To serve packaged plate dinners

Leave plates covered. Heat directly from freezer in a preheated 425° F. oven for 30 minutes. Remove foil and serve immediately.

Here are a few suggestions for ready-to-serve dishes made from leftovers.

Beef
Grind or mince, mix with vegetables and gravy, and make into flaky pastry turnovers, dinner or cocktail size.

Meat Loaf
Slice and freeze, separating each slice with a double thickness of waxed paper. To serve, unwrap slices and arrange on baking sheet. Spread with chili sauce and sprinkle with grated cheese. Broil 2 inches from heat until cheese is melted and meat is hot.

Chicken, Ducks, Lamb, Veal
Dice and add to a curry sauce.

Chicken
Dice and make into chicken pies.

Lamb
Grind and make into shepherd's pie.

Fish
Flake and add to CREAM SAUCE, WHITE WINE SAUCE, NEWBURG SAUCE, or CURRY SAUCE.

There are many recipes for curried dishes made from leftover chicken, duck, or lamb. Here is a really good one.

CURRY
(6 servings)

½ cup butter	2 tablespoons curry
4 cloves garlic, chopped	powder
4 medium onions, chopped	1 teaspoon black pepper
½ cup flour	1 teaspoon ground cumin
2 whole cooked tomatoes,	1 teaspoon ground
chopped	coriander
1 bay leaf	4 cups boiling water or
1 teaspoon cinnamon	chicken stock
6 cloves	3 cups diced cooked
2 teaspoons salt	poultry or meat

In heavy saucepan melt butter and in it sauté garlic and onions over moderate heat for 5 minutes, or until lightly browned. Stir in flour and cook, stirring, until flour is lightly browned. Add tomatoes and spices. Add water or chicken stock and whisk briskly over moderate heat until sauce is smooth and thickened. Reduce heat and cook over low heat for 25 minutes, stirring occasionally.

Stir in poultry or meat. Cool. Package, label, and freeze.

To defrost and serve

Reheat over simmering water for 30 minutes, stirring occasionally. Serve with chutney, chopped peanuts, and cooked rice.

Don't let roast-beef bones go to waste. Separate the bones from a leftover rib roast of beef into individual ribs, leaving as much meat on as possible. Freeze on baking sheet. When frozen, package and return to the freezer until you have accumulated enough for one rib per serving for your family.

Deviled roast-beef bones

Remove ribs from freezer 2 hours before cooking. Let defrost in wrappings at room temperature.

Preheat broiler to medium.

Coat ribs with prepared mustard or with dry mustard mixed with cream to a thick consistency. Roll the ribs in fresh bread crumbs to cover on all sides. Grill 6 inches from heat for about 20 minutes, turning frequently to brown the ribs on all sides.

FROZEN ASSETS FOR THE LUNCH BOX

Sandwiches are best when freshly made and wrapped in transparent film to keep them moist. However, there may be times when you want a vacation and must still provide for your family's lunch boxes. With a freezer you can do this nicely, preparing an entire week's luncheons in advance. Each item for the lunch box may be packaged and labeled separately so that the lunch-box set can make its own selections, or you can decide on the lunch-box combination and package each day's menu together in one package. If transferred to lunch box in the morning the foods will be thawed and ready to eat when lunchtime rolls around.

You'll want to prepare a variety of cakes or cupcakes, cookies, pies, tarts, desserts, and cold soups, but when all is said and done, sandwiches are the mainstay of the daily lunch box.

The don'ts: don't make sandwich fillings containing cooked egg whites, raw vegetables such as lettuce, celery, tomatoes, cucumbers, and don't use mayonnaise or salad dressing. It separates when frozen and soaks into the bread when thawed. That pretty much limits you to cheese, meat, fish, but with a little imagination you can differ the seasonings and come up with a variety of sandwiches that are interesting in flavor and texture.

Use a variety of breads. Whole wheat, rye, pumpernickel, graham—all breads, as well as white, freeze well. Here are some suggested fillings.

MEAT OR POULTRY

Diced or ground chicken, cream cheese, grated orange rind.
Chopped or ground ham and chopped peanuts or pecans.
Slices meat loaf, sliced stuffed olives.

Ground ham, chopped pickles, mustard.
Ground cooked chicken, cream cheese, and chopped almonds.
Chopped corned beef with chopped ripe olives.
Deviled ham and cream or cottage cheese.
Liverwurst and chili sauce or pickle relish.

FISH

Mashed boneless sardines, chopped hard-cooked egg yolks, and lemon juice.
Minced shrimp, lobster, or crab with cream cheese.
Flaked salmon, crushed pineapple, and chopped walnuts.
Flaked tuna, cottage cheese, and pickle relish.

CHEESE

Cream cheese and sliced stuffed olives.
Cream cheese, shredded dried beef, and horse-radish.
Cottage cheese, chopped peanuts, and apricot or strawberry jam.
Cream cheese, crushed pineapple, and chopped dates.

TO MAKE SANDWICHES FOR
THE FREEZER

1. Spread all slices with soft butter, spreading to the edges of the bread to prevent filling from soaking into bread when thawed.
2. Spread filling evenly on bread to insure even thawing.
3. Close sandwich and press slices firmly together.
4. Cut sandwiches into portions easy to handle for children or adults.
5. Wrap sandwiches immediately and tightly in freezer paper.
6. Label and freeze as part of a complete lunch or as an individual item.

FROZEN-FOOD MENUS

Entire meals—for emergency, for everyday use, for special holiday dinners, or for parties—can be prepared in advance and stored in your home freezer. Whether you prepare and freeze every dish for the menu or buy commercially frozen products to store in your freezer, you may like the idea of packaging every item for one meal together in a large bag and labeling the contents. Perhaps you will want to include on the label the menu and heating directions, or you might simply want to number the bag and keep on hand a logbook which lists not only the menu by number and the steps for preparing it, but any foods that you should have on hand to complete the meal, such as butter, cream, milk, salad greens, condiments, and coffee.

The following menus are meant to be only suggestions, for only you know the personal likes and dislikes, the favorite dishes, of your family. I hope they will provide inspiration in helping you plan your own meals and illustrate one way of getting the most value from your home freezer.

A WEEK OF FAMILY DINNERS FROM YOUR FREEZER

*The starred items cannot be frozen.

SUNDAY
 Fruit Cup
 Roast Pork
 Candied Sweet Potatoes
 Buttered String or Lima Beans
 Applesauce
 Brown-and-Serve Rolls
 Ice-Cream Roll

MONDAY
>   *Minestrone*
>   *Spaghetti with Tomato or Meat Sauce*
>   *Tossed Green Salad**
>   *Garlic French Bread*
>   *Angel-Food Cake*

TUESDAY
>   *Hungarian Goulash*
>   *Buttered Noodles*
>   *Hot Rolls*
>   *Salad**
>   *Ice Cream with Fruit Sauce*

WEDNESDAY
>   *Individual Chicken Pies with Whipped Potato Topping*
>   *Salad**
>   *Strawberry Tarts*

THURSDAY
>   *Vegetable Soup*
>   *Broiled Lamb Chops*
>   *French Fried Potatoes*
>   *Buttered Peas*
>   *Apple Pie with Cheese*

FRIDAY
>   *Tomato Juice*
>   *Fish Fillets Sautéed with Lemon Butter*
>   *Baby Lima Beans*
>   *Hot Rolls*
>   *Cucumbers in Sour Cream**
>   *Chocolate Cake*

SATURDAY
>   *Broiled Steak with Mushrooms*
>   *Baked Stuffed Potatoes*
>   *Buttered Broccoli*
>   *Fruit Salad*
>   *Cream Puffs*

A WEEK OF FAMILY SUPPERS FROM
YOUR FREEZER

*The starred items cannot be frozen.

SUNDAY
> *Vegetable Soup*
> *Salad**
> *Hot French Bread*
> *Chocolate Eclairs*

MONDAY
> *Frankfurters and Baked Beans*
> *Pumpernickel Bread*
> *Ice Cream*
> *Cookies*

TUESDAY
> *Beef Stew*
> *Salad**
> *Hot Rolls*
> *Butterscotch Pudding or Pie*

WEDNESDAY
> *Tomato and Clam Juice Cocktail*
> *Chicken à la King*
> *Corn Muffins*
> *Applesauce*
> *Cake*

THURSDAY
> *Sautéed Sausages*
> *Sweet-Potato Casserole*
> *Baking-Powder Biscuits*
> *Blueberry Pie*

FRIDAY
   Crab-Meat Newburg on Toast
   Salad*
   Lemon Ice
   Cookies

SATURDAY
   Hamburgers with Barbecue or Chili Sauce
   Potato Croquettes
   Salad*
   Baked Apples

HOLIDAY AND GUEST DINNERS
FROM YOUR FREEZER

One delightful way of casual entertaining is the casserole buffet supper. You can make your own favorite casserole such as chicken Marengo, chicken cacciatore, turkey Tetrazzini, beef Stroganoff, or any one of the stews and casserole dishes given in this book a week or two in advance and store casserole and all, well wrapped of course, in your freezer until the evening of your party. All you need to complement any of these meal-in-one dishes is a large tossed green salad, hot French bread, a bottle of good wine, and a glamorous dessert.

The greens for the salad can be washed, dried, and kept crisp and fresh in the refrigerator right in the salad bowl, covered with transparent film, and ready to be tossed with a good French dressing.

An hour before your guests arrive, remove casserole from freezer and put in a 350° F. oven to defrost and heat.

For dessert a baked Alaska is great, for it can be put into a hot oven directly from your freezer. Or you might prefer a large bowl of raspberry sherbet topped with peach halves or pineapple slices marinated in rum and freshly baked cookies. But no matter how fancy or simple your menu, with a home freezer as a silent partner your evening will be a happy one, you will have had fun at your own party, and you'll have a minimum of pots and pans to wash before you turn in for the night.

For those who like more formal entertaining, the home freezer can serve up more elaborate dinners as easily as a family one.

* The starred items cannot be frozen.

MENU NO. 1

Hot Consommé
Broiled Chicken with Tarragon Butter
Lima Beans in Cream
Saffron Rice
Hot Rolls
*Salad**
Peaches Thawed in Cognac
Petits Fours

MENU NO. 2

Fruit Cup
Roast Turkey with Chestnut Dressing
Giblet Gravy
Cranberry-Orange Relish
Sweet-Potato Puffs
Green Beans with Tiny Onions and Mushrooms
Hot Rolls
Plum Pudding with Hard Sauce

MENU NO. 3

Mushroom Soup
Roast Duck Bigarade
Wild Rice
Buttered Peas
Hot French Bread
*Salad**
Meringue Shells with Ice Cream

MENU NO. 4

Crab-Meat Cocktail
Veal Birds in White Wine
Buttered Broccoli
Baked Acorn Squash
*Avocado Salad**
Cherries Jubilee

MENU NO. 5
  Turtle Soup
  Broiled Shrimp
  Roast Beef
  Grilled Mushrooms
  Potatoes Duchesse
  *Endive and Beet Salad**
  Coupe de Marrons

QUICK MENU SUGGESTIONS FROM COMMERCIALLY FROZEN PRODUCTS

For those with limited freezer space, or little time to prepare your own dishes for "meals from the freezer," here are a few menu suggestions that can be composed from the wide variety of commercially frozen foods available today. Package each complete meal in a large bag, remove it when needed, and within 30 minutes you and your family can sit down to dinner.

* The starred items cannot be frozen.

MENU NO. 1
  Onion Soup
  Broiled Mixed Grill (Lamb Chops, Sausages, and Bacon)
  Succotash
  Hot Rolls
  Ice Cream with Raspberry Sauce

MENU NO. 2
  Hot Consommé
  Broiled Steak
  Green Beans
  French Fried Potatoes
  Hot French Bread
  *Salad**
  Cheesecake

MENU NO. 3
>*Tomato Juice*
>*Broiled Swordfish Steak*
>*Green Peas*
>*Cauliflower*
>*Brown-and-Serve Rolls*
>*Fruit Cup*
>*Cookies*

MENU NO. 4
>*Shrimp Cocktail*
>*Southern Fried Chicken*
>*Whole Kernel Corn*
>*Whipped Potatoes*
>*French Bread*
>*Asparagus Vinaigrette*
>*Apple Pie*
>*Ice Cream*

MENU NO. 5
>*Vegetable Soup*
>*Broiled Ham Steak*
>*Puréed Squash*
>*Spinach*
>*Parker House Rolls*
>*Fruit Salad*
>*Ribbon Ice-Cream Cake*

MENU NO. 6
>*Melon Balls*
>*Broiled African Lobster Tails*
>*Broccoli*
>*French Fried Potatoes*
>*Cole Slaw**
>*Peach Shortcake*

Part Two

PREPARING, PACKAGING, AND FREEZING FOODS

CHAPTER 1

Your Home Freezer

WHAT SIZE AND KIND OF FREEZER TO BUY

The space that you have available may well be the determining factor in the size of the home freezer you decide to buy.

The homemaker who lives in the average apartment may be only too happy to have a 4-cubic-foot freezer to squeeze into the last remaining wall space in her kitchen. She cannot hope to store in this a season's supply of fruits and vegetables. She cannot buy a side of beef or a dozen ducks when she finds a bargain. She can, however, keep on hand a few packages of her favorite commercially frozen foods, a few steaks, some broilers, a couple of loaves of French bread, and several ready-made dishes to warm up at a moment's notice.

If space is no problem, the next important consideration in selecting a freezer is how you intend to use it and your family's mode of life. Unless you live on a farm or in a rural town, miles from a shopping center, a small freezer is adequate for most family needs. Before you make your final choice, however, you should consider:

1. The number of people in your family.
2. The extent of entertaining that you do.
3. Whether you have your own garden and wish to freeze the surplus crops.
4. Whether you are working and have the responsibility of both earning a living and taking care of home and family.

In general you should figure 4 to 6 cubic feet of storage per person, depending on how you intend to use your freezer.

To help you make your decision, you should know that:

1 cubic foot of freezer space will accommodate 54 rectangular pint containers, 70 twelve-ounce packages of commercially frozen foods, or 12 frying chickens.

2 cubic feet will accommodate a loin or round of beef.

3 cubic feet will accommodate a quarter of beef.

There are three principal types of home freezers—in addition to the freezer section of two-door refrigerators. The freezer section of one-door refrigerators is not considered a freezer, for it rarely maintains temperatures low enough for the quick-freezing of foods. It will, however, keep commercially frozen foods solidly frozen for 2 to 3 days.

1. *The Chest-type Freezer* ranges in size from 2 to 18 cubic feet. It may be square or rectangular with a top opening. Most single-compartment chest freezers provide both freezing and storage in the same area. Those that have several compartments provide a separate area for freezing.

2. *The Upright Freezer* ranges in size from 6 to 20 cubic feet. It requires no more floor space than a refrigerator and has a front-opening door. This type of freezer usually includes several zero storage compartments, and some provide a special quick-freezing compartment.

3. *The Walk-in Freezer* is really suitable only for farms or for commercial use where more than 20 cubic feet of space is required. It is seldom practical for average-family needs. Some walk-in freezers have a chilling compartment, about 32° F., for holding meat, or for rapidly cooling freshly slaughtered animals. Others include a storage area for root crops and winter fruits.

Points to consider when shopping for your home freezer:

1. All-steel construction will give longer service.

2. The steel cabinet should be given some rust-resistant treatment before the exterior finish is applied.

3. Plastic door gaskets are resistant to grease and last longer.

4. Baked-on enamel does not chip and is easy to keep clean.

5. Rounded corners in the interior of the freezer are easier to clean.

6. The opening should be well insulated, and it should swing up or out easily, on ball-bearing hinges. It should close tightly and have a cushion gasket surrounding the opening to prevent warm air from leaking into the freezer.

7. Inorganic insulation from 3 to 4 inches deep is vitally important to the maintenance of a constant temperature with a minimum

of electric power. This is also important in the event that the power becomes interrupted. A well-insulated freezer will keep foods safely at zero temperature for as long as 36 hours with the electric current off.

8. A fast-freezing compartment is desirable, also frost-free freezers that require no defrosting are preferable.

9. Special features are the trademark of the different manufacturers, and it is up to you to decide which of these special features make one freezer more attractive to you than another.

10. Chest-type freezers require more floor space, but are more economical to operate. When an upright freezer is opened, cold air rushes out from all levels. It is, however, more attractive in the kitchen and takes up less space. Foods are more readily accessible in an upright freezer and therefore easier to organize and keep organized.

WHERE TO PLACE YOUR FREEZER

Before you buy your home freezer you will, naturally, give some thought to where you are going to put it.

The first choice is the kitchen, where you prepare the food to be frozen and later cook the frozen food. The temperature of the room does not affect the constant zero temperature within your freezer and certainly the kitchen is the logical place. Common sense would motivate you to select a spot away from the stove, radiator, or the direct rays of the sun.

The next best place would be the breakfast room, pantry, or porch, as close to the kitchen as possible.

Finally, the cellar or garage must be used if there is no room nearer the kitchen. Even so, a home freezer is worth these extra steps.

Check with your electrician to make sure that the electrical circuit for your freezer is not already overloaded. A level, solid floor is important.

If you are planning to remodel, or to build a new home, provide adequate space for a home freezer even if your present budget does not allow for one. It may not be long before it will!

HOW TO CARE FOR YOUR
HOME FREEZER

Specific directions for the care of your freezer are supplied by the company from which you buy it. The following are general:

A home freezer is the simplest of all household appliances to operate. The best care you can give it is to leave it strictly alone most of the time. It automatically controls the zero temperature in the storage compartment and below-zero in the quick-freeze compartment. When food to be frozen is placed in the freezer, the automatic control provides the additional refrigeration necessary to freeze it quickly.

Defrosting. Unless your freezer has non-frosting mechanism, it must be defrosted. How often your freezer must be defrosted depends on the moisture content of the air inside the freezer, how many times the door is opened to withdraw or put in packages, and how moisture-vaporproof your packaging of the food has been. But once or twice a year should be sufficient.

When frost accumulates to a depth of about ¼ inch, it should be scraped off with a smooth-edged, hard plastic or wooden paddle. Sharp tools or wire brushes should not be used. Remove the food from your freezer and wrap it in several thicknesses of paper. If your freezer has a drain, the frost may be melted easily by putting saucepans filled with boiling water in the freezer and repeating after 15 minutes if the frost has not melted. Otherwise, scrape the frost onto layers of newspaper so that it can be lifted out easily. Work as quickly as possible and return the frozen food as soon as the frost has been removed.

Cleaning. Once a year your freezer should be thoroughly cleaned, and the logical time to do this is in the spring, when your supply of frozen food is at its minimum. It is also logical to clean your freezer at a time when it needs defrosting as well. Turn off the current and place all the packages from the freezer in a box thickly lined with newspapers and dry ice. Defrost the freezer and wash each compartment with a solution of 2 tablespoons of baking soda dissolved in each quart of warm water. Soap or caustic solutions must never be used. Dry the inside of the compartments thoroughly before turning on the power, and return the food as soon as the interior reaches zero.

Does the motor need oiling? That depends entirely on the make of freezer you own. Most home freezers have units hermetically sealed with a lifetime of lubrication.

What happens if the power fails? DON'T OPEN THE DOOR UNTIL THE POWER IS RESTORED, or if the power remains off for more than 48 hours, open the door just long enough to put dry ice into the compartments. It is a wise precaution to locate a source of supply of dry ice near your home in case of emergency. Usually your local dairy or ice plant can supply you. Handle the dry ice with gloves and pack about 10 pounds into each compartment. Fifty pounds of dry ice will hold the temperature in a 20-cubic-foot cabinet with a full load of frozen food for about 4 days. If the freezer is only partially filled with frozen food, the danger point will be reached in 2 to 3 days. A 6-cubic-foot freezer needs only 15 pounds of dry ice to protect food in an emergency.

Dry ice is not really ice at all, for it contains no water. It is the harmless, non-toxic carbon dioxide gas, first liquefied, then frozen to a temperature of 109° *below zero.* As it melts and absorbs heat, it evaporates to its natural gaseous state, leaving behind it no moisture.

Should an alarm be installed? Definitely! Sometimes the door to your freezer is accidentally left open. A temperature-operated alarm sounds a warning if, for any reason, the temperature in your freezer rises to the danger point. Many freezers on the market today are already equipped with this device. Be sure to have the alarm batteries checked occasionally.

HOW MUCH WILL A FREEZER COST TO OPERATE?

That depends on many things—the cubic-foot capacity, the kind and thickness of insulation, the type of construction, the horsepower of the motor on the freezing unit, the quantity of foods frozen, the temperature of the food to be frozen, the length of time, how frequently the freezer is opened, and the temperature at which the cabinet is held for storage.

Here are a few rules for the most efficient and economical operation of your freezer:

1. Keep your freezer in a dry place away from sunny windows, radiators, and stoves.

2. Avoid freezing too large a quantity of food at one time.

3. Keep packages well organized in the most convenient place, so you can find them quickly and easily.

4. Defrost when necessary. Thick layers of frost inside your freezer reduce efficiency and make the maintenance of zero temperatures more difficult.

5. Chill all foods before putting them into your freezer. Warm foods raise the temperature inside the freezer and cause unnecessary use of electricity.

6. Two freezers are more economical than one. For instance, if you decide you need 20 cubic feet of freezer space, two 10-cubic-foot freezers are more economical than one large one. The use of one may be discontinued during periods when your supply of frozen foods is at a minimum. Again, one may be reserved for those foods that you intend to store for a considerable period. The other may be kept exclusively for foods such as butter, coffee, cream, bread, rolls, et cetera, that are used every day.

EQUIPMENT FOR HOME FREEZING

Except for a good supply of packaging materials, very little equipment other than that found in a moderately equipped kitchen is needed. You should have:

1. Sharp knives for slicing and preparing vegetables.

2. Measuring cups and spoons.

3. A large spoon or scoop.

4. A nest of bowls.

5. Two 6-quart cooking kettles with tight-fitting lids.

6. A square funnel, or a tin can with ends removed and sides flattened, for filling bags.

7. A carton holder for easier packaging and sealing.

8. A fine-meshed wire basket or cheesecloth for scalding vegetables.

9. A pitcher for syrup.

10. A thermostatically controlled hand iron, or a curling iron, for sealing packages.

11. A labeling pencil.

PACKAGING MATERIALS

Much of the success of home-frozen foods depends upon proper packaging materials and how foods are wrapped and sealed for storage, so the importance of this phase of freezing cannot be over-emphasized. There must be no exchange of moisture or air between the frozen food and the air inside the cabinet. Cold air is dry air and dry air will draw the moisture from the foods unless they are protected by moisture-vaporproof materials, which are readily available and which were designed expressly to exclude the air and prevent the escape of moisture from frozen foods.

The meaning of *moisture-vaporproof* should not be confused with the word waterproof. Ordinary waxed or oil papers, gift-wrap cellophanes, and ice-cream cartons, while waterproof, still permit the exchange of moist air through their pores and should not be used. It is false economy to buy improper wrappings and containers, for if the moisture is taken from the foods in zero storage that are not carefully wrapped in moisture-vaporproof wrappings, or if the covering becomes torn during storage, the foods will be dry and of inferior quality. They will lose flavor, color, and food value.

Loss of moisture in frozen foods also means that the food is exposed to the oxygen in the air. Exposure to oxygen hastens the rancidity of fats. Grayish-white spots are apt to develop on the surface of meat which is inadequately protected. This is known as "freezer burn." Actually, the meat has not been burned at all; rather, it has been robbed of its moisture, or dehydrated, and oxidation has taken place. Though still edible, the meat is definitely of poor quality.

Besides resisting the passage of moisture-vapor and protecting the food from contact with the air inside the freezer, packaging materials must protect the food from leakage and the possibility of an exchange of flavors between one food and another. Fish, butter, cheese, and pastries are all stored side by side, and if an exchange of flavors is permitted, the results could be disastrous. Butter, for example, will pick up other flavors if given the slightest opportunity.

Packaging materials should be odorless, tasteless, flexible, and easy to handle, seal, and label. They should be strong enough to stand considerable handling without cracking, durable enough to resist puncturing by bones or sharp edges, and they must not become brittle at zero temperature.

Packaging materials should be relatively inexpensive and economical of storage space. Square or rectangular cartons and plastic containers stack easily and use a minimum of space. They are available in pint and quart sizes, and you should select the size that is most suited to your family needs. A quart container will give you 6 to 8 servings of a vegetable or 8 to 10 servings of fruit. One cubic foot of freezer space will house about 24 rectangular or square cartons, but only 16 round or slope-sided cartons.

Briefly, here are the points to consider when you are shopping for packaging materials. They:

1. Must be moisture-vaporproof to protect the food from contact with the air inside the cabinet and loss of moisture, flavor, and odor.

2. Must protect the food from leakage and the possibility of an exchange of flavors.

3. Must be easy to handle and seal.

4. Must be strong and durable.

5. Should be fairly inexpensive.

6. Should use a minimum of storage space.

SHEET WRAPPINGS

Aluminum foil is easy to use. It is flexible and may be fitted snugly around the food, expelling the excess air, and does not require taping or heat-sealing. When two surfaces of aluminum foil are pressed tightly together, the package is sealed. It punctures easily and should be protected by an outside wrap, but it is excellent for wrapping roasts, poultry, large fish, and irregularly shaped foods.

Moisture-vaporproof cellophane needs an overwrap to protect it from puncturing. It's flexible and transparent for easy identification. Needs heat-sealing. It may be used to wrap steaks, chops, poultry, and fish.

Pliofilm is heavier and sturdier than cellophane. It is excellent for wrapping irregularly shaped foods and makes a handsome, air-free package because of its rubberlike quality. It needs a protective covering and heat-sealing.

Polyethylene is a plastic film that will stand more handling than either cellophane or Pliofilm. It is particularly strong and pliable and needs no overwrap.

Saran is an excellent transparent plastic film that clings closely to food, eliminating air pockets. It is moisture-vaporproof and pliable. Needs heat-sealing.

Laminated paper is made of two sheets of different materials held together by a flexible adhesive. It may be Pliofilm laminated to aluminum foil, or glassine or cellophane laminated to heavy paper. The lamination makes the paper moisture-vaporproof. Laminated papers are flexible and mold well to food. They are perfect for wrapping roasts. Ends and seams should be sealed with freezer tape.

CONTAINERS

There are many types of containers available for fruits, vegetables, soups, stews, juices, and cooked foods. Select the best size to suit your needs and number of servings. Be certain they are moisture-proof and leakproof. Durable plastic containers that are re-usable are a good investment.

When buying containers, consider these qualities:

Do they nest inside each other when not in use?

Do they stack easily on top of each other in the freezer?

Do they have lids with a good seal?

Do they permit easy labeling?

Are they easy to fill?

TYPES OF CONTAINERS FOR THE FREEZER

Aluminum Foil Containers

Baking Dishes (some can be put into a hot oven directly from freezer)

Drum and Tub Waxed Cartons

Glass Jars

Paper Bags lined with Pliofilm

Pie Plates

Plastic Bags

Plastic Containers, both pliable and rigid
Waxed Cartons with Cellophane Insert Bags
Waxed Cartons with Cellophane Covering

ADDITIONAL BASIC PACKAGING NEEDS

Outer wrappings give added strength to packages and prevent the moisture-vaporproof coverings from tearing during storage.

Stockinette material is a tubular, loosely knitted cotton fabric that may be stretched over odd-shaped foods for added protection.

Locker paper, butcher paper, nylon stockings, or *cheesecloth* may also be used as an overwrap. Polyethylene or laminated papers do not need this extra protection.

You should also have on hand locker tape—a special tape which will hold even in the zero temperatures of your freezer for any length of time. Use it to seal edges, to cover accidental punctures, and to attach labels. You will need a *heat sealer* of some type and a *china marking pencil* which will label clearly all types of papers and cartons.

HOW TO PACKAGE FOODS FOR
YOUR FREEZER

The way food is wrapped for the freezer is just as important in maintaining the quality of frozen food as the wrappings and containers that you buy. No matter how moisture-vaporproof the wrappings may be, if they are carelessly sealed so that the air can get in and the moisture of the food can get out, you might just as well have never wrapped it at all.

Whether packaging in containers or wrapping in paper, exclude as much air as possible from the package. Air pockets between the food and the packaging material collect moisture from the food. Package in amounts that are suitable for your family needs. Label accurately and informatively and freeze at once.

The *drugstore fold* is the easiest way to make a close, tight wrap with any suitable sheet wrapping and is recommended for irregularly shaped foods such as poultry and cuts of meat. Place the food in the center of a large sheet of flexible, durable paper. Bring the ends of the paper above the meat and fold them over and over downward in a lock seal, drawing the paper as tightly to the food as possible. Then fold the ends, fitting and pressing the paper close to the food to avoid air pockets. Use low-temperature locker tape to seal the edges of the folds.

The *butcher wrap* is also used for the inner and outer wrap of sheet wrappings, or for a single wrap if laminated paper is used. Place the food diagonally across one corner of a large sheet of freezer paper. Fold over the sides and roll the package over and over until the food is completely covered. Wrap tightly to exclude the air and keep the package flat. Seal the edges carefully with low-temperature locker tape.

Folding cartons with heat-sealing liners. Open the moisture-vapor-proof liner completely, including the corners, with the hand, and insert in the opened carton. The use of a block of wood on which to form packages is a time saver. Fill carton by means of a square funnel, or a tin can slightly flattened, to keep the top of the bag dry. The sealing edge must be perfectly dry and clean to have a perfect heat seal.

Press out air from liner and seal liner partway across close down to the packaged food. Press out remaining air and finish the seal. Then draw the iron upward toward the end of the bag. A wooden platform may be made to hold the package upright as you seal the liner. Another easy method of getting a seal close to the food is by resting a wide strip of heavy cardboard on top of the carton. Fold the bag over it at the point where the seal can be made snugly against the contents, press out the air from the liner, and move the iron over the cardboard. Use just enough heat and pressure to melt the plastic film or wax until it seals. Too much heat will scorch the liner and cause an imperfect seal.

Head space must be left in packing liquid or semiliquid foods to allow for expansion during freezing and to prevent bulging of containers, leaking, or breakage of glass. The more liquid the product, the greater the expansion and the more head space needed. Ideally, just enough space should be left so that the food will expand flush with the top, leaving no air pockets in the container, but this comes only by experience. In general, leave ½ inch head space for most foods and 1 inch for juices. If ordinary glass jars are used for freezing, leave 1 inch in pints and 1½ inches in quarts.

Plastic cartons. Simply fill and cover with the plastic cover. Follow manufacturer's directions for lifting edge of cover and pressing out air. Leave head space as above. Plastic cartons, while slightly more expensive than folding cartons, pay for themselves in a few months, for they may be used over and over again.

Labeling. Every package in your freezer should be identified as to the kind of food, the weight or the number of servings, the date of storage, and the intended use of the contents.

Freeze immediately. The more quickly packaged foods get into your freezer the better they will be when cooked. Check your freezing compartment to make sure it can accommodate the amount of food you are preparing. Freeze at one time only the number of packages advised by the manufacturer of your freezer. Place the packages in contact with the freezer lining, with air space between them.

WHAT CAN YOU FREEZE?

Practically every type of food can be preserved by freezing except vegetables to be eaten raw and crisp, like lettuce, celery, radishes, cucumbers, tomatoes, cabbage, onions, and green peppers. Tomatoes may be frozen as juice or purée, or in ready-made dishes. Cabbage may be frozen and used as a cooked vegetable, but it will not retain its crispness in the raw state.

Everything else freezes well—beef, lamb, pork, veal, and variety meats; chicken, ducks, turkeys, guinea hens, and geese; game birds, rabbits, squirrels, and venison; fish and shellfish; ice cream, sherbets, butter, cheese, and eggs; fruit juices and fruit purées; cakes, cookies, pies, puddings, bread, rolls, stews, soups, and ready-made dishes.

What should you freeze? Your freezer space is limited no matter what size you have, and if you are going to get the most from your freezer, every cubic inch must be strictly and wisely budgeted so that a variety of foods can be stored to satisfy the personal preferences of your entire family.

Your approach to daily living and where you live will affect your decision as to what and how much you want to freeze. If you have a garden, you will want to conserve the fruits and vegetables that cannot be eaten. Frozen fruits and vegetables are good, but they are never as good as when they are fresh, and for most city dwellers there is very little reason to freeze vegetables at all. Why freeze onions, turnips, beets, carrots, celery, green peppers? There is seldom a time throughout the year that these vegetables cannot be bought at your local vegetable store. Who would fill up her freezer with potatoes, just because she happened to have some spare time and felt in the mood to peel a peck? It makes sense to have a few packages of potato croquettes or French fried potatoes on hand. French fried onions are good too. But it makes no more sense to fill your freezer with potatoes or onions than to fill it with loaves of bread. Yet everyone should have a couple of loaves of French bread and a few packages of rolls and biscuits in the freezer for an emergency.

How difficult to resist filling the freezer with strawberries, raspberries, or peaches when they are in season! But resist you must, if you are going to use your freezer storage space to best advantage. It is easy to fill the space with the first products of spring—asparagus, peas, or strawberries—leaving little room for the broccoli and spinach which follow later. A fine crop of late vegetables or fruits and no place to put them can cause regret. Don't forget that you can always buy fruits and vegetables, as you need them, meticulously prepared and properly packaged and frozen by reliable commercial freezers.

Also, just because you are the proud owner of a home freezer, don't lose sight of the fact that there *are* other excellent ways (and in certain specific instances *better* ways) to preserve foods. Don't forget to make some of your fruit into jams and jellies. Dill your cucumbers; use your peppers and cauliflower in chowchow. Eat your fresh vegetables while they are in season. Buy the few frozen vegetables you need for winter use, or enjoy those root crops—beets, turnips, and parsnips—that keep well in a cool cellar.

Don't hoard large quantities of meat and poultry in your freezer. There is little to be gained. Let your freezer work for you by keeping the space in constant use. Store wise quantities of meat and poultry. Eat the foods from your freezer, use them up quickly, plan a constant turnover, and make replacements with a fresh supply.

Fish, like vegetables, are never as good as when they are strictly fresh. Eat lots of fish when it is in season and store only as much as you will consume in three or four months. So—

1. Be discriminating in the choice and selection of the foods you freeze. Freezer space is valuable—don't waste it.

2. Freeze only top-quality meats, poultry, and fish. Freezing does

not improve anything; it merely maintains whatever quality the food had before it was frozen.

3. Freeze only the amount of food that can be used in a few months, and use your supply constantly. Don't hoard for that rainy day that may never come.

4. Plan a constant turnover. No food improves with long storage and quality in some cases is lost after only a few months.

5. Save enough room for leftovers and for ready-made dishes.

PLANNING AND INVENTORY

Anticipate your fruit and vegetable needs

Plan in advance what you are going to freeze and how much, depending on the preferences of your family, to avoid overloading with the first crops of the season. Peak seasons for fruits and vegetables vary from one state to another. In New York State the seasons run approximately as follows:

May: Asparagus, rhubarb
June: Asparagus, sweet cherries, spinach, strawberries, turnip greens
July: Beets, blackberries, blueberries, carrots, sour cherries, sweet cherries, currants, gooseberries, kohlrabi, peas, raspberries
August: Apples, green-shell beans, snap beans, beets, blackberries, blueberries, carrots, chard, eggplant, peaches, peppers, turnips
September: Apples, lima beans, carrots, chard, sweet corn, cranberries, peaches, peppers, plums, prunes, winter squash, turnips, soybeans
October: Apples, broccoli, Brussels sprouts, cauliflower, cranberries, kale, soybeans
November: Broccoli, Brussels sprouts, kale

PLANNING YOUR FROZEN MEAT SUPPLY

A supply of meat can be put into the home freezer at any time of the year. The greatest supply, however, is available at the time when prices are lowest, normally during the late fall, winter, and early spring months. This is the time when farmers usually butcher. The harvest has been brought in and farmers have more time for butchering from November 15 to March 15. Also, at this time the weather is cold and the carcasses can be quickly chilled.

The logical way to fill the freezer with meat is once in the fall and again in early spring. Stocking up on meats only twice a year leaves more space for the seasonable fruits, vegetables, and poultry.

PLANNING YOUR POULTRY SUPPLY

Poultry is in season most of the year, but from May to November the supply is at its greatest:

Broilers—May to July
Fryers—June to August
Roasters and *Fowl*—June to November

ARRANGE THE FOODS IN YOUR FREEZER SYSTEMATICALLY

A well-organized freezer holds more packages. It may take a little more time than just throwing packages in haphazardly, but an orderly freezer is much more convenient to use. Bad planning often results in a scramble through the entire contents of the freezer in order to find a certain package, or it may mean that the last frozen are the first to be used, leaving some packages deep within the freezer much longer than they should be stored for best quality. Group the same kinds of foods together, assigning certain sections to vegetables, fruits, meats, poultry, and ready-cooked dishes. Place newly frozen packages at the bottom or back of their section so that the older ones will be the first used.

KEEP A RUNNING INVENTORY

An elaborate inventory is not necessary, but some system that will keep you informed at all times as to what and how much of the different foods you have on hand is absolutely essential if you are going to get the best use from your freezer.

214

An inventory:

1. Helps you keep a balanced assortment of foods in your freezer.
2. Helps you plan your menus.
3. Reminds you to use up packages that might otherwise be held too long and thus lose quality.
4. Warns you that certain items should be replenished.

Some like a series of recipe cards in a file box or a loose-leaf binder, each item with its own page or card. I prefer a good-sized slate blackboard and a piece of chalk. This is probably the simplest and most effective method of keeping an up-to-date record of the contents of your freezer.

Here are two examples of simple inventories:

Vegetables	DATE	IN	OUT	BALANCE
Asparagus	5/10/65	6	1-1-1-1	~~6~~ ~~5~~ ~~4~~ ~~3~~ 2
Spinach	6/4/65	6		6
Meat				
Porterhouse (for 4)	11/6/65	6	1-1	~~6~~ ~~5~~ 4
Round Steak (for 6)	12/15/65	4	1	~~4~~ 3
Venison Roast (7 pounds)	11/2/65	2		2
Poultry				
Ducks (6 pounds)	5/12/65	6		6
Chicken Fryers (3 pounds)	6/3/65	12	1-1	~~12~~ ~~11~~ 10

Instead of listing the date on which the food was frozen, you might prefer to list the date by which the food should be used for top quality. In this way you don't have to do any mental gymnastics every time you review your inventory.

	USE BY	NO. OF PACKAGES
Sausage Meat	3/15/65	~~8~~ ~~7~~ ~~6~~ ~~5~~ 4

HOW LONG CAN FOODS BE STORED
AT ZERO?

Many people have the misconception that a freezer preserves food indefinitely. *This is not true.* Freezing simply slows down the destructive action of the organisms that cause food spoilage—it does not destroy these organisms. The length of time that a food can be stored in your freezer without losing quality and flavor depends on the particular food, and the maximum storage times given throughout this book should be taken seriously if you are going to get the greatest enjoyment from your frozen foods.

No food should be kept longer than from one growing season to another, but most foods should be kept for much shorter periods. Your freezer should not be treated like a revered, almost untouchable hope chest. It should be made an active source of your daily food supply.

A great deal of research and experimentation has been done by the manufacturers of home freezers, by the United States Department of Agriculture, and by the many State colleges in order to determine the maximum storage life of various foods. As a result, we have learned that many factors affect the keeping qualities of food and that all foods do not have the same storage life.

We know that the variety and the maturity of fruits and vegetables and the speed and care given to them in their preparation is important.

We know that the proper scalding of vegetables is vital to their frozen life.

We have discovered that bacon and salt pork must not be kept in the freezer very long because the salt used in curing these meats accelerates the development of rancidity in the fat.

We know that ground and sliced meats have a relatively short storage life, because a greater amount of surface is exposed to the destructive chemical process of oxidation. Fat is the bad actor in zero storage and for this reason fat meat such as pork and fatty fish should not be kept longer than their recommended storage period.

CAN YOU REFREEZE FOODS?

In general, refreezing is not a good idea, as the food suffers a loss of flavor and quality. Completely thawed poultry, meats, and non-acid vegetables, which are subject to attack by harmful bacteria, should not be refrozen. Fruits and acid vegetables, however, are not prey to such bacteria and may be safely refrozen.

Any food only partially thawed may be refrozen.

When deciding whether to refreeze or not, remember:

1. If food is still firm and contains some ice crystals, it is safe to refreeze, although quality may be somewhat affected. Relabel, freeze quickly, and use as soon as possible.

2. If vegetables or cooked foods, such as stews or casseroles, are completely thawed, *but still very cold,* cook thoroughly and serve for lunch or dinner.

3. If poultry and meat is completely thawed, *but still very cold,* cook and serve or make into favorite cooked dishes and freeze the cooked dishes.

4. Baked goods may be refrozen many times, but each time they thaw they become a little staler.

5. Concentrated fruit juices refreeze safely.

6. Use thawed fruits for jams, jellies, and preserves.

CARE OF PURCHASED FROZEN FOODS

Correct handling of commercially frozen foods is as important as correct handling of those you freeze at home. Unfortunately you cannot control the care they get from manufacturer to store, or how they are handled in the store, but you can make sure that, once purchased, you get them home and into the freezer as soon as possible. The greatest damage to quality is if the frozen food is allowed to rise above zero temperature. Remember:

1. Make frozen foods the last shopping you do on your shopping trip.

2. Ask the store to give you insulated bags to put them in before leaving the store.

3. Put frozen foods in your freezer as soon as you get home.

4. Rotate frozen purchases, just as you would the foods you freeze yourself. The first in should be the first used.

5. Your ice-cube compartment in your refrigerator is not a freezer. This compartment maintains a maximum low of around 15° F. Use only for convenience until ready to cook within 3 days, sooner if possible for flavor can be lost even in that short time.

EQUIVALENT WEIGHTS OF FROZEN AND FRESH FOODS

When you buy frozen foods instead of fresh, you must consider the cost of food per serving and not the cost of food per pound. Remember that frozen foods are meticulously prepared and properly packaged for you. There is no waste. Frozen foods, on this basis, are not as expensive as they might seem. The following table from the Quick Frozen Food Association of Chicago shows the equivalent weights of frozen and fresh foods.

TABLE OF EQUIVALENTS

Vegetables	FROZEN EQUIVALENT TO:		FRESH
Asparagus	12 oz.	1	lb. 10 oz.
Green Beans	10 oz.	14	oz.
Wax Beans	10 oz.	14	oz.
Broccoli	10 oz.	1	lb. 6 oz.
Brussels Sprouts	10 oz.	1	lb. 4 oz.
Cauliflower	10 oz.	Med. Head	
Cut Corn	12 oz.	6	ears
Lima Beans	12 oz.	2	lbs.
Peas	12 oz.	2	lbs.
Peas and Carrots	12 oz.	2	lbs.
Mixed Vegetables	12 oz.	2	lbs.
Spinach	14 oz.	2	lbs. 8 oz.
Squash	16 oz.	1	lb. 6 oz.
Poultry			
Broilers and Fryers	2 lbs.	3	lbs. Undrawn
Roasters	3 lbs.	4	lbs. Undrawn
Fowl	2½ lbs.	3½	lbs. Undrawn
Turkeys	9 lbs.	12	lbs. Undrawn

Fish	FROZEN EQUIVALENT TO:		FRESH	
Cod and Haddock	1	lb.	3	lbs. Whole
Mackerel	1	lb.	1¾	lbs. Whole
Flounder (Sole)	1	lb.	4	lbs. Whole
Ocean Perch	1	lb.	5	lbs. Whole

FIFTEEN BASIC RULES FOR FREEZING

1. PLAN WELL
Freeze foods your family enjoys. Freeze the most popular in the greatest quantity. Freeze a well-balanced proportion of all foods according to your freezer space.

2. FOLLOW THE SEASONS
Freeze fruits and vegetables at their flavor peak. Consult your butcher for good buys of poultry and meat.

3. SELECT TOP QUALITY
You get nothing better out of your freezer than you put in. Freezing retains quality, but it does not improve it. *Don't waste freezer space with inferior foods.*

4. WORK QUICKLY
Prepare fruits and vegetables when they are as fresh as possible. Two hours from field to freezer is the perfect rule.

5. PREPARE FOODS CAREFULLY

6. PROCESS ONLY SMALL QUANTITIES AT A TIME
Handle only the amount that can be processed quickly and don't burden your freezer with too many unfrozen packages at one time.

7. FOLLOW DIRECTIONS
The instructions in this book are the result of the latest and most authoritative research on freezing.

8. CHILL FOODS BEFORE FREEZING
Scalded vegetables should be instantly cooled in ice water. Wash fruit in ice water.

9. PACKAGE IN MEAL-SIZE PORTIONS

10. PACKAGE FOODS CAREFULLY
Wrap snugly in moisture-vaporproof material and seal perfectly.

11. LABEL
Include type of food, weight or number of servings, and date of freezing.

12. FREEZE PACKAGED FOODS IMMEDIATELY

13. ORGANIZE FOODS IN FREEZER
Store all of one kind of food together. Foods to be used first should be readily accessible.

14. KEEP AN INVENTORY

15. OBSERVE RECOMMENDED STORAGE PERIODS
Plan a constant turnover of the contents of your freezer so that no food will have the opportunity to lose quality and flavor.

CHAPTER 2

Freezing Meat and Game

No other method of preservation retains the taste and texture of meat and game as well as freezing, providing it is fresh meat of good quality, is frozen as quickly as possible, and stored at a constant 0° F. or lower.

All meats, including specialties such as sweetbreads, heart, liver, tongue, and brains, freeze well. Often it is economical to buy a large portion of a carcass for use throughout the year, and sometimes it is possible to buy special meat or a specific cut of meat from your butcher at a real bargain. But any meat you buy for your freezer should be grade A quality, properly aged, cut, and boned, and packaged in the size most convenient for your family. Freezing seals in the original quality and flavor, it does not improve it. If you fill your freezer with inferior, tough meat, it will still be tough and dry and of poor quality when taken out.

SELECTING MEAT FOR YOUR FREEZER

Whether you purchase retail cuts, or buy an animal or portion of a carcass to be dressed for you, or do your own slaughtering and dressing, select fresh high-quality meats, moderately fat and well finished.

A good animal is thickly fleshed in the ribs, loin, and hindquarters. An ample layer of fat not only protects the lean meat from drying out during the freezing period, but adds flavor when the meat is cooked. Too much fat, however, should be avoided, as fat oxidizes quickly and rancidity is likely to occur. Veal rarely has surplus fat and is an exception to the general rule.

If buying a section of a carcass, separate steaks from roasts.

The less tender portions of the animal should be cut and packaged for braising or stewing, or ground for hamburgers and meat loaves. Plan to package meats in the right amounts to suit the size of your family, with only enough in each package for one meal.

HOW TO PACKAGE MEAT FOR THE FREEZER

Once meat has been cut, it should be packaged and frozen immediately. The meat should be shaped into its most compact form before it is wrapped, to avoid air pockets. Trim off the excess fat and wrap carefully and tightly in heavy moisture-vaporproof paper, pressing the paper firmly against the meat, again forcing out the air pockets. Keep packages as smooth as possible. The drugstore wrap is most effective. As the fold is formed, the paper can be pulled tightly against the meat. As the ends are folded, the air pockets can be pressed out. Seal the ends and seams with acetate tape and label with the kind of cut, number of pieces, and date of freezing.

Once packaged, freeze immediately at 0° F., leaving enough air around each package so that all sides are evenly exposed to the zero temperature. If your home freezer maintains a constant temperature of 0° F., and if several inches of air space are allowed around the packages, the meat will be frozen completely in 8 to 12 hours, and the more rapidly the meat is frozen solidly, the better its flavor and texture will be. So when you put a fresh supply of meat in your freezer try not to open the door for at least 12 hours. If you constantly keep opening the door of your freezer and letting in warm air, the meat may take 24 hours or longer to freeze and some quality will be lost.

Roasts and large cuts

Wrapping materials made especially for the freezer protect roasts and large cuts of meat properly against loss of surface moisture, oxidation, and rancidity. It is unwise to economize on wrappings for meat. If there are any protruding bones, pad them before wrapping the meat, to prevent the bones from breaking through.

Removing excess bones saves freezer space and makes it easier to package.

If Pliofilm, Saran, or aluminum foil is used, a stockinette over-wrap should be pulled snugly around the paper to protect it against tearing. Tie a knot in the stockinette tightly against the roast. Cut off and tie the end of the stockinette in a knot. Attach a tag or label. If one of the laminated papers is used, no overwrap is necessary. Wrap tightly, pressing paper tightly against all surfaces of the meat to remove air. The package should be smooth and firm when it is finished. Seal carefully.

Steaks and chops

Trim excess fat or bone. Package the number of steaks, chops, or cutlets needed for one meal in each package with two pieces of freezer paper between them. Keep the meat flat as you wrap it, packing the chops or steaks tightly together in neat, regular layers. Top-opening cartons stack well and conserve freezer space.

When frozen this way steaks or chops can be separated without thawing the entire package. If you do not need the amount of chops or steaks that you anticipated when you packaged them, one or more can be removed and the package resealed and placed again in the freezer.

Ground meat

Ground meat should never be refrozen; therefore it should be packaged in the right amount for a specific recipe. Omit all salt to avoid rancidity during storage. Pack the amount of ground meat you will need for a casserole firmly in a top-opening carton, pressing out any air pockets. Make meat loaves all ready to bake, wrap in moisture-vaporproof paper, and seal completely. Form ground meat into patties and pack the patties in layers, separating the layers with two sheets of freezer paper. Or wrap each patty separately and pack in a top-opening carton. Either way the patties may be easily separated for cooking directly from the frozen state, or a few may be cooked and the others returned to the freezer. Overwrap the cartons and heat-seal the edges and ends.

Meats for braising

Wrap large roasts for braising or boiling in the same manner as oven roasts. Cubed stew meat should be pressed firmly into rigid containers or cartons.

Variety meats

Prepare variety meats such as liver, tongue, heart, and kidneys as soon as they are chilled. Liver may be cut into slices of the desired thickness, the slices separated with two sheets of freezer paper, and packaged flat. Hearts may also be sliced. Variety meats should not be stored longer that 4 months.

Smoked meats

The keeping qualities of hams and bacon at zero temperature depend entirely on how well the meat was processed and the type of cure, but generally they should not be kept longer than a couple of months. It is important that these meats be wrapped tightly to prevent their drying out and to prohibit the transfer of flavor to other foods. Freeze bacon in 1- or 2-pound slabs rather than slices and slice after it is thawed.

If hams and bacon are fully cured and hung in a cool, dry room, they will keep for as long as 6 months, so there is little reason to occupy freezer space with them. However, the flavor of hams and bacon that are only mildly cured is delicate and delicious, and a mild cure may be used if these products are to be frozen.

Sausage

Spices and other seasonings such as black and red pepper, sage, and other herbs actually retard rancidity in sausage meat, but salt speeds up oxidation in any meat. The sausage may be completely seasoned, or the salt may be omitted and added before or during cooking. If salt is added, plan to use the sausage in a short time. Without salt, sausage meat may be safely stored in your freezer for as long as 6 months. Package in the same way as ground meat.

Bones and trimmings

Use these for soup stock. For recipes and freezing instructions see chapter on soups and stocks.

Label intelligently

It takes only a few seconds to write on the wrapper the type of meat, the number of servings, the date, and whether it is to be used for a specific purpose or a favorite recipe.

Keep meat cool during and after wrapping

If meat is wrapped in a warm room, it should be chilled in the refrigerator before it is frozen. Freeze only as much at one time as can be solidly frozen within 24 hours.

Rotate frozen meats

Organize meat in the freezer so that those that have been frozen longest will be the first used. There is no economy in using meat that is freshly frozen if the freezer holds similar cuts that have been frozen for several months.

SLAUGHTERING DOMESTIC ANIMALS AND LARGE GAME

Have a veterinarian inspect animals to insure that only healthy ones are slaughtered for food.

If you live on a farm and have proper equipment and cool, clean, adequate space, you will probably do your own slaughtering.

Detailed information can be obtained from your local extension office of the United States Department of Agriculture, but unless you have had experience it is wiser by far to enlist the services of an expert butcher. A good deal of fine meat can be spoiled when amateurs slaughter animals. Most locker plants not only sell meats, but have skilled services for slaughtering, butchering, chilling, aging, cutting, wrapping, and freezing.

On the farm, slaughtering is done from late fall to early spring, when the weather is cool enough to chill the carcass quickly and thoroughly. In warm months, unless adequate refrigeration is available, the meat will spoil at outdoor temperatures.

Feed should be withheld for 18 to 24 hours before animals are slaughtered, but plenty of water should be available. Slaughtering should be done in the evening so the carcasses can be hung in the cold night air, and only at a time when the weather is expected to remain at or a little below 40° F. The temperature should not rise above this; neither should it drop below the freezing point. The ideal temperature for slaughtering is between 33° and 38° F.

Chilling carcasses

Prompt and thorough chilling of slaughtered animals under sanitary conditions is imperative to prevent spoilage and to protect the meat from contact with undesirable odors. The body temperature of freshly slaughtered meat is around 100° F. and it must be reduced to between 33° and 38° F. within 24 hours.

Meat cut from warm carcasses is soft and will not hold its shape, resulting in ragged, unattractive cuts. If more than one carcass is hung, room must be left between them so that air can circulate as the carcasses cool. If the removal of body heat is not prompt and thorough, destructive molds, yeasts, and bacteria multiply with such speed that the flavor of the meat will be ruined and the flesh may become unfit for use. It must be kept in mind when cooling meat that warm flesh is most receptive to such odors as mildew, paint, and disinfectant.

A beef carcass should be split in half and washed thoroughly in plenty of lukewarm water. It will take 24 hours at 34° F. for the carcass of a 1000-pound steer to cool to an internal temperature of 38° F. at its thickest part. A clean skewer-type thermometer should be inserted in the thickest muscle to determine the internal temperature, for if the temperature is reduced to only 40° F., instead of 38° F., this small difference of just two degrees is apt to result in souring at the hip bone.

Hogs, calves, lambs, and mutton also require about 24 hours' chilling at 34° F.

Rapid chilling of pork at temperatures between 33° and 38° F. is most essential. Pork may sour in 12 hours if it is hung in a warm temperature, or if the carcasses are allowed to overlap so the cold air cannot circulate around them. Many hams are lost in curing because the hogs were slaughtered when the weather was too warm and the carcasses were not quickly and efficiently chilled to 38° F. or lower. To speed the chilling, the warm hogs should be split, the internal organs removed, and the leaf lard pulled out. Should the weather be below freezing, the carcasses should be wrapped in sheets and hung in a shed to protect them from freezing. And hang they must. Never lay them on the ground or floor.

The heavier and fatter the hog, the more carefully it must be handled. Rapid chilling cannot be overemphasized, but at the same time it must be thorough. Test the internal temperature of the large pieces of meat, such as the hams, with a meat thermometer. If the temperature is above 38° F., the carcass should be cut and the large pieces spread out during a second night to complete the chilling.

Freshly killed game needs even quicker attention than domestic animals, for spoilage starts immediately in the area of the wound. Large game, such as deer, moose, or antelope, should be bled promptly after they are killed and eviscerated. The body cavity must be wiped out with a clean cloth, but it should not be washed. If it is raining or snowing, the carcass chould be protected with canvas or burlap. If the weather is warm, the carcass must be covered with a sheet of cheesecloth to protect it from insects.

Aging

Young animals about 1 year old, such as pork and veal, do not need aging. They should be cut and packaged directly after cooling—especially pork, for pork fat becomes rancid quickly.

Variety meats, such as heart, liver, tongue, kidneys, and brains, should be chilled, cleaned, packaged, and frozen immediately.

Beef, lamb, mutton, and large game are improved in flavor and texture if they are allowed to age in a well-ventilated room at temperatures between 32° and 38° F. for 5 to 10 days.

Humidity is as important as temperature in the aging room. If the humidity is too low, the air will draw moisture from the meat and the carcass will become dry. If the humidity is too high, above 90 per cent, bacterial growth is apt to take place and the flesh will become slimy.

Aging breaks down the connective tissues and makes the meat more tender, but the length of time depends on the kind, quality, and size of the carcass, and an expert should be consulted.

The following aging periods are only approximate:

Beef	5 to 8 days
Large game	5 to 14 days
Mutton	2 to 3 days
Lamb	1 to 3 days

CUTTING AND BONING MEAT

This phase of preparing meat for the freezer is no job for the novice. You should employ an expert butcher. Most locker plants employ meat cutters or can direct you to one. Usually the charge for such services is reasonable, and it is good economics, in the overall picture, for someone trained in the profession can cut meat into uniform shape and thickness and can get the greatest number of desirable cuts.

It is wise, however, to direct the cutter as he works so that you will have the cuts which experience has taught you are most practical for your family.

Consider the size of your family and have the meat cut in family-size portions. Give thought to your preference in cooking and have the less desirable cuts, such as brisket, plate, and shank, cut into cubes for braising, or have them ground for meat loaves or patties. Consider the number of guests you entertain in your home and you will want to have some attractive guest-size cuts. Have your steaks cut good and thick. Thin steaks tend to dry out in several months' zero storage and also in cooking. Package roasts, chops, and steaks in meal-size portions, planning some extra-thick, succulent steaks, some choice roasts, a few double lamb chops, and so on, for special occasions.

Boning meat has become popular during the past few years for several reasons. Boned and rolled meat requires less space in your freezer, generally saving 25 per cent space, and in the case of lamb, it saves as much as 50 per cent. Less dehydration and oxidation can take place because of the snug, compact wrapping possible around the smooth surface of the rolled meat, which has no protruding bones to rupture the wrapping. When a roast is boned and rolled and tied, it may be cut into family-size portions and when cooked it may be carved more easily than a roast containing the bones. The bones may be used to make soup stock, and the stock may be frozen in convenient-size packages. The only disadvantage to boning meat is that it takes time and therefore increases the cost.

To help you direct the expert who cuts your meat, you must know and understand what he is doing. The following charts, given through the courtesy of the National Live Stock and Meat Board, show clearly the standard cuts made from a carcass or a portion of a carcass.

You will want to know too, if you purchase either a whole animal or a portion of one, how many pounds of meat, cut and trimmed, ready to be wrapped and frozen, you are going to realize from your purchase.

CUTTING BEEF

APPROXIMATE YIELD OF A WHOLE CARCASS

Live weight	750 pounds
Whole carcass	420 pounds
Dressed weight	338 pounds

TRIMMED CUTS FROM A WHOLE CARCASS

Steaks and oven roasts	40% of carcass weight, or 172 pounds
Pot roasts	20% of carcass weight, or 83 pounds
Stews and ground meat	20% of carcass weight, or 83 pounds
Total	80% of carcass weight, or 338 pounds

FOREQUARTERS WILL YIELD

Steaks and oven roasts	25% of carcass weight, or 55 pounds
Pot roasts	32% of carcass weight, or 70 pounds
Stews and ground meat	27% of carcass weight, or 59 pounds
Total	84% of carcass weight, or 184 pounds

HINDQUARTERS WILL YIELD

Steaks and oven roasts	58% of carcass weight, or 117 pounds
Stews and ground meat	18% of carcass weight, or 37 pounds
Total	76% of carcass weight, or 154 pounds

The approximate loss of 82 pounds between the weight of the carcass and the dressed meat is due to normal shrinkage, the loss of hide, fat, and meat trimmings, and the bones which are removed before the cuts are trimmed, and also the liver, tongue, and heart.

How the animal is cut depends a good deal on whether the animal was reasonably young, well fed, and well bred. If so, the rib and top round are satisfactory for steaks, and the rib and arm side of the chuck are usually tender enough to be oven-roasted. If the animal was old and thin, all these sections should be prepared for braising rather than roasting or broiling.

The best cuts for roasting are made from the rib sections of the carcass and the roast cut from the prime ribs, the standing rib roast, is a choice one. The bones may be removed, the meat rolled compactly and tied at 1-inch intervals with string. The roll may then be cut at intervals parallel to the string into family- or guest-size portions. The bones may also be removed from the rump, chuck, flank, plate, and neck to save freezer space.

Choice steaks cut from the loin, such as sirloin, porterhouse, T-bone, and club steaks, should not be boned. And before the round is sliced into steaks, it should be separated into three distinct parts in order to yield steaks of uniform tenderness. These parts are the top of the round, which is the most tender, the bottom of the round,

BEEF CUTS AND HOW TO COOK THEM

Retail Cuts	Wholesale Cuts	Retail Cuts

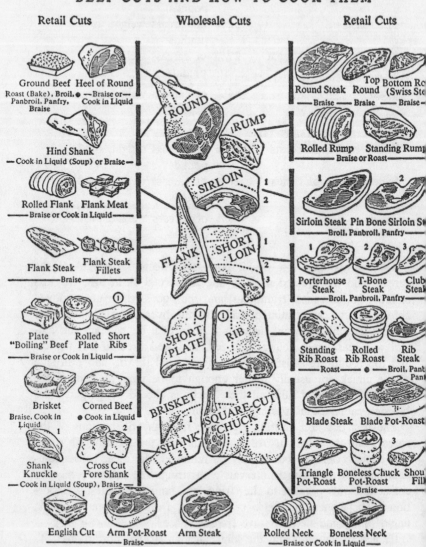

Ground Beef   Heel of Round
Roast (Bake), Broil, ●   —Braise or—
Panbroil, Panfry,   Cook in Liquid
Braise

Hind Shank
—Cook in Liquid (Soup) or Braise—

Rolled Flank   Flank Meat
—Braise or Cook in Liquid—

Flank Steak   Flank Steak Fillets
—Braise—

Plate   Rolled   Short
"Boiling" Beef   Plate   Ribs
—Braise or Cook in Liquid—

Brisket   Corned Beef
Braise, Cook in   ● Cook in Liquid
Liquid

Shank   Cross Cut
Knuckle   Fore Shank
—Cook in Liquid (Soup), Braise—

English Cut   Arm Pot-Roast   Arm Steak
—Braise—

ROUND   RUMP

SIRLOIN

FLANK   SHORT LOIN

SHORT PLATE   RIB

BRISKET   SQUARE-CUT CHUCK

SHANK

Round Steak   Top Round   Bottom Ro (Swiss Ste
—Braise—   —Braise—   —Braise—

Rolled Rump   Standing Rum
—Braise or Roast—

Sirloin Steak   Pin Bone Sirloin S
—Broil, Panbroil, Panfry—

Porterhouse   T-Bone   Club
Steak   Steak   Steak
—Broil, Panbroil, Panfry—

Standing   Rolled   Rib
Rib Roast   Rib Roast   Steak
—Roast—   ●   —Broil, Pant
Pan

Blade Steak   Blade Pot-Roast

Triangle   Boneless Chuck   Shou
Pot-Roast   Pot-Roast   Fil
—Braise—

Rolled Neck   Boneless Neck
—Braise or Cook in Liquid—

Courtesy of National Live Stock and Meat Bo

and the heel of the round. The steaks from both the bottom and top of the round should be sliced crosswise against the grain.

The less tender cuts from the shank, brisket, plate, flank, and neck are usually best when boned and ground or cubed for stews and casseroles. But save a slice of plate for boiled beef and get a pot roast from the arm.

Be sure to form ground meat for hamburgers into patties before freezing, so that they do not have to be thawed but can be broiled or sautéed directly from the freezer. One pound of ground meat, free of gristle and too much fat, makes four medium-sized hamburgers.

The heart and tongue may be frozen whole. The liver may be frozen whole or sliced before freezing.

CUTTING LAMB

APPROXIMATE YIELD OF A WHOLE CARCASS

Live weight	85 pounds
Whole carcass	41 pounds
Dressed weight	38 pounds

TRIMMED CUTS FROM A WHOLE CARCASS

Legs, chops, shoulders	75% of carcass weight, or 31 pounds
Breast and stew	15% of carcass weight, or 7 pounds
Total	90% of carcass weight, or 38 pounds

A leg of lamb is usually cut into two roasts. The best is the lower part, called "The Frenched Roast," which has part of the leg bone extending beyond the flesh. The upper part of the leg, called "The American Leg," is easier to wrap for the freezer, for it has no protruding bone. The bone is cut below the hock well into the leg meat. Other lamb roasts are cut from the shoulder, loin, and breast. The loin of the leg yields three large chops, but the best chops come from the loin itself. Rib chops are cut from the rack section, and Saratoga and shoulder chops come from the shoulder.

LAMB CUTS AND HOW TO COOK THEM

Retail Cuts   Wholesale Cuts   Retail Cuts

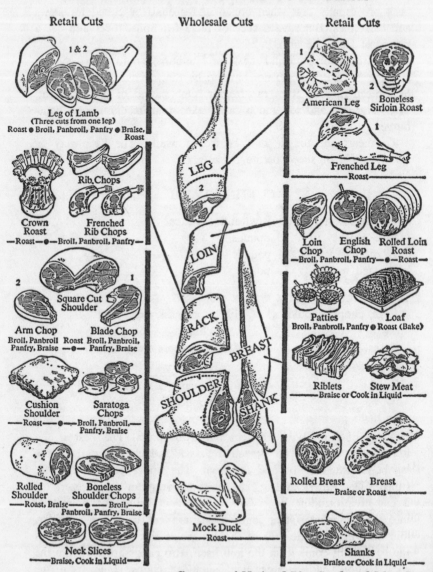

Leg of Lamb
(Three cuts from one leg)
Roast ● Broil, Panbroil, Panfry ● Braise, Roast

Rib Chops

Crown Roast
—Roast— ● —Broil, Panbroil, Panfry—

Frenched Rib Chops

Square Cut Shoulder

Arm Chop
Broil, Panbroil, Panfry, Braise

Blade Chop
Roast ●— Broil, Panbroil, Panfry, Braise

Cushion Shoulder
—Roast— ●

Saratoga Chops
—Broil, Panbroil, Panfry, Braise—

Rolled Shoulder
—Roast, Braise—

Boneless Shoulder Chops
● — Broil, Panbroil, Panfry, Braise

Neck Slices
—Braise, Cook in Liquid—

LEG

LOIN

RACK

BREAST

SHOULDER

SHANK

Mock Duck
—Roast—

American Leg

Boneless Sirloin Roast

Frenched Leg
—Roast—

Loin Chop   **English Chop**   **Rolled Loin Roast**
—Broil, Panbroil, Panfry—   —Roast—

Patties   **Loaf**
Broil, Panbroil, Panfry ● Roast (Bake)

Riblets   **Stew Meat**
—Braise or Cook in Liquid—

Rolled Breast   **Breast**
—Braise or Roast—

Shanks
—Braise or Cook in Liquid—

Courtesy of National Live Stock and Meat Board

A crown roast of lamb is a difficult cut to wrap and takes up valuable space. If you want one for a special occasion, do not plan to store it for long, unless you have plenty of room in your freezer.

The breast meat may be rolled for braising, diced for stew, or ground for lamb loaf or patties.

CUTTING PORK

APPROXIMATE YIELD FROM A WHOLE CARCASS

Live weight	225 pounds
Whole carcass	176 pounds
*Dressed weight	124 pounds

> * In addition to the dressed weight, a whole carcass will yield about 27 pounds of rendered lard.

TRIMMED CUTS FROM A WHOLE CARCASS

Fresh hams, shoulders, bacon, jowls	50% of carcass weight, or 90 pounds
Loins, ribs, sausage	20% of carcass weight, or 34 pounds
Total	70% of carcass weight, or 124 pounds

As with other meats, pork should be cut into meal-size portions. Roasts are cut from the hams, lower loins, and shoulders. The shoulder may be divided into the bottom butt and top shoulder, and each part may be trimmed, boned, and rolled into roasts.

Chops—loin, rib, and butterfly—are all cut from the upper loin.

The hams are usually cured, but fresh hams may be sliced and frozen for fresh ham steaks.

Bacon and salt pork are cut from the belly and jowl for curing. Bacon may be frozen, but it does not adapt itself to freezing as well as fresh ham. If the bacon is sliced before it is frozen, it may dry and become rancid in a short time. If a supply of bacon must be frozen in order to preserve it, cut it into 1- or 2-pound slabs and wrap each slab in moisture-vaporproof paper. Take out a slab as it is needed, let it thaw, and then slice.

Spareribs, cut from the belly, take up a lot of freezer space, but they are well worth it. They keep beautifully in frozen storage, and

PORK CUTS AND HOW TO COOK THEM

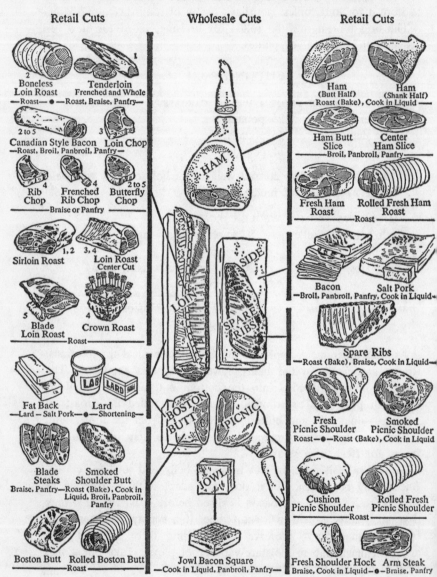

Retail Cuts   Wholesale Cuts   Retail Cuts

Boneless Loin Roast
—Roast—

Tenderloin Frenched and Whole
—Roast, Braise, Panfry—

Canadian Style Bacon
—Roast, Broil, Panbroil, Panfry—

Loin Chop
—Panfry—

Rib Chop

Frenched Rib Chop

Butterfly Chop
—Braise or Panfry—

Sirloin Roast

Loin Roast Center Cut

Blade Loin Roast

Crown Roast
—Roast—

Fat Back
—Lard — Salt Pork—

Lard
—Shortening—

Blade Steaks
Braise, Panfry

Smoked Shoulder Butt
—Roast (Bake), Cook in Liquid, Broil, Panbroil, Panfry

Boston Butt

Rolled Boston Butt
—Roast—

HAM

LOIN

SIDE

SPARE RIBS

BOSTON BUTT

PICNIC

JOWL

Ham (Butt Half)
—Roast (Bake)—

Ham (Shank Half)
—Cook in Liquid—

Ham Butt Slice

Center Ham Slice
—Broil, Panbroil, Panfry—

Fresh Ham Roast

Rolled Fresh Ham Roast
—Roast—

Bacon

Salt Pork
—Broil, Panbroil, Panfry, Cook in Liquid—

Spare Ribs
—Roast (Bake), Braise, Cook in Liquid—

Fresh Picnic Shoulder
Roast—

Smoked Picnic Shoulder
—Roast (Bake), Cook in Liquid—

Cushion Picnic Shoulder

Rolled Fresh Picnic Shoulder
—Roast—

Fresh Shoulder Hock
Braise, Cook in Liquid—

Arm Steak
—Braise, Panfry

Jowl Bacon Square
—Cook in Liquid, Panbroil, Panfry—

Courtesy of National Live Stock and Meat Boar

if they are packaged flat, layer upon layer, with two sheets of freezer paper between the layers, they will justify the space they occupy in your freezer.

Sausage meat is ground from the trimmings of the loin, blade, butts, bones, hams, and shoulders. It may be seasoned with salt, black pepper, red pepper, sage, or other herbs before it is frozen. Smoking prevents rancidity and drives off some of the moisture of the sausage meat. Fifty per cent fat and 50 per cent lean meat makes excellent sausage.

According to a recent letter from the United States Department of Agriculture, there is no information available to substantiate the report that the refrigeration of pork at 0° F. will insure the destruction of trichinella organisms that might be present in the meat.

Investigations have proved that once the trichinae larvae themselves reach a temperature of 0° F., they do not survive long and usually die in 24 hours. Once the larvae are embedded in the pork tissues, however, the period of refrigeration needed to destroy the parasites depends on the time required for all portions of the meat to reach a specified temperature.

It has been established that the trichinae are destroyed in pork not exceeding 6 inches in diameter that is subjected to −10° F. for a continuous period of 10 days, at −20° F. for 6 days, and at 5° F. for 20 days. Considering these facts, it seems most likely that small cuts of pork stored in a home freezer for a month or longer at 0° F. would be free of trichinae larvae, but until further experimentation determines the length of storage time for various cuts of pork, it would be wise to continue to cook all pork or foods containing pork until well done.

CUTTING VEAL

Veal needs no aging. It must be chilled promptly and should be cut, packaged, and frozen immediately after the body temperature is reduced to 38° F.

The calf should weigh from 110 to 200 pounds, and the carcass will yield from 80 to 90 pounds of roasts, chops, and ground and stew meat. Veal is cut in a manner similar to beef. The hindquarter is cut into the round, rump, loin, and shank and yields cutlets, round

VEAL CUTS AND HOW TO COOK THEM

Retail Cuts   Wholesale Cuts   Retail Cuts

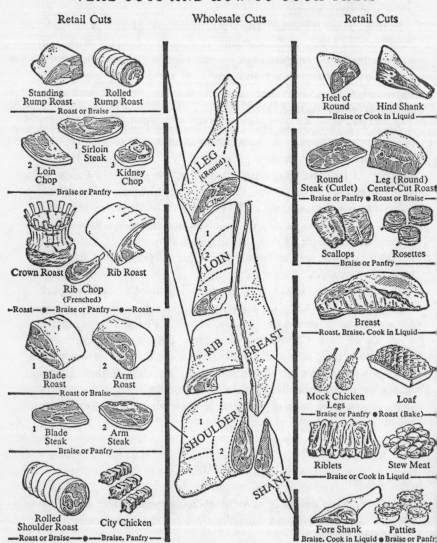

Standing Rump Roast   Rolled Rump Roast
— Roast or Braise —

2 Loin Chop   1 Sirloin Steak   3 Kidney Chop
— Braise or Panfry —

Crown Roast   Rib Roast
Rib Chop (Frenched)
► Roast — ● — Braise or Panfry — ● — Roast —

1 Blade Roast   2 Arm Roast
— Roast or Braise —

1 Blade Steak   2 Arm Steak
— Braise or Panfry —

Rolled Shoulder Roast   City Chicken
— Roast or Braise — ● — Braise, Panfry —

LEG (Round)
LOIN
RIB
BREAST
SHOULDER
SHANK

Heel of Round   Hind Shank
— Braise or Cook in Liquid —

Round Steak (Cutlet)   Leg (Round) Center-Cut Roast
— Braise or Panfry — ● Roast or Braise —

Scallops   Rosettes
— Braise or Panfry —

Breast
— Roast, Braise, Cook in Liquid —

Mock Chicken Legs   Loaf
— Braise or Panfry — ● Roast (Bake) —

Riblets   Stew Meat
— Braise or Cook in Liquid —

Fore Shank   Patties
Braise, Cook in Liquid ● Braise or Panfr.

Courtesy of National Live Stock and Meat Boar

steak, round roast, rump roast, rolled rump roast, sirloin steak, and loin and kidney chops. The forequarter is cut into shank, shoulder, breast, and rib and yields rib chops, rib roast or crown roast, blade and arm steaks and roasts, rolled shoulder, and ground and stew meats.

CUTTING VENISON AND OTHER LARGE GAME

Venison and other large game are cut in much the same way as beef or veal. Some states do not permit game to be stored for longer than 10 days, so you should familiarize yourself with the state laws in the locality in which you live. Consult your local game warden, or your state conservation department, for details.

COOKING AND THAWING MEAT

Frozen meat may be cooked while still frozen, when partially thawed, or when completely thawed. The exception is pork, which should never be cooked from the frozen state, because of the danger of trichinosis if the roast is not thoroughly cooked. Always defrost pork of any cut thoroughly, then cook until well done.

Whether to thaw or not to thaw beef, veal, and lamb before cooking is largely up to the homemaker. Small cuts are best cooked from the frozen state, as there is less loss of flavorful juices. Large roasts cook more evenly if thawed first. However, if some members of your family prefer rare meat and others like it well done, you might want to cook a small roast from the frozen state. There are also emergency occasions when it might be advantageous to place a frozen roast directly in the oven. Insert the meat thermometer when the roast is half cooked and completely thawed, otherwise you will break the thermometer. Continue cooking to the desired degree of doneness.

It takes approximately twice as long to cook meat from the frozen state and, naturally, uses more fuel. On the other hand waiting for a roast to thaw before putting it in the oven can often delay dinner.

So, if you plan to cook defrosted meats, be sure to allow sufficient time for the meat to thaw. Thaw meat in the sealed package to preserve moisture.

Complete thawing takes from 1 to 3 hours per pound at room temperature or about 5 hours per pound in the refrigerator. Thawing in the refrigerator is the preferred method because it is more uniform.

TIMETABLE FOR THAWING BEEF, VEAL, AND LAMB

	Refrigerator 40° to 50° F.	Room temperature 70° to 75° F.
Patties, ⅝ inch thick, and chops	6 to 8 hours	1 hour
Steaks, 1 inch thick	12 hours	2 to 3 hours
Roasts, small	3 to 4 hours per pound	1 to 2 hours per pound
Roasts, large	4 to 6 hours per pound	2 to 3 hours per pound

DEGREES FOR ROASTING MEAT

ROAST OF BEEF	INTERNAL TEMPERATURE
Rare	140° F.
Medium	160° F.
Well done	170° F.

ROAST OF LAMB	
Medium	175° F.
Well done	180° F.

VEAL AND PORK	
Well done	185° F.

GUIDE FOR COOKING MEAT*

CUT OF MEAT	METHOD OF COOKING	DEGREE OF DONENESS	*Approximate Minutes Per Pound* THAWED BEFORE COOKING	COOKED FROM THE FROZEN STATE
Standing rib	Roasting at	Rare	18	43
roast	300° F.	Medium	22	47
		Well done	30	55
Rolled-rib	Roasting at	Rare	28	53
roast	300° F.	Medium	32	56
		Well done	40	65
Pork-loin roast	Roasting at	Well done		
Center cut	300° F.		30 to 35	50 to 55
Rib or				
shoulder ends			50 to 55	70 to 75
Leg of Lamb	Roasting at 300° F.	Well done	30 to 35	40 to 45
Beef rump	Braising	Well done	30 to 35	50
Porterhouse	Broiling	Rare to		
steak		Medium		
1 inch thick			8 to 10	21 to 33
1½ inches thick			10 to 15	23 to 38
2 inches thick			20 to 30	33 to 43
Beef patties 1 inch thick	Pan-broiling	Medium	10 to 12	16 to 18
Sausage patties	Pan-broiling	Well done	15 to 25	22 to 28
Lamb chops ¾ to 1½ inches thick	Pan-broiling	Well done	10 to 20	15 to 25
Pork chops ¾ inch thick	Braising	Well done	35 to 40	50 to 55

* From *Meat and Cookery*, Committee of the National Live Stock and Meat Board.

CHAPTER 3

Freezing Poultry, Game Birds, and Small Game

Frozen poultry is one of the most successful of all frozen foods, providing the birds are of high quality and are stored at a constant 0° F. or lower. Freezing preserves the flavor and tenderness of poultry and game birds, but it cannot improve them or make tough fowl tender.

Freeze only the best. Grade A poultry are young, healthy, carefully raised birds. The body should be well fleshed in the breast, thighs, drumsticks, and back. There should be few pinfeathers and a layer of fat under the skin. Ducks and geese should be broadbreasted, deep-fleshed, and moderately but not excessively fat.

When the season for broilers, fryers, and roasters rolls around, allot a reasonable space in your freezer for them. When they are plentiful is the time to buy, for then they are at their cheapest and best. Prepare them for the freezer exactly in the same manner as if you were going to broil, sauté, roast, or fricassee them that day. You can do this yourself, or your butcher will clean, truss, and split them, or cut them in any way you wish. Fryers and broiler-fryers are usually disjointed or cut into serving pieces before freezing; broilers should be split in half down the back. Roasters should be trussed with wings and legs tied firmly to the sides of the bird.

Broilers should be not over 12 weeks old and should weigh from 2 to 2½ pounds.

Fryers are about 20 weeks old and weigh from 3 to 3½ pounds.

Roasting chickens should not be over 1 year old and should weigh from 4 to 5 pounds.

Fricassee chickens can be from 1 to 2 years old, reasonably fat, and weigh as much as 6 pounds.

Capons are from 8 to 10 months old, reasonably fat, and weigh from 7 to 10 pounds.

Baby turkeys are about 12 weeks old, weigh from 4 to 7 pounds, and may be split and broiled or stuffed and roasted.

Mature turkeys range in weight from 8 to 30 pounds and are at their prime for freezing from October to January.

Ducks are most plentiful in the spring. From 10 to 12 weeks old they are at their best and weigh from 5 to 6 pounds.

Birds for roasting are best at a certain age:

Chickens	5 to 9 months
Capons	7 to 10 months
Turkeys	5 to 9 months
Guineas	5 to 10 months
Geese	5 to 11 months
Ducks	4 to 6 months

PACKAGING POULTRY

Effective packaging of poultry is necessary to keep the flesh from drying out, to prevent freezer burn, and to keep the meat from being contaminated with other flavors. Without proper moisture-vapor-proof wrappings, dehydration is bound to take place at the low storage temperature and the birds will be tough and dry when they are cooked. Cut-up poultry takes less freezer space than whole birds and if freezer space is limited, it is wise to freeze only the choice pieces of meat, such as the breast and thighs. The backbones, wing tips, necks, and legs can be made into concentrated soup stock, and the stock frozen, or the cooked meat from the wings and drumsticks may be made into croquettes or creamed and the prepared dishes frozen. See Index for recipes.

Whole poultry

Once the bird is dressed it should be wrapped and frozen at once. If this is not possible, wrap the bird and place it in the refrigerator until it can be put in the freezer, but in any event no more than 1 hour should elapse from wrapping to freezing.

Clean cavity thoroughly and remove excess fat.

Trussing before freezing makes the carcass more compact, saves storage space, and improves the appearance of the cooked bird.

Fold the neck skin down over the back. Bend the wings around and lock them in back by twisting the wing tips over the forewings. Tie the center of a long piece of string around the leg joints, push the legs down, and tie them securely to the tail. Bring the ends of the string up the back of the bird, hitch them around the wings, and tie them over the neck skin in back.

Moisture-vaporproof Saran wrap, aluminum foil, laminated papers, Pliofilm, and polyethylene are all excellent protectors. Wrap the bird tightly, forcing out any air pockets which might form during the wrapping. Seal ends and seams with an acetate sealing tape, slip a stockinette over the bird if the wrapping needs this extra protection, and knot the ends close to the body of the bird. Slip a label between the paper and the stockinette for future identification.

NEVER stuff poultry before freezing.

Giblets

Chicken liver may be frozen with the bird, because it is quick-cooking. But the other innards should be packaged and frozen separately.

Broilers

Turkeys, as well as chickens and guineas, halved or quartered and ready for broiling, make valuable additions to the food supply in your freezer. It isn't necessary to wait for a special event in order to enjoy the flavor of turkey. Turkey is frequently an excellent buy in the non-holiday season. A portion of turkey to suit your family requirements may often take the place of a Sunday roast.

Wrap and freeze the giblets separately. Place two pieces of freezer paper between the two halves of chickens or other small birds so that they can be separated while still frozen. Then wrap the two halves securely in a moisture-vaporproof bag or paper. If you wish to package more than one broiler together, depending on the number of servings needed at one time, the halves may be nested with a double thickness of the paper between them. If the leg ends are sharp, wrap them so that they will not puncture the outer wrapping.

Turkey halves may be packaged separately for broiling or roasting. Envelop them compactly in moisture-vaporproof paper, excluding as much air as possible.

Cut poultry

Tender chickens, for frying or sautéeing; well-fattened birds past their prime for roasting, but suitable for braising or stewing; ducks and geese, and larger birds such as turkeys, can all be cut into serving pieces before they are frozen as an effective method of conserving space. Wrap each piece in a fold of freezer paper and pack tightly into a moistureproof carton that can be heat-sealed. Use small-, medium-, or large-size packages to suit your family needs. If you are freezing a large quantity of disjointed fowl, you might set aside and package certain choice pieces for special recipes.

PACKAGING GAME BIRDS AND SMALL GAME ANIMALS

Game birds, rabbits, and squirrels are packaged in the same manner as poultry. Some states do not permit game to be stored for more than 10 days, so it is wise to consult your state conservation department, or your local game warden, for details.

Label and freeze

Label each package of poultry or game with the kind, the method of preparation, the weight, the number of servings, the date frozen, and any other pertinent information that will be of help to you weeks or months later, when many of the things you think you will have remembered have been forgotten.

Freeze promptly

Freeze promptly at 0° F., leaving plenty of air space around each package to expose all sides to the zero temperature. When hard-frozen, stack compactly, and store at 0° F. or below.

PREPARING POULTRY, GAME BIRDS, AND SMALL GAME FOR THE FREEZER

There are six steps in the preparation of poultry for the freezer. They are: killing and bleeding, plucking, plumping, chilling, dressing, and packaging. In most instances the first five of these steps have already been done for you before you buy the birds. Or you can have the birds prepared for you on order, as most locker plants will not only kill and dress poultry and cut them according to your specifications, but package them too, if you wish.

But for those who raise their own chickens, turkeys, and ducks, I am including information about the first five steps in preparing poultry for the freezer.

Killing and bleeding

For 2 weeks before the birds are to be killed, they should be restricted to an enclosed area where they are allowed access to all the food they want to consume. At this time, fish meal or fish oil should be eliminated from their diet and milk should be added to the daily rations. The fat is more evenly distributed through the flesh of milk-fed fowl than corn-fed birds.

The birds should be starved for 16 to 24 hours before they are killed, but plenty of fresh water should be available to help empty the crop and intestines. The fowl will then be much easier to clean, without any danger of the flavor of the flesh being spoiled.

Thorough bleeding is essential for fine-flavored meat and long storage life. Improperly bled birds have dark, reddened skin usually on the hips and wing tips, which detracts from their appearance. Congealed blood deteriorates rapidly and therefore lessens the storage time in the freezer for maximum flavor.

There are several satisfactory methods of killing birds to insure complete bleeding. A commonly used method of killing chickens and turkeys involves bleeding by severance of the jugular vein followed by braining, which involves piercing the medulla or back part of the brain through the mouth or eye. Braining, if correctly done, tends to loosen the feathers and facilitates plucking. It is not usually done to ducks and geese. Regardless of the method used to kill the birds, they should be hung to insure proper bleeding.

Hang the bird securely by the feet, head down. Grasp the head and cut through the jugular vein on the left side of the throat with a very sharp knife. Then, to brain, insert the knife blade in the cleft of the roof of the mouth, run it back in a line between the eye and ear, and give it a quarter turn.

Some people like to hang the bird in a suspended funnel to kill it, as the bird cannot struggle and there is no opportunity for it to break or bruise its wings.

Plucking

All kinds of poultry may be dry-plucked, although this is more difficult than scalding, especially with geese. If the bird is to be dry-plucked, the feathers must be removed immediately, for they set quickly. Keep the bird in the hanging position until it is thoroughly bled, but start plucking at once. Remove the tail feathers and large wing feathers first. Then continue with the breast, sides, thighs, and legs. Finally, pick out the back feathers, the soft feathers on the neck, and the small feathers on the wings.

An easier method of plucking is to let the bird hang until it is thoroughly bled and then scald it. To scald, select a container large enough so that the bird can be completely covered with water with the exception of the feet. The temperature of the water should be from 130° to 145° F., but no hotter. Too hot water damages the tender skin of young birds, and the skin will tear as the feathers are removed. Plunge the bird in the hot water for 30 seconds, or until the wing and tail feathers pull out easily, moving it up and down to agitate the water and force the water through the feathers to the skin.

Once scalded, remove the wing and tail feathers first, then the leg feathers, and lastly the feathers on the body. Work quickly and rub the feathers off the body rather than pluck them. Start at the neck and work down. When all the feathers have been carefully removed, grasp the bird, neck in one hand, feet in the other, and turn it from side to side over a smokeless gas flame to singe off the hair feathers.

Ducks and geese are best scalded in water at a temperature just below the boiling point and just long enough to loosen the feathers. The ducks should be agitated vigorously during the scalding to force the water through the oily feathers to the skin. Geese may be scalded and then wrapped in a heavy sack or blanket for a few minutes to hold in the heat and to achieve an even scald. Trial will determine the correct temperature and the length of scalding time, as both over- or underscalding may result in the tearing out of small pieces of skin with the feathers during the plucking.

Plumping

After poultry has been plucked, the skin often has a loose appearance. If the bird is plunged for 7 to 10 seconds in water heated to 195° F., the slack will be taken up and the bird will have a nice plump appearance. Plunge the bird immediately into a bath of cold water for a couple of minutes after plumping.

Chilling

The quick removal of body heat is important once the bird is plucked and singed. This can be done before or after the bird is dressed or drawn. Chilling first hardens the fat and makes the poultry easier to draw. On the other hand, many authorities agree that the sooner the bird is eviscerated, the better will be the flavor of the flesh. Poultry may be chilled under refrigeration for 12 hours or overnight, or if no refrigeration is available, the body heat may be removed by placing the birds in ice water for 2 hours, or until they are completely chilled, replenishing the ice as it melts.

Dressing whole birds

Before a bird is drawn, the pinfeathers should be removed. This can be done quite neatly by using a strawberry huller, if you have one, or tweezers; otherwise catch the pinfeathers between thumb and a paring knife.

Scrub the skin in cold water with a brush or rough cloth and rinse the bird well. The bird is now ready to be drawn.

1. Cut off the feet. Grasp the leg and bend it back so that the skin is taut over the front leg joint. Cut across the front, bending back the leg to dislocate the joint, and cut across the back skin.

2. Cut out the oil sac in the tail.

3. Cut off the head.

4. Slit the neck skin down the center back to the shoulders and sever the neck at this point. Removing the neck makes it easier to remove the gullet, or esophagus, the crop, and the windpipe.

5. Loosen the crop, which is attached to the skin near the base of the neck, and the windpipe and esophagus, which are attached to the neck skin, by inserting the fingers into the neck opening and moving them around the cavity as far down as possible. Pull the crop, windpipe, and esophagus out as far as possible, cut them off at a point where they enter the body, and discard. Birds may be drawn through either a vertical or horizontal incision.

6. (a) To draw a bird through a vertical incision, place the bird on its back and make an incision to the abdomen starting three inches above the vent. Continue the incision toward the tail and encircle the vent, cutting all around about ¾ inch from the center of the vent.

(b) To draw the bird through a horizontal incision, place the bird on its back and make a horizontal incision about 4 inches long just behind the breastbone. In this case a separate cut must be made around the vent in order to free the intestines so that the viscera can be removed.

7. Remove the viscera by inserting a forefinger into the opening and circle it around the intestines. Now hold the carcass firmly with one hand and insert the other hand through the opening and locate the gizzard near the center of the viscera. Grasp the gizzard firmly and draw the entrails completely out of the cavity.

8. Remove the lungs, making sure they are completely removed. This is important, as they contain blood. They are located in two sections, one on each side of the backbone over the ribs.

9. Make sure the heart is removed. It is found just under the wishbone.

10. Rinse out the cavity with cold water, or wipe it with a damp cloth, and drain thoroughly.

11. Detach the heart, liver, and gizzard from the other entrails.

12. Discard the heart sac, cut off the blood vessels, and wash the heart to remove blood.

13. Cut out the gall sac from the liver, being very careful not to break it, and discard any part of the liver that might be stained green by contact with the gall bladder. Should the bladder break, you will not only have to discard the liver but any part of the chicken that it might have touched.

14. Make a slit in one side of the gizzard, being careful not to cut the inner sac. Force the slit open with the thumbs and pull the gizzard gently but firmly away from the sac. Discard the sac with the intestines and remaining viscera.

15. Wash the giblets in cold water and drain them well.

Dressing broilers

Broilers are dressed by splitting the birds up the back.

1. Cut off the head and feet of young chicken not over twelve weeks old.

2. Slit the skin from shoulder to tail along the right side of the backbone.

3. With heavy kitchen shears, cut along this line from the tail to the shoulders. With a sharp knife, cut from the tip of the tail up to and encircling the vent ¾ inch from the center of the vent.

4. Spread the bird open at the back, lay it flat on the table, flesh down, and remove the viscera, lungs, and kidneys.

5. Rinse the cavity of the bird with cold water, or wipe it with a damp cloth.

6. Prepare the giblets (see Dressing Whole Birds).

Broilers may be left split, still joined at the breastbone, or they may be separated into halves or quarters. The backbone may be completely removed before the broilers are packaged for the freezer.

Dressing frying chickens

Chickens weighing about 3 to 3⅓ pounds are perfect for deep-fat frying or for sautéeing. They may be drawn, or dressed, at the same time they are cut into serving portions. Use a very sharp knife.

1. Cut off the wings at the joints and either remove the wing tips

to use in making soup stock or slip the tip of each wing under the second joint to fasten it securely in place.

2. Remove the legs, pulling each leg in turn away from the body of the bird so the skin is taut. Sever the skin and flesh down to the thigh joint and free the leg at the hip. Separate the drumstick from the thigh.

3. Separate the back from the breast by cutting from one wing joint to the other, encircling the bird around the vent.

4. Place the bird on the table. Grasp the vent end with one hand and the top of the breastbone with the other and gently pull the breast end up. The breast will snap away from the wing joints and it may be cut into two parts, or if the breast section is quite large, smaller pieces may be cut, as desired.

5. Grasp the vent end of the back with one hand; slip the forefinger of the other hand under the entrails and lift them out.

6. Remove the lungs from the backbone of the chicken, and wash the back with cold water or wipe it with a damp cloth.

7. Prepare the giblets (see Dressing Whole Birds).

The back may be halved, but there is so little meat on it that it does not pay to take up freezer space with this part of the bird, or the neck. Make concentrated soup stock instead, and freeze the stock.

What have you got from one fryer? Two wings, two thighs, two drumsticks, two pieces of breast meat, and the giblets.

Dressing fricassee and stewing chickens

Large chickens for braising, poaching, or stewing should be cut up the same as fryers to conserve freezer space.

Dressing game birds

Wild fowl of all kinds—pheasant, grouse, quail, wild geese, wild ducks, and guinea hens—are prepared in the same manner as domestic fowl. They should be properly bled right after they are bagged, and a wise hunter will also chill the birds instead of stuffing them into a hunting bag.

Pluck game birds in the same manner as other poultry, rather than skin them. Skinning causes loss of flavor and drying of the flesh. The birds should be scalded and plucked as soon after killing as possible. Remove as much of the shot as possible and roll them in melted paraffin to remove the pinfeathers and down.

Game birds should be drawn as soon as possible after they have been shot. If there is no time to do the complete job, remove the craw and intestines so that the flavor of the meat will not be spoiled by the partly digested food. This applies especially to wild ducks, which might have been feeding on strongly flavored water plants and fish. In any event, clean them thoroughly as soon as possible, for the flesh of game birds deteriorates rapidly, particularly in the wounded areas.

All game birds should hang at a temperature just above freezing for at least 48 hours before they are packaged for the freezer.

Game birds may be prepared for roasting or cut up for sautéeing, depending on how you wish to use them.

Many states limit the period for storage of game. For this information consult your local game officials.

Dressing small game animals

Rabbits, squirrels, and other small game animals should be dressed as soon as possible after they are shot. Immediately after killing them, behead them, bleed them thoroughly, and hang them in an airy place at a temperature a little above freezing for 48 hours. Then skin and dress them. Wipe them with a cloth dipped in scalding water and cut them into serving pieces, as with frying chickens. Sometimes, to save freezer space, only the thick back and hindquarters, known as "the saddle," are frozen. Use the rest, while fresh, for stews or casseroles.

HOW TO BONE A BIRD

Squab, chickens, capons, and turkeys may all be boned before they are frozen to conserve freezer space. The boned poultry may be rolled, or made into galantines or ballotines before they are frozen, ready for the most important occasions. The entrails are removed as the bird is boned.

Remove the head and the feet. Cut off all but the first joint of the wings and the neck, but keep the skin of the neck as long as possible. With a very sharp pointed knife, or a boning knife, cut a straight line down the back from neck to tail. Cut off the tail.

Now begin to scrape and cut the flesh from the backbone down to the shoulder blade, being careful not to pierce the skin. When you come to the leg and wing joints, cut through the joints. Proceed in the same manner on the other side and the meat will be free from the carcass and the entire carcass with the entrails may be lifted out, leaving the fleshy part of the bird and the skin intact. Scrape the flesh from the thigh bone, cut through the leg joint, and pull out the thigh bone. Continue to scrape the flesh from the leg and wing bones and draw the bones out of the flesh.

THAWING FROZEN POULTRY

Poultry can be cooked directly from the hard-frozen state in case of an emergency, but unthawed roasters cook less uniformly and of course cannot be stuffed. It requires longer cooking at moderate temperatures in order to let the heat penetrate.

It's better by far to thaw poultry in the sealed package to preserve moisture, and to cook it soon after it is thawed. The skin of an unwrapped bird becomes dry when exposed too long to the air. Thawing in the refrigerator is also preferred for a whole bird because it is more uniform, but you must plan approximately 5 hours per pound for refrigerator thawing; only half or one third that time if thawed at room temperature. When necessary, thawing time may be speeded up by placing the sealed package in cold running water, but only until the poultry is pliable.

If you plan to dip poultry parts into eggs and crumbs or into a flour mixture before cooking, it must definitely be thawed and the pieces dried well on paper toweling before they are coated.

TIMETABLE FOR THAWING POULTRY

	Refrigerator 40° to 50° F.	Room Temperature 70° to 57° F.	Cold Running Water
3 lb. cut-up fryer	10 to 15 hours	4 to 5 hours	
5 lb. roaster	20 to 30 hours	5 to 6 hours	
4 to 10 lb. turkey	1 to 2 days	6 to 12 hours	4 to 6 hrs.
10 to 20 lb. turkey	2 to 3 days	12 to 18 hours	6 to 8 hrs.
20 to 24 lb. turkey	3 to 4 days	18 to 24 hours	8 to 12 hrs.

COOKING FROZEN POULTRY

Roasting poultry

Rub the inside of the bird with salt and pepper. Fill the cavity, if desired, with your favorite stuffing. Do not pack it tightly, as the filling must have room to expand. As it expands it absorbs some of the juices as they cook out of the meat and for this reason any bird is juicier and the flesh is more flavorful and succulent if the bird is not stuffed. Rather put in the cavity a few sprigs of parsley, a small stalk of celery, and an onion, quartered, or a few shallots. Some like a clove of garlic or a spray of tarragon or thyme. Bake the dressing separately, so that it will not rob the flesh of its moisture and flavor.

Close the cavity with skewers, or sew it up with kitchen thread, and truss the wings and legs close to the body. Rub the skin generously with butter and sprinkle it with salt and pepper. Place the bird on a rack in a shallow roasting pan, breast down, for half the cooking period, to keep the breast meat moist, then turn it for the rest of the roasting time to brown the breast. Baste occasionally with the pan drippings to keep the skin moist. For a rich, brown color, add 1 teaspoon tomato paste to the drippings in the pan ½ hour before the bird is done and baste frequently. To test for doneness, insert the prongs of a fork in the thigh. If the juice that runs out is clear and has no pink tinge, the bird is done.

To roast half a turkey

Half a turkey is generally a better size for the average family and may be roasted beautifully. Season the cavity with salt and pepper and place the turkey, cut side down, in the roasting pan. If dressing is desired, mound about 4 cups of seasoned bread crumbs on the bottom of the roaster and place the bird over the crumbs. Brush the skin with melted butter and roast the turkey in a slow oven (325° F.), basting occasionally, until it tests done. A 6-pound half turkey, thawed, will require about 2½ hours roasting time. Allow an extra ½ hour if roasted from the frozen state.

TIMETABLE FOR ROASTING THAWED POULTRY

BIRD	POUNDS DRESSED WEIGHT	DEGREES F. OVEN TEMP.	APPROXIMATE HOURS ROASTING
Chicken	4 to 5	350	1½ to 2
Duck	5 to 6	350	2 to 2½
Goose	10 to 12	325	3 to 4
Guinea	2 to 2½	350	1½
Turkey	6 to 9	350	2 to 2½
	10 to 13	325	2½ to 3½
	14 to 17	300	4 to 5
	18 to 25	275	5½ to 7

To roast unthawed birds

Allow 30 minutes longer cooking time for a 4- to 5-pound chicken or duck, 1 hour longer for a 6- to 8-pound capon or turkey, 1½ hours longer for a 10-pound goose or turkey.

Broiling poultry

Thaw broilers in the refrigerator overnight.

Brush thawed split broilers with melted butter and sprinkle them with salt and pepper. Place them on a preheated oiled broiler rack skin-side down and broil 5 inches from the flame. Turn the birds frequently and brush them with melted butter each time they are turned. Broil for 25 to 50 minutes, depending on the thickness and tenderness of the meat, or until the skin side is golden and the juice that runs from the thigh when it is pricked with a fork has no tinge of pink. A little finely chopped fresh herb, such as tarragon, thyme, parsley, chervil, or chives, heated with the basting butter will add a subtle flavor.

Broilers may be broiled without preliminary thawing in exactly the same manner as the thawed halves. Allow half again as much broiling time.

Frying

Poultry that is to be fried in hot deep fat should be thawed completely, or the outside will be brown and crisp while the center is still cold. Some like to steam the pieces first until tender, especially if the bird is not so young as it should be for frying. When thawed, wipe the pieces dry and dip them in a batter made by beating 1 egg lightly and stirring in ¾ cup milk, 1 cup flour, and ½ teaspoon salt. Fry the pieces a few at a time in deep fat (350° F.) for 15 to 20 minutes, depending on the size and age of the bird and whether or not the pieces were presteamed. Drain on absorbent paper and sprinkle with salt and pepper.

Sautéeing

Poultry may be sautéed or pan-fried directly from the frozen state, or partially or completely thawed. Dredge the pieces in flour and brown them on all sides in hot butter. When brown, reduce the flame, cover the skillet tightly, and sauté for about 30 minutes, or until done. A little wine or stock, a clove of garlic, chopped parsley, some finely chopped onion or shallots, a few tomatoes, peeled and quartered, a leaf of sweet basil—any or all may be added for infinite variations. Allow half as much cooking time for the thawed chicken as the frozen.

Fricasseeing

Older birds need long, slow cooking in liquid or steam to tenderize them. Cut-up chicken or other poultry may be removed from the freezer, dredged with seasoned flour, and browned slowly in hot butter without any preliminary thawing. The browned pieces of poultry are then transferred to a casserole. Enough water or stock is added barely to cover them, the casserole is covered tightly, and the bird is baked in a moderate oven (350° F.) for 2 to 3 hours, or until the pieces are tender. Vegetables may be added when the bird is partially cooked. Tomato juice or wine may be substituted for part of the water or stock.

Stewing

Stewing differs from fricasseeing in that the pieces are not browned, but are cooked in seasoned liquid for 2 to 3 hours, or until tender.

CHAPTER 4

Freezing Fish and Shellfish

Freshly caught fish should be iced or refrigerated until it can be prepared for the freezer. Speed is essential, for fish is an extremely perishable food. It deteriorates rapidly from the moment it leaves the water and within a few hours bacteria from air and water begin their work of contamination. Packing fish in ice or refrigerating them merely retards the bacterial action, as the particular organisms which attack fish can survive at lower temperatures than those which attack meat.

The storage period for fish is relatively brief. One to three months is the maximum, and the more fatty a fish, the shorter the storage period. Fatty fish such as salmon, mackerel, and herring should not be stored more than 6 weeks. Fortunately there are more varieties of lean than fatty fish, and these retain their quality and flavor for as long as 3 months, but the sooner eaten, the better the flavor will be.

Some sections of the country have limits on the length of time fish can be stored, so consult your local game warden before packaging fish for your freezer.

Fatty fish include, among others: barracuda, bonito, butterfish, catfish, eel, herring, kingfish, mackerel, millet, pilchard, pompano, rockfish, rosefish, salmon, shad, squid, tuna, whitefish.

Lean fish include, among others: bass, blowfish, bluefish, blue runner, burbot, cod, crevallé, croaker, flounder, fluke, gar, grouper, grunt, haddock, halibut, lingcod, muskellunge, perch, pickerel, pike, pollack, porgy, red drum, red snapper, scrod, sea trout, sheepshead, smelt, snook, sole, spot, sunfish, swordfish, trout, weakfish, whiting, wolf fish.

PREPARING FRESHLY CAUGHT FISH
FOR THE FREEZER

Fish should be prepared for the freezer as soon as possible after they are caught and in exactly the same way as if they were going to be cooked immediately. Small fish may be left whole and pan-dressed—scales, entrails, and fins removed. The backbone may also be cut out and, to save freezer space, the head and tail are usually discarded. Large fish are generally filleted, or are cut crosswise into steaks an inch or more thick.

It is not an unpleasant task to clean and dress a fish. It can be done quickly and easily with no more equipment than a sharp, strong knife. If you anticipate a busy fishing season, a fish scaler is helpful, but not essential.

To clean
and pan-dress a whole fish

1. Wash the fish quickly in cold salted water, using 1 tablespoon salt to each quart of water.
2. Place the fish on several thicknesses of strong paper and grasp the head firmly. Scrape the scales off from tail to head with a sharp knife held at an almost vertical angle, or a fish scaler.
3. "Run" the dorsal and pelvic fins. This means cut down into the flesh on either side of the fins, then pull them out. Never cut off the fins with scissors.
4. Slit the entire length of the belly from head to vent and remove the entrails.
5. Cut off the head, including the pectoral fins, and the tail.
6. Dip the fish quickly in cold salted water and remove the clotted blood and any remaining membranes.

To bone a fish such as a pike or bass

Insert a very sharp knife with a pointed blade into the flesh on one side of the backbone and cut from head to tail close to the bone. Turn the fish over and cut from head to tail on the other side. Lift out the entire backbone of the fish and pull out any small bones that remain.

To fillet a flat fish such as flounder or fluke

1. Cut through the flesh along the back of the fish on one side of the dorsal fin from tail to head.
2. Cut across the fish just behind the head down to the backbone.
3. Turn the knife flat and cut off the flesh from the backbone from head to tail. The knife runs along the rib bones and the fillet is cut off in one piece.
4. Turn the fish and repeat the process on the other side.

To skin the fillets

Loosen the skin at the broad end of the fillet. Hold the flesh firmly against the table or a board, grasp the skin firmly, and strip it off.

Or, place the fillet skin-side down. Cut through the flesh to the skin ½ inch from the tail end. Hold the free end of the skin firmly against the table. Flatten the knife on the skin and pull the knife forward, cutting the flesh from the skin.

To remove fishy odor from hands and utensils, rub the fish knife and your hands well with moistened salt, rinse off the salt with hot water, then wash thoroughly with soap or detergent.

PACKAGING FISH FOR THE FREEZER

Before packaging, lean fish—whole, steaks, or fillets—should be dipped for 20 seconds in cold salted water, made by dissolving 1 cup salt in 1 gallon ice water. Fatty fish should not be treated with a salt solution.

Whole fish

Wrap whole fish individually in moisture-vaporproof paper. If whole fish are small, several or enough for one meal may be packaged together, individually wrapped, in a top-opening carton or bag. Seal and label.

Whole fish may be stuffed with a favorite forcemeat before they are frozen, but the time of storage for even a lean fish should then be limited to 1 month.

To glaze a whole fish

Whole fish has a tendency to dry out in frozen storage. An excellent way to prevent this is to place the fish on a tray and put it in the freezer until it is frozen. Then dip the fish in ice water several times, chilling it between dips. The water will freeze on the fish almost immediately and a layer of ice ¼ inch thick can be quickly built up to encase the fish in a glacial shroud. Wrap the ice-encrusted fish in moisture-vaporproof paper, seal the edges with acetate tape, label, and store in the freezer.

Fillets and steaks

Pack fillets and steaks in layers in top-opening cartons with two sheets of freezer paper between layers so they will separate easily when taken from the freezer. Close the carton, label, overwrap with moisture-vaporproof paper, and heat-seal all open edges with a warm hand iron, or seal with acetate tape.

To freeze

Freeze fish the moment it has been wrapped at 0° F. Store at a constant zero temperature, or below.

Fish soups

Use the fish heads, bones, and leftover scraps of flesh to make a good chowder or fish stew or a concentrated fish stock (see Index). Pour the soup, stew, or stock into leakproof cartons or glass jars, leaving 1 inch head space, seal, and freeze.

HOW TO COOK FROZEN FISH

Frozen fish is cooked just like fresh fish. It is best when cooked from the thawed or partially thawed state. Hard-frozen fish is likely to spatter and stick to the pan. Cook partially thawed fish a little longer and at slightly lower temperature than fresh fish. Hard-frozen fish may be poached or stewed directly from the frozen state.

To thaw, place the unopened package on the shelf in the refrigerator to defrost. A 1-pound package of frozen fish will thaw in 8 to 10 hours in the refrigerator. The same quantity will thaw in about 3 hours at room temperature, but there is less loss of juices and flavors if the fish is thawed slowly. Once thawed or partially thawed, cook while it is still cold, or still contains some ice crystals.

It is very difficult to give absolutely accurate cooking times for fish, since so much depends on the thickness, freshness, and texture of the particular fish. But the surest way is to cook the fish until the flesh flakes easily when tested with a toothpick or the prongs of a fork. Just be careful not to dry it out by overcooking.

Broiling

Broiling is one of the simplest methods of cooking whole fish, fillets, or steaks. Whole split fish and fillets should be broiled on one side only and not turned, since the turning is apt to break the fish into pieces.

Don't use a broiler rack. Rather, use a shallow, flat pan. Heat both the broiler and the pan to 450° F. Oil the hot pan generously with olive oil and place the fish on it, skin-side down. Dot the surface of the fish with butter and broil the fish 4 or 5 inches from the flame, basting it several times with butter, until it is golden brown and the flesh flakes easily.

Whole fish and fish steaks need broiling on both sides and should be basted frequently with butter, or a mixture of melted butter and white wine. They should be turned carefully with two large spatulas. Large whole fish that are thick through the center should be split and broiled open with frequent bastings of butter, or cooked in another manner—perhaps baked or poached.

Serve broiled fish simply, with a wedge of lemon, or with melted butter mixed with plenty of chopped parsley and lemon juice.

Broiling time

In general, small whole fish, such as weakfish, sea bass, or flounder, require 3 to 8 minutes' broiling on each side. Fish steaks 1 inch thick will take 4 or 5 minutes' broiling on each side. Whole fish, split, take from 8 to 14 minutes. Fillets need from 5 to 8 minutes. If fish is broiled from the frozen state, the broiling time must be doubled.

Baking

Baking is the best method of cooking large fish, although small whole fish, fish fillets, and steaks may be cooked in the oven. The fish should not be turned, even a large one, as the heat of the oven will cook it evenly from both the top and the bottom.

Preheat the oven to 450° F. Oil the baking pan, or line it with lettuce leaves, to prevent the fish from sticking. Place fish in the pan and butter the surface generously. Bake, basting frequently with butter, or a mixture of melted butter and white or red wine, until the fish is delicately brown and the flesh flakes easily.

Baked fish may be served with parsley-butter or lemon-butter sauce, with tomato sauce, cream sauce, egg sauce, wine sauce, or hollandaise.

Fish ranging from 4 to 8 pounds are excellent stuffed and baked. If the fish was frozen unstuffed, it must be thawed before it can be stuffed and skewered. A favorite bread stuffing may be used. A vegetable stuffing of thinly sliced onions, shallots, or scallions, sliced tomatoes, and chopped parsley gives flavor to fish without robbing it of its natural juices. Season the stuffing with salt and pepper and add plenty of butter. The fish may be basted with tomato juice, or with fresh or sour cream.

Baking time

Allow approximately 12 minutes per pound for baking thawed fish. If baking fish from the partially frozen state, about 15 minutes per pound should be allowed.

Sautéeing or pan-frying

Sautéeing is one of the best ways to cook small fish or fish fillets, and plenty of butter or fat is needed to keep the fish from drying out over the brisk heat. Sauté the fish until it is golden brown on both sides and just until the flesh flakes easily. Be careful not to overcook. Fish does not need tenderizing by long cooking; quite to the contrary, overcooking is apt to make it tough.

The fish may be dipped in egg yolk beaten with a little milk and rolled in flour or bread crumbs. When cooked, sprinkle the fish with salt and pepper and serve with a wedge of lemon and several sprays of water cress.

Sauté Meunière is a favorite way to serve sautéed fish. When cooked, remove the fish to a hot platter and sprinkle it with salt, pepper, and lemon juice. Add butter and plenty of chopped parsley to the pan, cook until the butter begins to foam, and pour over the fish. Garnish with lemon slices.

Sauté Amandine is another favorite. Sauté the fish in butter until it is golden and the flesh flakes easily. Remove to a hot serving platter and sprinkle with salt, pepper, and lemon juice. Add more butter to the pan and some shredded blanched almonds. Cook, stirring, until the almonds are golden and pour almonds and butter over the fish.

Sautéeing time

Sauté thawed small fish or fish fillets for 3 to 5 minutes on one side, turn, and continue to sauté on the other side for another 3 minutes. Add 2 minutes' cooking time on each side for partially thawed small fish or fillets.

Frying

Dip small fish or fillets in flour, then in beaten egg, and roll them in bread crumbs or corn meal. Fry a few at a time in hot deep fat (380° F.) for 3 to 5 minutes, or until golden brown, and drain on absorbent paper. Sprinkle the fish with salt and pepper and serve with tomato sauce, *sauce diable,* or tartar sauce. The fish should be thawed before they are fried.

Poaching

Any fish, whether it is whole or cut into fillets, is at its best when poached in court-bouillon, or cooked in seasoned water just below the boiling point. It is the ideal way for salmon, whether you plan to serve it hot or cold. The court-bouillon may be strained and used as the base for a wine sauce, or gelatin may be added, and broth chilled and used for fish aspic.

To make a court-bouillon you need fish stock, which you may have frugally concentrated from the head, bones, and trimmings of fish, and then frozen, or else you must buy the bones and trimmings from your fish dealer and simmer them in 2 quarts of water for about 20 minutes to extract the flavor.

At any rate, into your fish poacher, or any kettle that is large and long enough to hold your fish, put about 2 quarts of good fish stock, or enough to cover the fish, and add 1 cup wine, red or white, 1 onion stuck with 2 cloves, 4 peppercorns, ½ bay leaf, 4 sprigs of parsley, a pinch of thyme, and salt to taste. Bring the stock to a boil and simmer for 10 minutes.

Tie the fish in cheesecloth and tie the ends into loops so it will be easy to lift the fish from the pan when it is cooked. Lower it gently into the liquid and poach the fish until the flesh flakes easily. Be careful not to overcook, and do not let the liquid boil. Lift the fish from the kettle, unwrap, and roll it onto a warm serving platter. Remove the skin carefully and serve the fish hot with a hot lemon-butter-parsley sauce, or with any favorite fish sauce. Or chill the fish and serve it simply with mayonnaise, the platter beautifully garnished with watercress, sliced tomatoes, and cucumbers. Or coat it with mayonnaise *chaud-froid,* glaze it with aspic, and serve mayonnaise on the side. The fish may be elaborately embellished with little cutouts of black olive or truffles.

Fish fillets may be poached in court-bouillon either flat or rolled and tied. The rolls may be stuffed with a fish forcemeat. Once the fish is cooked and removed to a serving dish, the court-bouillon may be thickened with egg yolks, or with flour rubbed to a paste with butter, to make the sauce. Finish the sauce with heavy cream, pour it over the fillets, and sprinkle with parsley.

Poaching time

Large fish need from 6 to 10 minutes per pound poaching time, and fillets require about 1 minute per ounce. Double the poaching time if the fish is poached from the hard-frozen state.

HOW TO FREEZE SHELLFISH

Lobsters

Select only live lobsters. Small lobsters, 2 pounds or less, are the most delicate. Larger ones are apt to be tough. Plunge them into boiling salted water or court-bouillon (see Index) and simmer them from 10 to 20 minutes, depending on their size. Cool and split. Discard the intestinal vein and the sac behind the head and put two halves together again to form a whole lobster. Wrap in Saran, Pliofilm, or aluminum foil, overwrap, and freeze to serve cold, when thawed, with mayonnaise or remoulade or ravigote sauce. Or remove the meat from the tail and claws, pack the meat in cellophane-lined cartons, leaving ½ inch head space, and freeze for use in lobster Newburg, or other cooked lobster dishes. Thaw completely before serving cold in salad or sea-food cocktail.

Shrimp

Shrimp are best frozen uncooked in the shell or unshelled.

Wash uncooked shrimp thoroughly in cold water. If desired, remove shell and intestinal vein that runs down the back. Rinse and drain. Package in cartons with two layers of freezer paper between layers of shrimp. Wrap the carton in moisture-vaporproof paper, seal, and freeze. Thaw just enough to be able to separate shrimp from paper.

To freeze cooked shrimp, simmer the shrimp in boiling salted water or court-bouillon (see Index) for 10 minutes. Cool them in the cooking liquor, shell, and devein. Pack cooked in cartons, leaving ½ inch head space. Overwrap, seal, and freeze promptly. Do not plan to store for more than 1 month. Freeze cooked shrimp only for convenience, as they tend to toughen during long storage at zero temperature. Thaw completely to serve cold in salad or shrimp cocktail.

Crabs

During the warmer months from May to October, crabs shed the hard shells that begin to pinch a little as the crustaceans grow one size larger. For 2 to 3 days the hard-shelled crab is a soft-shelled crab and if caught at this particular time in its life, it is entirely tender and edible, including the new embryo shell.

Soft-shelled crabs

Cut off the head, about ¼ inch behind the eyes. Squeeze gently to force out the green bubble behind the eyes which contains a bitter fluid. Lift the soft shell where it comes to a point at each side and cut off the white gills with kitchen scissors. Peel back the apron and cut it off. Dip crabs in cold salted water and package in cartons with two layers of freezer paper between layers of crabs. Overwrap the carton with moisture-vaporproof paper, seal, and freeze. Thaw just enough to be able to separate crabs from paper, or about 15 minutes.

Broil partially thawed soft-shelled crabs under moderate heat for about 15 minutes on one side and 10 on the other, basting frequently with melted butter. Serve sprinkled with lemon juice and parsley. Or sauté in butter from the partially thawed state for about 10 minutes on one side and 6 on the other, and serve with lemon-butter sauce, with shredded almonds browned in butter, with finely chopped mixed herbs such as tarragon, chives, and parsley wilted in butter, or with *sauce diable*.

Hard-shelled crabs

Wash hard-shelled crabs in cold water. Drop them into boiling water containing 1 teaspoon salt for every quart of water and simmer them for 15 minutes. Drain and cool thoroughly. Remove the edible meat from the body and claws and pack it into moisture-vaporproof cartons, leaving ½ inch head space. Seal and freeze.

Defrost the crab meat and serve it very cold as salad or cocktail with mayonnaise, or a more highly seasoned sauce such as remoulade, ravigote, or Russian dressing.

Oysters and clams

Oysters and clams must be handled very rapidly and carefully. Wash the shells in cold running water to remove any external sand. Shuck the bivalves, saving the liquor, and discarding any dead or injured ones. Wash them in a brine made of 2 tablespoons salt dissolved in a quart of cold water, and drain. Package the oysters or clams in liquid-tight containers and fill the containers to within ½ inch of the top with the liquor. Seal and freeze quickly.

Oysters and clams may be thawed and served cold with a cocktail sauce, or may be used in soups and chowders or baked sea-food casseroles.

CHAPTER 5

Freezing Vegetables

To freeze or not to freeze

Vegetables that you enjoy raw and crisp, such as salad greens, radishes, green peppers, celery, tomatoes, cucumbers, cabbage, and onions, do not retain their crispness when frozen. They may, however, be frozen for use in favorite cooked dishes, if you wish.

Most of the rest that are normally cooked before they are served freeze well and retain much of their nutritive value, color, flavor, and goodness if the rules for freezing are strictly followed. But, like any processed food, frozen vegetables are never as good, nor should you expect them to be, as garden vegetables cooked in a small amount of water until barely tender and served in a matter of minutes from the time they were picked from the vine or plucked from the earth.

Many vegetables such as carrots, onions, turnips, beets, celery, and potatoes are available most of the year, so there is little reason to freeze them. When root cellars and cold-storage warehouses are exhausted, a new crop begins to arrive in northern markets from the Carolinas, Texas, Florida, and California. Our southern states keep our markets supplied with a large variety of green vegetables, which can be easily prepared and quickly cooked, so there is little economy in freezing them in quantity.

As a matter of fact, I can think of only two reasons why anyone should monopolize valuable freezer space with quantities of home-frozen vegetables.

1. If you and your family are inordinately fond of a vegetable such as zucchini that is in season for only a short period during the year and is not frozen by commercial freezing companies.

2. If you have a surplus of choice vegetables from your own farm or garden that would go to waste if you did not freeze them.

And I do mean CHOICE, for you get out of your freezer only the quality that you put in. The finest, tenderest, most flavorful vegetables are the ones to freeze. Immature vegetables that have not developed their maximum flavor and overripe ones that have lost flavor, are tough or mushy, will never improve in quality in your freezer.

If you don't have a surplus of choice vegetables from your farm or garden, if you can't arrange with a local farmer to supply you with your favorite vegetables freshly harvested, it is wiser by far to depend on the commercially frozen products to supply your daily needs. Commercial plants can do a better job with vegetables than you can and, generally, at a lower price if you take into consideration your time.

SELECTING AND PREPARING VEGETABLES

Select only well-ripened, tender choice vegetables in quantities that you can handle with ease. Don't overestimate your energy or time.

Prepare vegetables as carefully as you would for the table. Wash thoroughly in several changes of cold running water. Discard any unripe, discolored, or damaged portions. Peel when necessary. Sort according to size or cut into uniform pieces so that the scalding will be exact and the packages will be uniform.

Scalding or blanching

If vegetables are not carefully and exactly scalded or blanched, they lose color and develop an off flavor in several weeks.

Scalding retards the action of enzymes, those chemical agents that are present in all living material. Enzymes are essential to the growth and ripening of vegetables, but once maturity is reached and the vegetable is harvested, the enzymes speed up the oxidation of the vegetable cells, causing a rapid loss of vitamins, color, and flavor.

It is important to understand that scalding does not destroy enzymatic action. It simply retards the work of the organisms that cause spoilage. Storing at a constant zero temperature further discourages the enzymes, yet slowly and inevitably their job of destruction continues. As each month goes by, frozen vegetables will lessen in flavor—imperceptibly if they are prepared and scalded with care, but no frozen vegetable should be stored longer than from one growing season to another. The sooner they are eaten after freezing, the better they will be.

There are two methods of scalding, one in boiling water, the other in steam:

Scalding in boiling water in the home kitchen is generally preferable to steam scalding. Leafy vegetables *must* be scalded in boiling water for uniform results. The flavor of broccoli, on the other hand, is slightly better if the broccoli is steam scalded.

Some authorities prefer steam scalding. The premise upon which they base their reasoning is that boiling water dissipates vitamins and minerals to a greater extent than steam. On the other hand, more uniform results are obtained by vegetables being bathed on all sides and agitated in boiling water.

Water scalding

Scald only 1 pound of any vegetable at a time in 1 gallon of rapidly boiling water. Larger quantities of vegetables in this amount of water would reduce the temperature of the water so drastically that the exact scalding time listed for each vegetable would be affected and inferior products might result.

Use a large kettle with a tight-fitting cover. Bring 1 gallon of water to a rapid boil, so that when 1 pound of vegetables is added the temperature of the water will not drop more than 10 degrees.

Place 1 pound of vegetables in a fine-mesh wire basket with a lid, or tie them loosely in cheesecloth. Immerse the vegetables in the boiling water, cover tightly, and start counting the scalding time immediately.

The water may be re-used, but be sure to bring it back to a vigorous boil each time before adding another pound batch and renew the water with boiling water from a tea kettle as it boils away.

Steam scalding

Use a large utensil with a tight-fitting cover, preferably a pressure cooker with the petcock open. Place a rack in the kettle and add enough water to reach the rack (about 2 or 3 inches) but not touch the vegetables. Keep the water boiling vigorously during the steaming period.

Place 1 pound of prepared vegetables in a fine-mesh wire basket. Place the basket in the kettle, cover tightly, and start counting scalding time as given for individual vegetables. In general, steam scalding time increases water scalding time by one half. A colander with small perforations may be used, or the vegetables can be tied loosely in cheesecloth.

All blanching times are for 1 pound of vegetables. At 5000 feet or more above sea level, scald all vegetables 1 minute longer.

Cooling

Vegetables should be cooled immediately after scalding to stop further cooking, which might make them mushy. Quick, effective cooling to 60° F. or lower results in better frozen products.

Fill the sink, or a large pan, with ice water. Leave the vegetables in the basket or cheesecloth in which they were blanched, lower the basket or cheesecloth into the ice water, and move it back and forth for several minutes, or until thoroughly cool. A good rule is to cool the vegetables for the same length of time as they were blanched. Renew the supply of ice as it melts. Drain thoroughly to remove excess water.

PACKAGING VEGETABLES

Package vegetables in moisture-vaporproof cartons, plastic containers, or bags in the size that is best suited to your family needs, but be careful not to bruise them. A pint carton will yield 3 large or 4 small servings of most vegetables. A quart container will yield 6 generous or 8 small servings. Containers larger than quarts are not recommended. For a family of two, package vegetables in small bags containing just enough for two servings and enclose several of the small bags in a larger one.

Vegetables expand a little when freezing, but do not require as much head space as fruits or purées. Leave ½ inch head space in pint cartons and ¾ inch in quart cartons for tightly packed vegetables. Loosely packed foods such as broccoli or cauliflower need no head space.

Press out as much of the air as possible from the containers and seal tightly. Wipe the edges of the bag with a dry cloth to remove any moisture that would prevent a complete seal with a warm iron.

Vegetables such as asparagus or corn-on-the-cob may be wrapped in freezer paper and sealed.

Label packaged vegetables clearly with the kind of vegetable, the variety, the date packed, and any special information.

FREEZING VEGETABLES

Freeze packaged vegetables as soon as possible. Put them one by one in the refrigerator until all the packages are ready. Then transfer them to the freezing compartment of your freezer. Spread the packages evenly against the freezer plates or coils, but keep them far enough apart from one another so that the air can move between them. After 24 hours, the frozen vegetables may be put in the storage compartments.

COOKING FROZEN VEGETABLES

Whether fresh or frozen, vegetables are best when they are cooked quickly in a tightly covered container, with a small amount of water, until just barely tender. Since frozen vegetables have already been partially cooked, they need only about half the cooking time required for the fresh product. Care should be taken not to overcook them.

Break the frozen vegetables into several chunks and put the chunks in a saucepan with from ¼ to ½ cup boiling water and a little salt. Cover and cook over a brisk heat until the chunks can be separated with a fork to allow the water and steam to circulate, reduce the heat, and simmer until tender.

272

If you cook more than one package of a frozen vegetable at a time, use a wide pan so that one package need not be placed upon another. A large skillet with a tight-fitting lid is a perfect cooking kettle and is superior to a deeper saucepan smaller in diameter.

Cook only the amount of vegetables to be eaten at one meal. Large packages may be cut in half with a sharp knife while still frozen and the unused portion wrapped and returned to the freezer.

Beets, squash, pumpkin, sweet potato, and vegetable purées that have been completely cooked before freezing should be heated to serving temperature in a saucepan placed over boiling water.

Corn-on-the-cob must be thawed before it is cooked. If frozen ears were dropped into boiling water, the kernels would be cooked before the cobs defrosted. Thaw the ears at room temperature in their wrappings.

Oven-cooked vegetables take longer, but this method is excellent if an oven meal is being prepared.

Break the frozen vegetables into chunks and place the chunks in a buttered casserole. Sprinkle with salt and pepper and dot with bits of butter. Cover the casserole tightly and cook in a moderate oven (350° F.) for 30 minutes. The vegetables are butter-steamed in their own juice.

COOKING TIME FOR VEGETABLES

It is almost impossible to give the exact cooking time for frozen vegetables, as it will vary with the variety and the maturity of the vegetable and the size of the pieces. The amount of water will also vary with the cooking time.

The following is approximate:

2 CUPS OR 1 POUND	AMOUNT OF WATER IN CUPS	TIME OF COOKING AFTER WATER RETURNS TO BOIL IN MINUTES
Asparagus, spears	½ to 1	5 to 8
Asparagus, cut	¼ to ½	3 to 4
Beans, lima	½ to 1	7 to 15
Beans, green	¼ to 1	10 to 15
Broccoli	¼ to ½	6 to 8

2 CUPS OR 1 POUND	AMOUNT OF WATER IN CUPS	TIME OF COOKING AFTER WATER RETURNS TO BOIL IN MINUTES
Cauliflower	½	4 to 6
Corn, cut	¼ to ½	5 to 6
Corn-on-the-cob	to cover	4 to 5
Peas	¼ to ½	5 to 7
Soybeans	½ to 1	10 to 15
Spinach	¼ to ½	4 to 6

FREEZING AND COOKING
ALL KINDS OF VEGETABLES

ASPARAGUS

1 crate (24 pounds) yields 20 pints
1 to 1¼ pounds yield 1 pint
Harvest, prepare, and freeze within 2 hours.
Avoid using iron utensils, as they discolor asparagus.
Select young, tender asparagus with thick, compact tips.

Wash thoroughly, discard the woody portion of the stalks, and sort into 3 groups according to the thickness of the stalks. The flavor of frozen asparagus is improved if the scales on the stalks are removed with a vegetable peeler. Any sand which lurks under these scales is also eliminated. Leave the stalks in lengths to fit the package, or cut stalks into 2-inch pieces.

Scald in boiling water or steam with the tips up:

	BOILING WATER	STEAM
Small stalks	2 minutes	4 minutes
Medium stalks	3 minutes	5 minutes
Large stalks	4 minutes	6 minutes

Cool in ice water and drain.

Pack into freezer containers or wrap in freezer paper, alternating tip and stem ends.

Seal and freeze.

Ways to serve: Serve cooked asparagus with melted butter or hollandaise sauce.

Leftover cooked asparagus makes a delicious salad if marinated in the refrigerator for a few hours in French dressing with a sprinkling of finely chopped onion and parsley.

Asparagus au gratin

Arrange stalks of cooked asparagus on thin slices of freshly made toast. Pour over the asparagus a few tablespoons of CREAM SAUCE and sprinkle with fine dry bread crumbs mixed with an equal amount of grated cheese. Dot generously with butter and bake in a hot oven (450° F.) until the sauce is bubbling and delicate brown. This makes a delicious luncheon dish.

Asparagus polonaise

Cook 1 pound frozen asparagus according to standard instructions. Sauté ½ cup soft fine bread crumbs in ½ cup hot sweet butter, stirring constantly, until the crumbs are golden brown. Stir in 1 hardcooked egg, finely chopped, 2 tablespoons finely chopped parsley, and salt and pepper to taste. Arrange the asparagus on a hot serving platter and pour the sauce over it.

BEANS, GREEN OR WAX

1 bushel (30 pounds) yields 30 to 40 pints

⅔ to 1 pound yields 1 pint

Avoid using iron utensils, as they discolor beans.

Select only tender, crisp, stringless beans of bright color.

Wash thoroughly, discard immature, bruised, or discolored beans, and sort for size. Cut off stem ends and tips. Leave whole, or cut into 1-inch pieces, or slice lengthwise into thin strips for Frenched beans.

Scald in boiling water or steam:

	BOILING WATER	STEAM
Whole beans	3 minutes	4 minutes
Cut beans	2 minutes	3 minutes
Frenched beans	1 minute	2 minutes

Cool promptly in ice water and drain.
Pack into freezer cartons or bags, leaving ½ inch head space.
Seal and freeze.

Green beans niçoise

2 onions, thinly sliced
½ green pepper, finely diced
1 cup stewed tomatoes
1 bouquet garni of 4 sprigs parsley, 1 stalk celery with the
leaves, and 1 bay leaf, all tied together
1 pound French-cut frozen string beans, cooked until barely
tender in a small amount of water
3 tablespoons butter
Salt and pepper
1 tablespoon finely chopped parsley

Simmer the onions and green pepper in the tomatoes with the
bouquet garni for about 20 minutes, or until the vegetables are
tender. Discard the *bouquet garni*. Toss the string beans with the
butter and salt and pepper, pour the tomato sauce over them, and
sprinkle with the chopped parsley.

BEANS, LIMA

1 bushel in the pods (32 pounds) yields 12 to 16 pints
2 to 2½ pounds yield 1 pint
Select young lima beans with plump pods.
Shell the beans and sort them according to 3 sizes.
Scald in boiling water or steam:

	BOILING WATER	STEAM
Baby beans	2 minutes	4 minutes
Medium beans	3 minutes	5 minutes
Large beans	4 minutes	6 minutes

Discard any beans that turn white during the scalding, for this means that they are overmature and contain too much starch for a good frozen product.

Cool in ice water and drain.

Pack into pint freezer cartons or bags, leaving ½ inch head space. Seal and freeze.

Lima beans in cream

Cook 1 pound frozen lima beans according to standard instructions. Drain and sprinkle with salt and pepper. Add 2 tablespoons finely chopped parsley and ½ cup heavy cream, cover, and keep the beans hot until ready to serve.

Lima beans and mushrooms

Cook 1 pound frozen lima beans according to standard instructions. Drain, sprinkle with salt and pepper, and combine with 1 cup sliced mushrooms sautéed until tender in butter.

BEET GREENS. See GREENS

BEETS

1 bushel without the tops (52 pounds) yields 35 to 40 pints
1¼ to 1½ pounds yield 1 pint
Select deep red, young beets not larger than 3 inches in diameter.
Wash the beets and sort them according to size. Trim the tops, leaving ½ inch of the stems.
Cook in boiling water until tender:

Small beets	25 to 30 minutes
Medium beets	45 to 50 minutes

Cool in ice water and slip off the skins.

Small beets not over 1½ inches in diameter may be frozen whole. Larger beets should be sliced or diced or quartered.

Pack in freezer cartons or bags, leaving ½ inch head space for cut beets. Whole beets need no head space.

Glazed beets

Defrost 2 cups precooked, frozen tiny beets over boiling water. Heat 3 tablespoons butter in a saucepan, add the beets, and shake over moderate heat for about 3 minutes until they are coated with butter. Sprinkle the beets with 1 tablespoon sugar and continue to shake the pan for another minute or so, until the beets are glazed.

Beets with sour cream

Cook 1 pound frozen beets according to standard instructions. Drain and press through a fine sieve.

In a saucepan placed over boiling water whisk 1 cup heavy sour cream with 2 tablespoons butter until the mixture is hot and creamy. Add the beet purée, salt, pepper, and a dash of cayenne, and mix thoroughly.

BROCCOLI

1 crate (25 pounds) yields 24 pints
1 pound yields 1 pint
Select compact, dark green heads with tender stalks.

Soak broccoli for ½ hour in a solution of 4 teaspoons salt dissolved in 1 gallon of cold water to remove any insects. Wash in clear, cold water, discard the large leaves and any tough portion of the stalks, and split the stalks lengthwise, so that the heads are not more than 1½ inches wide.

Scald in boiling water or steam:

BOILING WATER	STEAM
3 minutes	5 minutes

Cool in ice water and drain.

Pack in freezer cartons or bags, arranging the heads in opposite directions. No head space is necessary. Or wrap in moisture-vapor-proof paper.

Seal and freeze.

Ways to serve: Serve broccoli hot with hollandaise sauce or *mousseline.* Serve it cold with French dressing or *sauce vinaigrette.*

Broccoli amandine

Cook 1 pound frozen broccoli according to standard instructions. Drain the broccoli and arrange on a warm serving platter. Pour over ¼ cup butter mixed with 2 tablespoons lemon juice and sprinkle with ½ cup finely shredded toasted almonds.

BRUSSELS SPROUTS

1 bushel (32 pounds) yields 16 pints

2 pounds yield 1 pint

Select firm, compact, bright green sprouts.

Soak the sprouts for ½ hour in a solution of 4 teaspoons salt dissolved in 1 gallon of cold water to remove any insects. Remove the coarse outer leaves and discard any wilted or discolored sprouts. Wash the sprouts in clear, cold water and sort into 3 sizes.

Scald in boiling water:

Small heads	3 minutes
Medium heads	4 minutes
Large heads	5 minutes

Cool quickly in cold water and drain.

Pack Brussels sprouts in freezer cartons or bags, allowing 5 to 6 heads per serving, depending on their size. No head space is necessary.

Seal and freeze.

Brussels sprouts sautéed with grated onion

Cook 1 quart frozen Brussels sprouts according to standard instructions and drain. Melt 4 tablespoons butter in a skillet. Add the Brussels sprouts and 1 tablespoon grated onion and shake the skillet over moderate heat for 3 minutes. Sprinkle with 2 tablespoons finely chopped parsley and serve.

Brussels sprouts with crisp bacon

Sauté 6 slices of bacon, diced, until crisp and drain on absorbent paper. Pour off all but 2 tablespoons of the fat in the skillet and in the remaining fat sauté 1 small onion, finely chopped, until it is tender. Add 1 quart frozen Brussels sprouts, cooked according to standard instructions and drained, and shake the skillet over the heat for 1 minute. Turn into a serving dish and garnish with the crisp bacon.

CABBAGE

Frozen cabbage is not suitable for use in coleslaw or salads.
Select solid, green heads with crisp leaves.
Discard the coarse outer leaves and cut the head into wedges, or shred rather coarsely.
Scald in boiling water:

Wedges	3 minutes
Shredded cabbage	1½ minutes

Cool in ice water and drain.
Pack cabbage in freezer cartons, leaving ½ inch head space.
Seal and freeze.
Ways to serve: Serve frozen cabbage cooked with caraway seeds and tossed in butter, or:

Cabbage sweet and sour

Stew 1 tablespoon finely chopped onion in 2 tablespoons butter and ¼ cup water for 3 minutes. Add 2 cups frozen, shredded cabbage, cover, and cook for 10 minutes. Add 1 sour apple, thinly sliced, ½ teaspoon salt, a little more water if necessary, and simmer for about 10 minutes, or until the cabbage is barely tender. Add 2 tablespoons each red wine and brown sugar and simmer for 5 minutes longer.

CARROTS

1 bushel without the tops (50 pounds) yields 40 to 50 pints
1 to 1¼ pounds yield 1 pint
Select young, small or medium, bright orange carrots.
Wash the carrots, scrape, and sort for size. Leave the small carrots whole. Cut the others into ¼-inch cubes, thin slices, or lengthwise strips.
Scald in boiling water or steam:

	BOILING WATER	STEAM
Whole, small carrots	4 minutes	5 minutes
Lengthwise strips	3 minutes	4 minutes
Diced or sliced carrots	2 minutes	3 minutes

Cool in ice water and drain.
Pack carrots into freezer cartons or bags, leaving ½ inch head space for cut carrots. Alternate large and small ends of whole carrots compactly; for these no head space is necessary.
Ways to serve: Serve carrots hot, tossed with butter and plenty of finely chopped parsley, or cold, marinated in *sauce vinaigrette.*

Glazed whole carrots

Cook 1 pound small whole frozen carrots according to standard instructions until barely tender. Drain and add ¼ cup butter, ¼ cup brown sugar, and a dash of salt and continue to cook, stirring frequently, until the carrots are glazed and golden.

Carrots and peas

Prepare carrots and peas separately.
Cool and mix them in any desired proportions.
Package and freeze.

CAULIFLOWER

12 medium-sized heads (24 pounds) yield 24 pints
1 pound yields 1 pint
Select compact, snow-white heads.
Cut the heads of cauliflower from their thick bases and surrounding leaves and break or cut them into flowerets about 1 inch across.
Soak the pieces for ½ hour in a solution of 4 teaspoons salt dissolved in 1 gallon of cold water; wash in clear, cold water and drain.
Scald in boiling water or steam:

BOILING WATER	STEAM
3 minutes	5 minutes

Pack compactly into freezer cartons or bags, leaving no head space.
Seal and freeze.

Cauliflower fritters

Thaw frozen cauliflower and sprinkle the flowerets with salt, pepper, and lemon juice. Dip the flowerets into fritter batter and fry them a few at a time in hot, deep fat until golden. Drain on absorbent paper and serve hot.

Cauliflower polonaise

Cook 1 pound frozen cauliflower according to standard instructions with 1 tablespoon lemon juice and a generous dash of nutmeg. Drain, turn into a serving dish, and pour over ½ cup fine dry bread crumbs, sautéed in butter until golden. Sprinkle with finely chopped parsley.

CELERY

Select crisp, tender stalks.
Wash celery thoroughly, trim, and cut the stalks into 1-inch lengths.
Scald in boiling water for 3 minutes.
Cool in ice water and drain.
Pack into freezer cartons or bags, leaving ½ inch head space.
Seal and freeze.

Celery casserole

Cook 1 pound frozen celery according to standard instructions and drain. Stir in 1 cup MORNAY SAUCE and turn the celery into a buttered casserole. Sprinkle the celery with fine dry bread crumbs mixed with 1 tablespoon grated cheese and brown in a hot oven, or under the broiler flame.

Celery parmigiana

Cook 1 pound frozen celery according to standard instructions with 1 small onion, chopped, 1 clove, and 2 slices of bacon, diced, and drain. Put a layer of celery in a buttered shallow casserole, cover it with tomato sauce, and sprinkle with grated Parmesan cheese. Repeat the layers until the celery is used, ending with sauce and cheese. Bake the celery in a preheated hot oven (400° F.) for 10 minutes.

COLLARDS. See GREENS

CORN-ON-THE-COB

Select only the most tender, succulent ears.
Husk the ears and remove the silk, wash the corn, and sort it according to size.
Scald in boiling water:

Small ears 1¼ inches or less in diameter	6 minutes
Medium ears 1¼ to 1½ inches in diameter	8 minutes
Large ears over 1½ inches in diameter	10 minutes

Cool immediately and thoroughly in ice water and drain.
Wrap each ear in moisture-vaporproof paper, seal, and freeze.
When frozen, several ears may be packed in a bag, a carton, or stockinette.
Ways to serve: Thaw corn-on-the-cob for 2 hours at room temperature in the unopened wrappings. Drop into boiling water, cover, and simmer for 10 minutes.

CORN, WHOLE KERNEL
AND CREAM-STYLE

1 bushel in the husks (35 pounds) yields 20 to 24 pints
Select freshly picked sweet corn with full, regular kernels. The kernels should be golden and shiny and when one is ruptured with the thumbnail, the milk should spurt out.
Husk the ears, remove the silk, and wash the corn.
Scald the corn-on-the-cob in boiling water for 3 to 4 minutes.
Cool the corn in ice water and drain.
For whole kernel corn, cut the kernels from the cob close to the cob. *For cream-style corn,* cut the corn from the cobs at about the center of the kernels. Scrape the cob with the back of the knife to remove the heart of the kernel and the corn juice.

Package in freezer cartons or bags, leaving ½ inch head space. Seal and freeze.

Ways to serve: In a saucepan, combine 2 cups frozen whole-kernel corn, ¾ cup heavy cream, 1 tablespoon paprika, salt, and a pinch of cayenne. Cover the saucepan and cook over boiling water for about 20 minutes, or until the corn is thawed. Stir in 2 table-spoons sweet butter and serve.

Corn pudding

Thaw 2 cups cream-style frozen corn and mix with 1 cup cream, salt, pepper, and 2 tablespoons melted butter. Stir in 3 lightly beaten egg yolks and fold in 3 egg whites, stiffly beaten. Turn pudding into a buttered baking dish and bake in a preheated moderate oven (350° F.) for 40 minutes.

EGGPLANT

1 bushel (33 pounds) yields 33 pints
1 pound yields 1 pint
Select firm, ripe eggplants about 6 inches in diameter.
Overmature eggplants are not good for freezing.

Peel one eggplant at a time, cut into slices ½ inch thick, and drop slices into a solution of 3 teaspoons lemon juice and 1 quart water. Work quickly to prevent discoloration.

Blanch the slices in boiling water or steam:

BOILING WATER	STEAM
4 minutes	5 minutes

Cool in 1 gallon of ice water to which is added the juice of 1 lemon. Rinse in ice water and drain.

Reshape the eggplant, putting two pieces of freezer paper between the slices. Wrap the reshaped eggplant in moisture-vapor-proof paper.

Seal and freeze.

Eggplant parmigiana

*1 eggplant, thawed in its
wrappings
1 cup olive oil
1½ cups tomato sauce*

*4 tablespoons grated
Parmesan cheese
½ pound Mozzarella cheese,
thinly sliced*

Drain eggplant slices on absorbent paper and sauté in the hot olive oil until brown on both sides. Drain again on absorbent paper.

Place a layer of eggplant in a casserole and cover with some of the tomato sauce. Sprinkle sauce with some of the Parmesan and cover with a layer of the Mozzarella. Repeat layers until all eggplant is used, ending with Mozzarella. Bake in a preheated hot oven (400° F.) for 15 minutes.

Deep-fried eggplant

Thaw the eggplant in its wrapping. Dip slices in fritter batter and fry as you would the fresh vegetable.

GREENS

(beet greens, collards, kale, mustard greens, spinach, Swiss chard, turnip greens)

1 bushel (12 pounds) of collards, mustard greens, Swiss chard, or turnip greens yields 12 to 14 pints

1 bushel (15 pounds) of beet greens yields 15 pints

1 bushel (18 pounds) of kale or spinach yields 18 to 20 pints

Select young, tender greens.

Discard bruised and imperfect leaves and cut off tough stems before washing. Wash greens thoroughly in several changes of cold water to remove all the sand.

Scald only ½ pound at a time in 1 gallon boiling water. Twirl the container several times during the scalding to separate the leaves.

Beet greens, kale, mustard greens, turnip
    greens, Swiss chard, spinach   2 minutes
Collards   3 minutes

Cool immediately in ice water and drain.

Pack greens into freezer cartons or bags, leaving ½ inch head space. Do not press compactly into containers.

Seal and freeze.

Ways to serve: Beet greens, mustard greens, collards, and Swiss chard are best cooked according to standard instructions, drained, and tossed with salt, pepper, and butter. Kale is delicious tossed with diced bacon, sautéed until crisp. Add 1 small onion, finely chopped, to the water in which the frozen kale is cooked. Spinach is excellent cooked as a spinach soufflé, or in the following ways:

Spinach parmesan

Cook 1 pound frozen spinach according to standard instructions and drain. Add ¼ cup butter, salt and pepper to taste, a pinch of nutmeg, and 3 tablespoons grated Parmesan cheese and mix well.

Spinach purée

Cook 1 pound frozen spinach according to standard instructions and drain. Rub spinach through a fine sieve and mix the purée with 1 cup hot CREAM SAUCE. Season mixture with salt, pepper, and nutmeg and keep hot over simmering water until serving time.

HERBS

Select garden-fresh herbs.

Rinse under cold water and discard stems and any discolored leaves.

Pack leaves tightly into small glass jars (empty baby-food jars are perfect). Seal tightly.

Place jars in saucepan and cover with water. Bring water to a boil and simmer for 30 minutes. Cool jars and store in freezer.

KALE. See GREENS

KOHLRABI

Select young, mild-flavored, small to medium-sized kohlrabi.
Discard the tops and roots of kohlrabi. Wash and peel.
The small roots may be left whole, or all may be cut into ½-inch cubes.
Scald in boiling water or steam:

	BOILING WATER	STEAM
Whole kohlrabi	3 minutes	5 minutes
Cubes	2 minutes	3 minutes

Cool in ice water and drain.
Pack whole kohlrabi into freezer cartons or bags, or wrap in moisture-vaporproof paper. Pack cubes into freezer cartons or bags, leaving ½ inch head space.
Seal and freeze.
Ways to serve: Serve kohlrabi hot, mixed with CREAM SAUCE, or cold, marinated in French dressing or *sauce vinaigrette*.

MUSHROOMS

10 pounds yield 20 pints
Select fresh, white, cultivated mushrooms.
Wash mushrooms briefly. If they are white they will need little washing. Wiping with a damp cloth is sufficient. Discard tough portion of the stems. Sort according to size. Leave whole the small button mushrooms not larger than 1 inch across. Slice the rest.
Sauté ½ pound mushrooms at a time in 4 tablespoons hot butter for 4 to 5 minutes, or until almost cooked. Turn them into a flat dish and cool over cracked ice.
Or soak the mushrooms for 5 minutes in a solution of 1 tablespoon lemon juice and 6 cups cold water.

Steam:

Whole mushrooms not larger than 1 inch across	5 minutes
Tiny buttons, or quartered mushrooms	3 minutes
Sliced mushrooms	4 minutes

Cool promptly in ice water and drain.

Pack in freezer cartons or bags, leaving ½ inch head space in the packages containing the sliced mushrooms.

Seal and freeze.

Mushrooms in cream

1 scallion, chopped	*1 pound frozen, sliced*
1 small onion, chopped	*mushrooms*
2 tablespoons olive oil	*Salt and pepper*
2 tablespoons butter	*½ cup heavy cream*

Sauté the scallion and onion in the oil and butter until the onion is golden in color. Add mushrooms, sprinkle with salt and pepper, cover, and cook over a low heat for 15 minutes. Add cream and continue to cook for 3 minutes longer, stirring constantly.

MUSTARD GREENS. See GREENS

OKRA

Select tender, young, green pods.

Wash thoroughly, rinse, and sort for size. Cut off the stems without cutting into the seed cells, as this would let the juices leak out during the scalding.

Scald in boiling water:

Small pods	3 minutes
Large pods	4 minutes

Cool in ice water and drain.

Leave whole or slice crosswise.

Pack compactly in freezer cartons or bags, alternating top and tip ends, leaving ½ inch head space.

Seal and freeze.

Ways to serve: Cook frozen okra and serve it with lemon and butter or creamed. It may be sautéed or French-fried, or combined with onion, corn, and tomatoes in a stew.

Okra au gratin

1 pound frozen okra	1½ tablespoons butter
1½ cups CREAM SAUCE	¼ cup grated Parmesan
¼ cup bread crumbs	cheese

Cook okra according to standard instructions, drain, and turn it into a buttered baking dish. Pour cream sauce over the okra, sprinkle with bread crumbs, dot with butter, and sprinkle with cheese. Bake in a preheated moderate oven (375° F.) for about 20 minutes, or until sauce is bubbling and crumbs are brown.

PARSLEY. See HERBS

PARSNIPS

1 bushel (50 pounds) yields 40 to 50 pints

Select young, small to medium-size parsnips with a small center core.

Discard tops, wash, and peel. Cut lengthwise into ¼-inch-thick strips or cut into ½-inch cubes or slices.

Scald in boiling water for 2 minutes.

Cool in ice water and drain.

Pack in freezer cartons or bags, leaving ½ inch head space.

Seal and freeze.

Parsnip croquettes

Cook 1 pound frozen parsnips in a small amount of boiling salted water with 1 teaspoon sugar in a tightly covered saucepan until tender but not mushy. Put parsnips through a ricer and add enough hot cream to make a thick purée. Stir in 2 egg yolks, lightly beaten, and 2 tablespoons melted butter, and correct the seasoning. Spread mixture on a platter to cool. Form into small croquettes. Dip croquettes in flour, then in 1 egg beaten with 1 tablespoon milk and 1 tablespoon olive oil, and then in fine dry bread crumbs.

Fry the croquettes in hot, deep fat or sauté in butter until golden. Drain on absorbent paper and serve on a hot platter decorated with fried parsley.

PEAS, GREEN

1 bushel in the pods (30 pounds) yields 12 to 15 pints
2 to 2½ pounds yield 1 pint
Harvest early in the morning and freeze within 1 hour from the vine.

Select young, bright green, plump pods with sweet, tender peas. Shell the peas, discarding any overmature, immature, or wrinkled peas.

Scald in boiling water or steam:

BOILING WATER	STEAM
1½ minutes	2 minutes

Cool promptly in ice water and drain.

Package in freezer cartons or bags, leaving ½ inch head space. Seal and freeze.

Ways to serve: Peas are at their best when cooked in a small amount of salted water and tossed with butter and parsley and, if you like, a little heavy cream. They may be combined with mushrooms or tiny whole cooked onions and CREAM SAUCE, or served sprinkled with finely chopped fresh mint.

Peas French style

1 pound frozen peas	1 teaspoon sugar
8 tender lettuce leaves,	¼ cup water
shredded	Salt and pepper
10 small white onions	Butter

In a saucepan or baking dish put peas, lettuce leaves, onions, sugar, and water. Cover dish tightly and cook peas gently for about 15 minutes, or until tender. Season with salt and pepper, add a good lump of butter, and serve hot.

PEPPERS, SWEET

1 bushel (25 pounds) yields 20 quarts (21 pounds)

3 peppers (⅔ pound) yield 1 pint

Select firm, crisp, brightly colored peppers with glossy skin and thick walls.

Wash peppers thoroughly, cut out stems, and remove the seeds. Leave whole or cut into ½-inch strips or rings, or halve, slice, or dice according to use.

Scald peppers in boiling water or steam:

	BOILING WATER	STEAM
Whole or halves	3 minutes	4 minutes
Slices or dice	2 minutes	3 minutes

Cool in ice water and drain.

Pack in freezer cartons or bags, leaving ½ inch head space, or pack small amounts in envelopes made by heat-sealing freezer paper on three sides, then package several envelopes in pint cartons or bags.

Seal and freeze.

Peppers Roman style

Sauté 1 small onion, sliced, in 1 tablespoon of butter and 1 tablespoon olive oil until the onion is golden. Add 3 tomatoes, peeled and chopped, or 1 cup stewed tomatoes, and cook for 5 minutes. Add 1 pound frozen, sliced peppers and salt and pepper to taste. Cover skillet and cook peppers slowly for 30 minutes, stirring frequently.

PIMIENTOS

Select crisp, thick-walled, deep red pimientos.

Roast the pimientos in a hot oven (450° F.) for 20 minutes, or until skin blisters, and wash off the charred skins under cold running water.

Follow instructions given for SWEET PEPPERS.

Pack pimientos into freezer cartons or bags, leaving ½ inch head space.

Seal and freeze.

Thaw pimientos for use in salads and sandwich fillings, or as a garnish.

POTATOES, FRENCH-FRIED

Do not store longer than 6 weeks.

Select uniform potatoes.

Peel, wash, and cut lengthwise into ¼-inch-thick slices. Cut across the slices at ¼-inch intervals to make regular julienne strips. Soak strips in cold water for 5 minutes, drain, and dry them on a towel. Fry the potato strips in hot deep fat (370° F.) until pale gold. Drain on absorbent paper.

Spread the fried potatoes in a flat pan and chill over cracked ice.

Package compactly in freezer cartons, leaving ½ inch head space.

Cool and freeze.

Ways to serve: Remove frozen potatoes from the carton and plunge into deep hot fat (400° F.) for 2 minutes. Or place on a cooky sheet and bake in a preheateed hot oven (425° F.) for 15 to 20 minutes, basting several times with a little melted butter.

POTATOES, SWEET

10 pounds yield 16 pints
Do not store over 3 months.
Bake large sweet potatoes in a preheated moderate oven (350° F.) for 1 to 1½ hours, or until tender.
Cool potatoes, peel, and cut into halves or quarters, or slice ½ inch thick. Dip the slices in lemon juice and roll them in brown sugar.
Pack potatoes flat in layers, or stack, with a double layer of freezer paper between the layers or slices.
Or mash the potatoes and mix the purée with 2 tablespoons lemon juice or ¼ cup orange juice per pint. Package in moisture-vaporproof containers, leaving 1 inch head space.
Seal and freeze.

Candied sweet potatoes

Remove potato slices from their container and spread on a generously buttered shallow pan. Dot each slice with butter, sprinkle with a little salt and pepper, and bake in a preheated moderate oven (350° F.) for about 30 minutes. Or sauté the slices a few at a time in hot butter until brown and the sugar is caramelized. Blaze with warm rum or cognac, if desired.

PUMPKIN

10 pounds yield 12 pints
Select full-colored mature pie pumpkins.
Wash, cut into quarters, and discard the seeds and stringy fibers. Place the quarters in a low-sided baking pan containing ½ inch hot water and bake in a preheated moderate oven (350° F.) for about

40 minutes, or until tender. Remove the pulp from the rind and mash or rub through a sieve or food mill.

Cool the pumpkin purée in a pan placed over cracked ice, stirring occasionally.

Pack into freezer cartons or bags, leaving ½ inch head space. Seal and freeze.

Pumpkin-pie mix

Pumpkin-pie mix may be prepared according to your favorite recipe and frozen within a pie shell, or in a moisture-vaporproof, liquid-tight container. If the latter, save freezer space by leaving out the milk and cream from the recipe. This can easily be added when the mix is thawed.

RUTABAGAS

Select young, medium-size rutabagas.

Cut off the tops, wash, and peel. Cut into ½-inch cubes.

Scald in boiling water for 2 minutes.

Cool in ice water and drain.

Or cook in boiling water until tender. Drain and mash, or rub through a sieve or food mill and cool by stirring the purée in a saucepan over ice water.

Pack in freezer cartons or bags, leaving ½ inch head space. Seal and freeze.

Ways to serve: Cook cubed rutabagas according to standard instructions and toss with salt, pepper, butter, and parsley. They are also good tossed with diced bacon, sautéed until crisp and golden.

Thaw the rutabaga purée in a saucepan placed over boiling water and whip until smooth with cream, butter, and salt and pepper to taste. Or combine the rutabaga purée with an equal amount of fluffy mashed potatoes.

SAUERKRAUT

Pack into freezer containers.
Seal and freeze.

SOYBEANS

Select bright green, plump pods.
Wash the pods and drain.
Scald the beans in the pods in boiling water for 5 minutes.
Cool in ice water and squeeze the soybeans out of their pods.
Pack in freezer cartons or bags, leaving ½ inch head space.
Seal and freeze.
Ways to serve: Cook soybeans according to standard instructions and serve hot, tossed with butter and salt and pepper, or cold, marinated in French dressing.

SPINACH. See GREENS

SQUASH, SUMMER, OR ZUCCHINI

1 bushel (40 pounds) yields 32 to 40 pints
1 to 1¼ pounds yield 1 pint
Select young squash with tender skin and small seeds.
Wash the squash thoroughly and cut into ½-inch-thick slices or cubes.
Cook 1 pound squash in ½ cup water, without salt or seasonings, in a tightly covered saucepan for 5 minutes, or until tender. There should be little or no water left in the saucepan when the squash is cooked.
Cool by placing saucepan over cracked ice and stir frequently. The squash may be mashed if desired.
Package in freezer cartons or bags, leaving ½ inch head space. Seal and freeze.
Or dip sliced squash or zucchini into lemon juice and roll in

fine dry bread crumbs. Sauté the slices in hot melted butter until very pale gold and tender. Package the slices in layers in a freezer carton, separating each layer with two layers of freezer paper. Seal and freeze.

Zucchini sauté

Remove squash slices from the carton and sauté slowly in hot butter until brown. Sprinkle with salt, pepper, and freshly chopped parsley.

Zucchini casserole

1 pound frozen, sliced zucchini	2 eggs, lightly beaten
4 tablespoons butter	2 tablespoons grated Parmesan cheese
1½ cups CREAM SAUCE	Salt and pepper

Sauté zucchini slices in butter until golden on both sides. Combine cream sauce, eggs, cheese, and salt and pepper to taste and fold in zucchini. Turn mixture into a buttered casserole and bake in a preheated moderate oven (375° F.) for 30 minutes.

SQUASH, WINTER

10 pounds yield 12 pints
Select mature, hard-shelled varieties with firm flesh.

Cut or break the squash into pieces and discard the seeds and stringy fibers. Place pieces in a shallow-sided baking pan containing ½ inch hot water and bake in a preheated moderate oven (350° F.) for about 40 minutes, or until tender.

Or cook 1 pound squash in ½ cup water in a tightly covered container for 20 minutes, or until tender.

Scrape the pulp from the rind and mash, or rub through a sieve or food mill.

Cool the purée by placing it in a saucepan over cracked ice and stir frequently.

Pack into freezer cartons or bags, leaving ½ inch head space. Seal and freeze.

Ways to serve: Thaw squash purée in a saucepan placed over boiling water, season with salt and pepper and butter, and serve as a vegetable.

The thawed purée may also be used to good advantage in pies, puddings, and soups.

Hubbard squash purée

Thaw 2 cups squash purée over boiling water and beat into it 2 tablespoons melted butter, 2 teaspoons brown sugar, ¼ teaspoon ground ginger, and salt to taste. Beat in enough hot heavy cream to make a fluffy mixture. Turn into a serving dish and sprinkle with chopped parsley.

SUCCOTASH

Prepare corn and lima beans separately.
Cool and mix in equal proportions.
Package and freeze.

SWISS CHARD. See GREENS

TOMATO JUICE. See FRUIT JUICES

TURNIPS

Select small or medium-size firm, tender turnips with a mild flavor.

Remove tops, wash turnips, peel them, and cut into ½-inch cubes.

Scald in boiling water or steam:

BOILING WATER	STEAM
2½ minutes	3½ minutes

298

Cool in ice water and drain.

Pack in freezer cartons or bags, leaving ½ inch head space. Seal and freeze.

Ways to serve: Cook 1 pound frozen turnips according to standard instructions. Drain well and turn into a skillet containing 3 tablespoons hot butter. Cook for a few minutes, stirring constantly, then sprinkle with 1 tablespoon sugar and continue to cook, stirring, until the turnips are nicely glazed.

Or mash cooked turnips and put in a casserole. Sprinkle generously with grated Parmesan cheese, and brown under the broiler flame.

TURNIP GREENS. See GREENS

VEGETABLE PUREES

When you are preparing vegetables for freezing you can, if you wish, cook some until tender and purée them for baby food or for cream soups.

Puréed squash, pumpkin, and sweet potato are all excellent for pies. Tomato purée can be used in many ways; in soups, tomato sauces, gravies, and casseroles.

Package purées in quantities to suit your various needs. Baby foods may be frozen in paper cups or ice-cube trays, then wrapped in moisture-vaporproof paper, and stored. Small amounts of tomato purée may also be frozen in the same way.

CHAPTER 6

Freezing Fruits, Fruit Purées, and Fruit Juices

Freezing, better than any other method of preservation, captures the tree- or vine-ripened fresh flavor of fruits, and retains their bright color and texture. Happily, no other home method of preservation is as easy as freezing fruits.

Whole fruits, fruit juices, and purées are unusually easy to pack for year-round use in desserts and salads and for cold drinks, puddings, ice cream, and ice-cream toppings; and, if you wish, for jelly and jam making in midwinter, when there is more time for homemaking than during the carefree summer and busy, holiday-packed fall and early winter months.

Fruits need no scalding, but are simply packed dry, with sugar or in sugar syrup.

If your freezer is a small one, you may wish to store only the fruits that your family is especially fond of. Or you might choose to freeze some of the more exotic fruits that reach our markets at various times of the year, such as persimmons, papaya, or fresh figs, which are not packed by commercial freezing companies, depending upon the reliable frozen-food companies to supply your daily needs of orange juice, strawberries, peaches, raspberries, apples, et cetera.

SELECTION IS IMPORTANT

Fruits ripened on the bush or tree or vine have more flavor and better color for freezing. Select or pick the fruits that are fully ripe, yet firm. Overripe fruits will freeze to a mush and those that are not ripe enough lack flavor and sweetness. And be sure to taste fruits before you buy them. Blushing peaches and luscious ripe-red berries may look beautiful and yet be watery and tasteless to the bite.

PREPARATION

Fruits and berries lose quality very quickly if they are allowed to stand at room temperature for any length of time. If a delay is unavoidable, store them on trays in the refrigerator until the first free moments. Even then, don't keep the fruits waiting too long for frozen storage.

Work with a small amount of fruit at a time. Clean and sort it carefully and very gently, for all fruits bruise easily. Discard all parts that are blemished, overripe, or green. Wash the fruit carefully in cold running water. It should not be allowed to soak in water, for berries, in particular, will readily exchange valuable and flavorful juice for water. The juices will leach out and water will fill the cells, dissipating the wonderful fruit flavor. Extremely cold water or ice water is best for washing fruit. It helps to prevent "water logging" and keeps the fruit firm. Drain off all the excess water and stem, pit, peel, hull, or slice fruit in exactly the same manner as you would prepare it for the table.

Larger fruits are generally sliced before they are packed for freezing either mixed with dry sugar or covered with a sugar syrup. The amount of sugar used depends on the tartness of the fruit, the way you plan to serve it, and personal taste.

Some fruits may be packed without sugar or sugar syrup, but usually they are not so satisfactory. For fruits, like vegetables, contain chemical substances called enzymes that continue their work of destruction after the product is harvested. While vegetables are scalded to retard the enzymatic action, fruits are packed with sugar. The sugar performs the same service to fruits as the boiling-water bath does to vegetables—it slows down the action of the enzymes. In addition to this the syrup, whether it is prepared and poured over the fruit or formed by the juice drawn from the fruit combining with the dry sugar, keeps the air away from the fruit and retards oxidation.

Dry pack

The few exceptions to the sugar-pack rule in freezing fruits are: cranberries, boysenberries, gooseberries, loganberries, raspberries, blueberries, strawberries, blackberries, currants, youngberries, and rhubarb. These are fruits that can be washed and prepared without danger of rupturing the skin and that do not darken easily upon exposure to the air. The dry-pack method of packing fruit is usually used for fruits that are to be made into pies, puddings, or preserves.

Wash the fruit carefully and sort it, cutting away any bruises or blemishes and discarding any fruit that is overmature or underripe. Drain the fruit thoroughly between layers of absorbent paper to remove surface moisture. Place fruit, without crowding, in a jellyroll pan, and freeze for about 2 hours, or until marble-firm.

Pour the frozen fruit in moisture-vaporproof containers. Berries and cut rhubarb remain loose and easy to measure when the time comes to cook them. Seal and label each package with the name of the fruit, the date of storage, and the way it is to be used, and return to freezer.

Dry sugar pack

Fruits packed in dry sugar are excellent for making into pies or for other cooking purposes because they are less liquid. Dry sugar is especially suitable for juicy fruits that are sliced or crushed, as the natural fruit juices quickly blend with the sugar to form a protective syrup.

Wash the fruit carefully, sort, and drain it. Prepare the fruit as you would for the table. Work with a small amount of fruit at a time. Spread about 1 quart of fruit in a large, flat pan and sift sugar over, distributing it as evenly as possible. Four parts of fruit to 1 part of sugar by weight or volume gives adequate protection and is not too sweet for most palates and purposes. The sugar may vary, however, according to the tartness of the fruit. Anywhere from 3 to 5 parts of fruit to 1 part of sugar is the recommended proportion.

Fruit and sugar are best measured by a kitchen scale, but lacking this, the weight must be estimated on the basis that 1 cup tightly packed fruit weighs about as much as 1 cup sugar. For a 4-to-1 pack, then, you should measure 4 cups or 1 quart tightly packed fruit to 1 cup sugar.

Mix the sugar through the fruit gently with a wooden spoon until each piece is coated with sugar.

The sugar may be added to the fruit as the fruit is packed. Fill the package about ¼ full and sprinkle in ¼ of the sugar. Continue to fill the container in this way, shaking the container occasionally to distribute the sugar through the fruit.

Package sugared fruits in liquid-tight, moisture-vaporproof containers, leaving ½ inch head space. Be certain that the top seal on the bags is complete so there is no danger of the juice leaking out. Label with the name of the fruit, the date of storage, the quantity of sugar added, and the way in which you propose to use it. Freeze and store.

Syrup pack

Syrup pack is used for packing fruits that have little juice of their own and is especially valuable for those particular fruits, such as peaches, apricots, plums, and pears, that quickly discolor when the flesh is exposed to the air.

Forty per cent sugar syrup is generally sweet enough for any fruit; however, a higher or lower percentage may be used according to individual taste. A less sweet syrup is better for mild-flavored fruits such as cantaloupe balls or pineapple wedges, because the sugar does not mask the delicate flavor, while a heavier syrup may be preferred for very sour fruits such as sour cherries.

Place the prepared fruit in liquid-tight, moisture-vaporproof containers and cover it with syrup, leaving ¾ inch head space for expansion during freezing. Each pint of fruit will require about ⅔ cup of syrup.

SUGAR SYRUPS

Add the required amount of sugar to boiling water and stir until the sugar is completely dissolved. Chill the syrup in the refrigerator until ready to use, but do not store for longer than 2 days.

PERCENTAGE OF SYRUP	AMOUNT OF SUGAR	AMOUNT OF WATER
20% (very light)	1 cup	4 cups
30% (light)	2 cups	4 cups
40% (medium)	3 cups	4 cups
50% (heavy)	4 cups	4 cups
60% (very heavy)	6 cups	4 cups
65% (very heavy)	6¾ cups	4 cups

Part of the sugar used to make a sugar syrup may be replaced by white corn syrup. As a matter of fact, many fruits are superior in flavor packed in the sugar and corn syrup mixture rather than in all-sugar syrup. Dissolve the sugar in the water, add the corn syrup, and mix well.

HOW TO PREPARE SYRUP
WITH CORN SYRUP AND SUGAR

PERCENTAGE OF SYRUP	AMOUNT OF SUGAR	AMOUNT OF CORN SYRUP	AMOUNT OF WATER
40% (medium)	2 cups	2 cups	5 cups
50% (heavy)	3 cups	2 cups	4 cups

Honey may also be used to replace ¼ of the sugar in the syrup for freezing fruit, but the honey will impart a distinctive flavor to the fruit and should be used only if the family likes honey flavor, as it may mask the flavor of the fruit.

CONTROLLING DISCOLORATION

Many of the light-colored tree fruits such as apples, peaches, pears, plums, cherries, apricots, and nectarines have a tendency to turn dark when their cut surfaces are exposed to the oxygen in the air during preparation or frozen storage, or, more frequently, when the fruit is thawed. This can be partially prevented by slicing the peeled fruit directly into a container partly filled with syrup. But the most effective way to prevent discoloration is by the use of ascorbic acid.

How to use ascorbic acid

Ascorbic acid is another name for vitamin C, which is one of the major vitamins essential to good health. It not only prevents fruit from oxidizing, but enriches its vitamin C content. Ascorbic acid may be purchased from your drugstore in powdered or crystalline form and is better than tablets, which contain a filler. To use ascorbic acid, simply add it to the syrup just before the syrup is combined with the fruit. Stir only enough to dissolve the powder and stir gently to avoid mixing air into the syrup. Use 1 teaspoon ascorbic acid in 1 quart of prepared syrup.

To use ascorbic acid with dry sugar packs, dissolve ¼ teaspoon ascorbic acid in 2 tablespoons cold water and drip the solution over 1 pint of fruit before adding the sugar.

How to use citric acid or lemon juice

An alternative method to the ascorbic-acid treatment of fruit is the use of citric acid or lemon juice, but it is less effective than ascorbic acid and adds tartness to the fruit. Citric acid in powder or crystals is available at your drugstore.

Dissolve 4 teaspoons citric acid in 1 gallon of cold water and immerse the sliced fruit in this solution for 1 minute. Drain the fruit well before packing it, whether with dry sugar or in sugar syrup. Five tablespoons lemon juice may be substituted for the citric acid.

PACKAGING FRUITS

Any moistureproof, liquid-tight containers that can be sealed, or glass jars are good for packaging fruits. Select the size container that is best suited to your needs. A quart-size container will supply fruit for a well-filled 9-inch pie. A quart of strawberries or peaches will make 4 generous individual or 1 large shortcake. If used as an ice-cream or pudding topping, 1 pint of fruit will serve from 4 to 6 people.

Pack the fruit firmly into the container, but don't use enough pressure to crush the fruit that you want to remain whole, and leave ½ inch head space for dry packs and ¾ inch head space for syrup packs.

Seal the packages tightly and label each package, with either waterproof ink or a china marking pencil, with the name of the fruit, the date of storage, the quantity of sugar or the percentage of syrup added to the fruit, and the intended use. Freeze immediately.

HOW TO USE FROZEN FRUITS

Frozen fruits are ready to be served as soon as they are thawed and if the fruit was carefully selected and prepared for your freezer, the flavor is almost the same as that of fresh fruit.

Always thaw fruit in the sealed container in which it was frozen to preserve the best color, and turn the container several times during the thawing to keep the fruit bathed in the juice. On the refrigerator shelf a 1-pound package of fruit will thaw in 6 to 8 hours. At room temperature it will defrost in 2 to 3 hours. To thaw fruit quickly, place the package in cool running water for 30 minutes. Fruit packed with dry sugar will thaw a little more quickly than that packed with syrup.

Frozen fruit loses texture and flavor very quickly after it is thawed. So it is best to cook any leftover frozen and defrosted fruit and serve it in a compote, pudding, or other cooked dessert.

Serve berries while they still contain a few ice crystals. And the texture of peaches and most other fruits is better when they are served very cold. On the other hand, the flavor is improved by more complete thawing.

Most frozen fruits may be used in the same way as fresh fruits. They make excellent desserts served alone, or combined with ice cream. Or they may be used in pies, shortcakes, puddings, muffins, cobblers, upside-down cakes, or made into jams, jellies, and preserves.

Pies and tarts

For a 9-inch pie, or for 8 tarts, thaw 1 quart of frozen fruit only long enough to be able to separate the pieces. If the fruit was packed without sugar, add the amount of sugar called for in the recipe you are using. If the fruit was packed with dry sugar in the proportion of 4 parts fruit to 1 part sugar, no sugar at all should be added. If the fruit was packed in syrup, drain off the syrup, measure ½ cup, and add it to the quart of fruit in the pie. Reserve the remaining syrup to use in fruit drinks, compotes, or fruit sauces.

Frozen fruits develop more juice than fresh, so add a little more thickening to pies and tarts made with the frozen product.

Muffins and pancakes

Thaw frozen berries or other fruit just long enough to be able to separate the pieces and add to the flour mixture before stirring in the liquid.

Upside-down cake

Thaw frozen fruit in its container just long enough to be able to separate the pieces and arrange it in a buttered baking dish. Prepare a cake batter according to your favorite recipe, pour it over the fruit, and bake.

Jellies, jams, and preserves

Whole fruit, fruit juices, or purées need not be defrosted, but may be emptied directly into the cooking utensil. Follow a good recipe and make allowance for the sugar added to the fruit before it was frozen.

DETAILS OF HOME-FREEZING FRUITS

APPLES FOR PIE

Since winter apples keep beautifully if carefully stored in a cold room, there is little point in filling up the freezer with them, unless there happens to be a real shortage and you and your family just can't get along without apple pie.

Select only firm, ripe sour apples in prime condition for eating.

Peel, core, and cut apples into slices for pie. Small apples should be sliced into eighths and large ones into twelfths. Peel only a few apples at one time, as the cut surfaces of apples discolor rapidly on exposure to the air. The browning may be prevented in either of two ways:

1. Drop the apple slices directly into a solution made by dissolving 3 teaspoons salt in 2 quarts cold water, or 3 tablespoons lemon juice or 2 tablespoons citric acid dissolved in 2 quarts cold water. Remove the apples from the solution after 1 minute and drain. Then scald the slices in steam for 90 seconds and cool in ice water.

2. Submerge the apple slices for 5 minutes in a solution made by dissolving 1½ teaspoons sodium bisulphite in 1 gallon of cold water. Be sure to mix the solution in an earthenware, glass, stainless-steel, or enameled container. Drain the apple slices on absorbent paper. Package without sugar, or sugar may be added in the proportion of 1 pound sugar to 4 pounds fruit. Seal and freeze immediately. A quart of apple slices makes a 9-inch pie.

APPLESAUCE

1 bushel (48 pounds) yields 23 to 25 quarts

Either winter or summer apples may be used to make delicious applesauce.

Select fine-flavored apples.

Stem the apples, cut away any bruises or bad spots, and cut them into eighths. Put them in a saucepan with only enough water to prevent the apples from sticking to the bottom of the pan and bring to a fast boil. Reduce the heat and simmer for about 10 minutes, or until the apples are mushy. Force the apple pulp through a food mill or sieve and stir in sugar to taste.

If you wish to peel and core apples before cooking, you will not need to purée them in a food mill, but you will lose the flavor imparted to the applesauce by the skin.

Cool applesauce over ice water, package, and freeze promptly.

Apple compote

Peel, core, and slice apples and stew them in sugar syrup in the usual way. A stick of cinnamon may be added, or any other favorite spice. Cool the stewed apples, package with the syrup, and freeze.

Baked apples

Bake apples according to your favorite recipe, filling the centers with raisins or nuts, brown sugar, butter, and spice. Cool them over ice water and wrap individually in freezer paper. Package as many as you will need for one meal in a carton, seal, and freeze. Defrost in a moderate oven (350° F.) for 30 minutes, basting them occasionally with a little melted butter and sherry or rum.

APRICOTS

1 crate (16 pounds) yields 10 quarts

Select tree-ripened fruit, brightly colored, richly flavored, with no trace of green and with easily removable pits.

Wash apricots thoroughly and remove stems. Plunge about 12 apricots at a time in boiling water for 30 seconds to loosen the skins. Remove and plunge into ice water to cover for 1 minute. Peel apricots, cut into halves, and remove the pits.

Pack the apricot halves in containers and cover with 40 to 50 per cent syrup to which has been added ¼ teaspoon ascorbic acid to each cup of syrup (see Index.) Place a crumpled piece of freezer paper on the fruit under the top of the container to keep it submerged in the syrup.

Seal and freeze at once.

AVOCADOS (*purée only*)

Select avocados that are just ready to be eaten. They should not be hard or mushy. The small dark-skinned Calavos have a nuttier and better flavor than the large bright-green avocados.

Wash avocados, cut in half, and remove pits. Scoop pulp from rind and mash with 2 teaspoons lemon or lime juice and 1½ teaspoons sugar for each avocado. Refill the shell with the purée, wrap individually in moisture-vaporproof paper, and freeze immediately.

Avocados prepared in this way are delicious served for dessert and very colorful too if a fluted border of whipped cream is piped all around near the shell. Sprinkle the center with finely chopped pistachio nuts.

Do not store longer than 1 month.

The velvety smooth texture of avocado purée lends itself to creamy frozen desserts, ices, and ice creams. The avocado gives a delicate nutty taste to the ice cream, blends well with other fruit flavors, and because of the large amount of oil in the pulp, adds richness to the cream.

Avocado Pineapple ice

2 cups pineapple juice
¾ cup sugar
½ cup lemon juice

Pinch of salt
1 ripe avocado

Combine pineapple juice and sugar, heat to just below boiling point, and cool. Stir in lemon juice and salt. Pour mixture into a refrigerator tray and freeze to a mush. Cut the avocado in half, peel, and remove the seed. Mash the fruit to a pulp and beat it into the frozen mixture. Return to the freezing compartment and freeze until firm. Serve for dinner, or pack in moisture-vaporproof cartons and store for not more than 2 weeks.

BERRIES

(blackberries, boysenberries, dewberries, loganberries, youngberries, and nectarberries)

A 24-quart crate (36 pounds) yields 24 to 26 quarts

Select firm, sweet, plump, fully ripened berries with fine flavor. If the berries are from your own garden crop, do not pick them after a heavy rain, or during extremely hot weather.

Pick over the berries and discard any that are bruised, underripe, poorly colored, badly formed, or overseedy. Wash a few at a time in ice water and drain in a colander, or on absorbent paper.

Syrup pack. Place the berries in moisture-vaporproof, liquid-tight containers and cover them with a 40 to 50 per cent syrup, leaving ¾ inch head space. Berries packed in syrup are good for a dessert sauce or an ice-cream topping.

Sugar pack. Sprinkle 5 parts berries with 1 part sugar and mix lightly with a wooden spoon until the fruit is coated with the sugar. Use for pies or in the making of preserves.

Package and freeze immediately.

A quart of berries makes a 9-inch pie.

BLUEBERRIES

A 24-quart crate (36 pounds) yields 24 to 26 quarts

Select large, tender-skinned blueberries with a sweet flavor.

Wash blueberries thoroughly and discard the leaves and berries that are immature or shriveled and drain.

Dry pack. This is the best method if the blueberries are to be used in pies, muffins, or pancakes. Quick freeze on jelly-roll pans.

Sugar pack. Place blueberries in a dish, sprinkle with sugar in the proportion of 5 parts berries to 1 part sugar, and mix well, crushing them slightly. For use in blueberry shortcake, as a fruit sauce, in ice creams and frozen desserts, or as an ice-cream topping.

Package, seal, and freeze.

CANTALOUPE (*also papaya*)

6 large cantaloupes yield 10 quarts
Select firm-fleshed but well-ripened melons with fine flavor. The deep yellow varieties are best.

Cut the melons in half and discard the seeds. Scoop out the flesh with a French potato-ball cutter, or peel the melons and cut the flesh into uniform slices or cubes.

Dry pack. Arrange in layers, separating each layer with two pieces of freezer paper, so that the pieces may be easily separated for serving, before they are completely thawed, in fruit cups or salads.

Sugar pack. Mix 10 pounds cut melon with 2 cups sugar and 1⅔ cups white corn syrup.

Package in moisture-vaporproof containers, seal, and freeze.

CHERRIES, SOUR

1 bushel (56 pounds) yields 18 quarts
Select tender-skinned, bright-red cherries with a characteristic tart flavor.

Wash the cherries in ice water, stem, and pit.

Sugar pack. Mix 1 pound sugar with 4 pounds cherries.

Package in moisture-vaporproof, liquid-tight containers, seal, and freeze promptly.

Frozen sour cherries are delicious made into pies and cobblers. Frozen cherry juice is excellent in punches and sherbets.

CHERRIES, SWEET

1 bushel (56 pounds) yields 19 quarts
Select firm, fully ripe, tree-ripened cherries with rich flavor.

Wash the cherries in ice water, stem, and pit if desired, depending on how you wish to serve them.

Syrup pack. Whether pitted or whole, cherries should be packed in a 40 to 50 per cent syrup to which is added ¼ teaspoon ascorbic acid to each cup of syrup. Sweet cherries are excellent for an ice-cream sauce, if slightly crushed, or for cherries jubilee.

Package in moisture-vaporproof, liquid-tight containers, seal, and freeze immediately.

COCONUT

Unsweetened coconut, grated and mixed with its own milk, makes an excellent frozen product for use in curry sauces, desserts, cake frostings, or ice creams.

Or 1 part sugar may be added to every 8 parts shredded coconut. Stir in the coconut milk for extra flavor.

Package in moisture-vaporproof, liquid-tight containers, seal, and freeze.

CRANBERRIES

1 pound yields 1 quart

Select deep red, glossy-skinned cranberries with a mealy texture.

Wash and sort cranberries and discard any that are soft or poorly formed. Drain.

Dry pack. Cranberries need no sugar or syrup. Freeze until solid on jelly-roll pans. Package in moisture-vaporproof cartons or heat-sealing bags and return to freezer.

Jellied whole cranberries or favorite cranberry sauce or relish may be packed and frozen.

CURRANTS

2 quarts (3 pounds) yield 2 quarts

Select bright-red, well-ripened berries.

Stem the currants, wash, and drain.

Dry pack is good for jelly making later in the season, when you might like to combine the currants with apple or raspberry juice.

Sugar pack for use in pies, tarts, and cobblers. Crush the currants lightly and mix 3 parts fruit with 1 part sugar.

Package, seal, and freeze.

FIGS

Select figs with tender skins and flesh that is soft.

Wash figs carefully and discard any that are split or show signs of internal rot or souring.

Figs may be peeled, if desired, halved, sliced, or left whole.

Syrup pack. Cover figs with a 40 to 50 per cent syrup.

Package according to family needs in moisture-vaporproof, liquid-tight containers, allowing 3 or 4 figs per serving.

Seal and freeze immediately.

GOOSEBERRIES

Select fully matured, ripe berries with just a little red color.

Wash the gooseberries in cold water, drain, and remove the stems and blossom ends.

Dry pack, freezing until hard before packaging.

Sugar pack. Mix the gooseberries with 1 part sugar to 3 parts berries.

Package, seal, and freeze.

GRAPEFRUIT AND ORANGE SECTIONS

All varieties of oranges freeze well. Select them for their fine flavor.

Thin-skinned grapefruits that section easily are preferable, but again it is better to select grapefruit for flavor and sweetness.

Chill the fruit in the refrigerator. Peel, removing all the white skin, and cut the sections free from the membranes. Discard seeds.

Dry pack. Package in layers with two sheets of freezer paper between the layers so the sections may be separated, while still partially frozen, for use in fruit cups and salads. Grapefruit sections may be sprinkled with sugar to taste, if you wish.

Sugar pack. Use 1 part sugar to 12 parts fruit. Orange and grapefruit sections may also be packaged in combination with other fruits, such as cantaloupe, grapes, papaya, unpitted cherries, watermelon, and pineapple.

GRAPES

Select firm, ripe table grapes with tender skins and sweet flavor.
Wash, sort, discard any soft or shriveled grapes, and drain.
Dry pack purple grapes.
Sugar pack red and green grapes. Cover with 35 to 40 per cent
syrup for use in fruit cocktails and salads.

Concord grapes for pie

Separate pulp and hulls. Simmer pulp for 5 minutes, press through
a fine sieve, and discard seeds. Simmer hulls for 20 minutes to
soften, combine puréed pulp and hulls, and stir in 1 part sugar to 3
parts by weight of the combined pulp and hulls.

Package in moisture-vaporproof, liquid-tight containers in quart
size, which is sufficient for a 9-inch pie.

HUCKLEBERRIES. See BLUEBERRIES

PEACHES (*also nectarines*)

1 bushel (48 pounds) yields 24 quarts
*White peaches do not make as good frozen products as the yellow
varieties.*

Select peaches that are just right for eating. They should be juicy,
tree-ripened fruit with firm, fine-grained flesh. The freestone types
with red-colored pit cavities make the most attractive frozen product.

Place 12 peaches in a wire basket and plunge them into boiling
water to cover for 30 seconds, then plunge them into ice water and
peel. Slice the peaches directly into cold syrup in moisture-vaporproof, liquid-tight containers. The syrup should be made in advance
by dissolving 3 cups sugar in each 4 cups water. Chill the syrup and
when ready to use, gently stir 1 teaspoon ascorbic acid into each
quart of the syrup.

Press the fruit down in the container and add enough cold syrup to cover, leaving ½ inch head space in pints and 1 inch in quarts. Place a crumpled piece of freezer paper on top of the fruit, under the container top, to hold the fruit under the syrup.

Seal and freeze.

Frozen peaches make delicious pies, shortcakes, and upside-down cakes. They may be served as fresh fruit or as an ice-cream topping when only partially thawed.

Peaches and nectarines that are crushed or puréed without first being poached in syrup should also be mixed with ascorbic acid (½ teaspoon per pint of purée) to retain their color during frozen storage. Stir the ascorbic acid into the purée with 1 part sugar to 3 parts purée. Stir gently until the sugar is dissolved, being careful not to whip in any air. Delicious for ice creams, mousses, soufflés, and filling for tiny, thin pancakes.

PEARS

2 dozen (8 pounds) yield 4 quarts

Select tender, juicy, fine-fleshed pears.

Peel, halve, and core pears. Slice lengthwise about ½ inch thick directly into cold syrup in moisture-vaporproof, liquid-tight containers. The syrup should be from 40 to 50 per cent, and should contain ¼ teaspoon ascorbic acid per cup.

Or the sliced pears should be immersed in boiling syrup for 2 minutes, then packed in containers and covered with cold syrup, leaving ½ inch head space in pints and 1 inch head space in quarts. Place a crumpled piece of freezer paper over the fruit, under the lid of the container, to keep fruit covered with syrup.

Seal and freeze.

After thawing, pears can be used in pies, cobblers, fruit cocktail, or salads.

PINEAPPLE

1 pineapple (3 pounds) yields 3 pint cartons or 12 to 14 slices

Select ripe pineapple with a fragrant odor and sweet flavor.

Cut pineapple into slices ¾ inch thick, remove outer skin and eyes from each slice, and cut out the core.

Sugar pack. Add 1 part sugar to 5 parts fruit.

Package, seal, and freeze.

Shredded pineapple or cubes may be packed in a light syrup for use in dessert sauces.

PLUMS AND PRUNES

1 crate (20 pounds) yields 8 quarts

Select fully ripened plums.

Wash and sort plums. Discard any that are bruised or damaged, immature, or overripe. Cut plums in half, remove pits.

Syrup pack. Drop directly into moisture-vaporproof, liquid-tight containers containing a 40 to 50 per cent syrup with ¼ teaspoon ascorbic acid added to each cup.

Sugar pack. Add 1 part sugar to 5 parts fruit.

Seal and freeze.

RASPBERRIES, RED

A 24-quart crate (36 pounds) yields 24 to 26 quarts

Select large, ripe berries.

Raspberries are exceptionally fragile and care must be taken in handling them or they will bruise. Wash only a few at a time in ice water and drain them on absorbent paper.

Dry pack. Freeze on jelly-roll pan before packaging.

Sugar pack. Pack berries directly into moisture-vaporproof, liquid-tight containers. Use 1 cup sugar to 4 cups berries. When the container is ¼ full, add ¼ of the sugar and continue to alternate layers of berries and sugar until the container is full. Raspberries will make their own syrup when sugar is added.

Seal and freeze promptly.

RHUBARB

15 pounds yield 11 quarts

Select tender, deep red-colored stalks early in the spring before the rhubarb has become tough.

Wash rhubarb well under running water and cut the stalks into 1-inch pieces.

Dry pack. Rhubarb does not need sugar or sugar syrup. Simply freeze on jelly-roll pans, then pack in moisture-vaporproof cartons or bags.

Sugar pack. Rhubarb may be packed with 1 part sugar to every 4 or 5 parts rhubarb. Use liquid-tight containers.

Seal and freeze.

Rhubarb may also be stewed or steamed according to your favorite method, sweetened to taste, and frozen. Pack in moisture-vaporproof, liquid-tight containers leaving ½ inch head space.

Seal and freeze.

STRAWBERRIES

A 24-quart crate (36 pounds) yields 30 quarts

Select ripe-all-over, sound, firm berries with slightly tart flavor.

Wash berries, a few at a time, in ice water, drain, and remove hulls.

Strawberries may be frozen whole in sugar syrup, or as a purée or juice, but for the fullest, finest flavor, strawberries should be sliced or crushed and mixed with dry sugar.

Sugar pack. Slice the strawberries into a bowl and crush lightly, if desired. Sprinkle with 1 cup sugar to 4 cups fruit and toss with a wooden spoon until the berries are coated with sugar.

Syrup pack. Whole strawberries hold shape better if they are packed in 40 per cent sugar syrup, as this method is less likely to bruise the delicate fruit. The flavor of whole strawberries packed in syrup is not as good, however, as the sliced sugar-packed berries. The syrup contains water which dilutes the strawberry flavor.

Pack berries in moisture-vaporproof, liquid-tight containers, leaving ½ inch head space in pint containers and 1 inch head space in quarts. Place a crumpled piece of freezer paper on top of the berries under the container lid to keep them immersed in the syrup.

Seal and freeze.

WATERMELON

Any thoroughly ripened watermelon is excellent for freezing for fruit cups or fruit salads, but the red-ripe center of the watermelon is best. Prepare and freeze watermelon according to the directions for cantaloupe.

FRUIT JUICES

Most fruit juices, including cranberry, cherry, grape, raspberry and strawberry, apple, and citrus and tomato juice, make excellent frozen products and retain their fresh flavor from one season to another. They make refreshing drinks thawed and served cold, or they can be made into fruit juices, ice creams, and sherbets, or boiled up with sugar and made into clear and sparkling jelly.

Orange and Grapefruit need only be squeezed to extract the juice. The juice is then packed into liquid-tight containers and frozen. Select fully ripe fruit and chill thoroughly in refrigerator. Cut fruit in half, ream out juice, and strain through a stainless-steel or plastic strainer or cheesecloth. Pour juice into containers, leaving 1 inch head space, and freeze immediately.

Apples as well as citrus fruits need no heat treatment. Extract the juice from sound winter apples, pour into moisture-vaporproof, liquid-tight containers, allowing 1 inch head space, and freeze at once. The secret of really fresh-flavored golden apple juice is in the speed with which it is handled and put in the freezer. Fermentation starts almost immediately, and if the juice is allowed to remain at room temperature for even an hour, it begins to darken and develops a "cider" flavor.

Cherries, Grapes, and Berries must be heated to extract the juice. Select fully ripe, flavorful fruit. Wash, sort, and drain fruit and put it in a stainless-steel or aluminum preserving kettle. Crush fruit with a potato masher and heat very gradually to between 160° and 170° F., stirring occasionally, to soften the fruit and release the juices. Strain juice through a muslin jelly bag and cool by floating the saucepan containing it in ice water. Sweeten juice with from ½ to 1 cup sugar per gallon, or sweeten to taste. Pour the juice into moisture-vaporproof, liquid-tight containers, leaving 1 inch head space for expansion during freezing, and freeze immediately.

Apricots, Peaches, and Rhubarb must also be heated to extract the juice, and since these are drier fruits than cherries or berries, a little water should be added. Wash, sort, and drain the fruit. Put it in a stainless-steel or aluminum kettle and add about ½ cup water for each pound of fruit.

Bring the fruit to a simmer, mashing occasionally with a potato masher, and simmer very gently for 10 minutes. Strain juice while hot through a jelly bag and cool by floating the saucepan containing it in ice water. Sweeten the juice to taste, pour into moisture-vapor-proof, liquid-tight containers, leaving 1 inch head space for expansion, and freeze immediately.

Tomatoes should be fully ripe and sound. Wash, core, and quarter, discarding any green portions. Heat tomatoes slowly in a stainless-steel or aluminum kettle until juice begins to boil and press juice and pulp through a fine sieve. Cool juice over ice water and add 2 tablespoons salt to each gallon of juice, or salt to taste. Other seasonings such as pepper and celery salt, or herbs such as fresh marjoram, garlic, or thyme, may also be added to taste. Pour the seasoned juice into moisture-vaporproof, liquid-tight containers and freeze immediately.

FRUIT PUREES AND APPLESAUCE

Fruit purées or "sieved" fruit pulp retain their quality for long periods of frozen storage and can be used in many ways, in ice creams, sherbets, and other frozen desserts; in puddings, cake frostings, pie- and tart-shell fillings; in fillings for sweet rolls or breakfast rings; in whips, beverages, confections, and so on. A little purée may be cooked with sugar to make a small batch of fresh jam.

Berries, peaches, plums, apricots, cherries, and grapes are some of the best fruits for purée, and the making and freezing of them takes little time.

Select fully ripe fruit of the finest flavor. Actually the fruit can be too mellow for canning and still produce the best flavor for a purée. It must, however, be perfectly good.

Wash and sort the fruit and trim away any blemishes or overripe spots. Mash the fruit pulp and deal with it in the same manner as if you were making fruit juice, except that instead of straining the juice through a sieve you must press both juice and pulp through a fine sieve, or put it through a food mill. Heat in a stainless-steel or aluminum kettle those fruits, such as cherries and plums and guavas, that need heating in order to start the juices flowing; soft fruits such as cantaloupes, papayas, persimmons, mangoes, and berries need nothing except mashing and being pressed through a sieve.

Mix the purée with a small amount of sugar to taste, cool over ice water, and package in moisture-vaporproof, liquid-tight containers, leaving ¾ inch head space. Freeze immediately.

Strawberry Purée. Select fully ripe strawberries of fine, sweet flavor. Wash, drain, and hull. Press through a fine sieve. Don't force through the very last of the pulp as this contains most of the seeds and is apt to give an off flavor to the purée. Five quarts of whole fresh fruit make about 6 cups of purée.

Other Berry Purées. Wash and pick over berries and press them through a fine sieve. Four quarts of whole fresh berries make about 6 cups of purée.

Cantaloupe Purée. Peel and slice fully ripe cantaloupes, discarding the seeds, and press the flesh through a fine sieve. Six pounds of whole melons make about 6 cups of purée. Papayas, persimmons, and ripe mangoes may be puréed in the same way.

Cranberry Purée. Wash and pick over the berries. Cook in a little water in a tightly covered saucepan until the skins burst, and press both cranberries and juice remaining in the pan through a fine sieve. Three quarts of whole fresh cranberries make about 6 cups of purée.

Concord Grape Purée. Wash and stem the grapes. Place in a stainless-steel or aluminum kettle and crush with a potato masher. Cover kettle, bring grapes to a simmer, and heat until the juice begins to flow and the seeds are loosened from the pulp. Press through a fine sieve. Six pounds of fresh grapes make about 6 cups of purée. Cherries, plums, and guavas may be puréed in the same way.

Peach, Apricot, and Nectarine Purées. Select fully ripe, full-flavored fruit. Peel, trim away any bruised spots, quarter, and discard pits. Drop fruit into boiling syrup made by dissolving 1 cup sugar in 8 cups water and simmer for 3 minutes. Press fruit through a fine sieve and cool the purée over ice water. Six pounds of whole fruit make about 6 cups of purée.

Rhubarb Purée. Wash rhubarb and cut stalks into 1-inch pieces.

Heat in a saucepan placed over boiling water until rhubarb is soft and press through a fine sieve. Cool the purée over ice water. Four pounds of cut rhubarb make about 6 cups of purée.

PACKAGING FRUIT PUREES

Combine 6 cups fruit purée with from 1½ to 2 cups sugar, depending on the tartness of the fruit and personal taste. Stir the purée until the sugar is completely dissolved.

Package in moisture-vaporproof, liquid-tight containers, or in glass jars, leaving 1 inch head space for expansion during freezing.

BLENDED FRUITS FOR YOUR FREEZER

If you have an electric blender, blended fruits have more flavor and nutritional qualities to offer than fruit purées, because they usually contain both the skin and the pulp. They are strained only when it is necessary to remove the seeds.

Blueberry Purée. Bring to a boil 1 pound of blueberries (about 3 cups) and ¼ cup water. Turn berries and juice into glass container of a blender, cover, and blend for about 1 minute, or until mixture is smooth. Stir in ⅓ cup sugar and cool the blended fruit over the ice water. Package in moisture-vaporproof, liquid-tight containers and freeze. Makes 2½ cups.

Peach or Apricot Purée. Blanch 1½ pounds of peaches for 1 minute in boiling water. Dip into cold water, peel, halve, and pit. Bring to a boil 3 cups water and 1 cup sugar and cook the peach halves in the syrup for 3 minutes. Place peaches in the glass container of a blender, cover, and blend for about 1 minute, or until fruit is a smooth purée. Add ⅓ cup sugar and stir until sugar is dissolved. Cool the blended fruit over ice water, package in moisture-vaporproof, liquid-tight containers, and freeze. Makes about 2⅔ cups.

Plum Purée. Bring to a boil 1 pound halved, pitted ripe plums (about 2½ cups) and ¼ cup water and cook for 2 minutes. Turn plums and their juice into the glass container of a blender, cover, and blend for about 1 minute, or until the plums are smooth. Add ¼ cup sugar and stir until sugar is dissolved. Cool the blended fruit over ice water, package in moisture-vaporproof, liquid-tight containers, and freeze. Makes about 2½ cups.

Rhubarb Purée. Bring to a boil 1 pound cut rhubarb stalks (about 3 cups) and ½ cup water, cover, and cook for 2 minutes. Turn rhubarb and juice into the glass container of a blender, cover, and blend for about 1 minute, or until rhubarb is smooth. Stir in ½ cup sugar and stir until the sugar is dissolved. Cool the blended fruit over ice water, package in moisture-vaporproof, liquid-tight containers, and freeze. Makes about 2⅔ cups.

Strawberry Purée. Wash and hull 1 pound strawberries (about 3½ cups). Put them in the glass container of a blender and add 2 tablespoons water. Cover and blend for about 1 minute, or until fruit is smooth. Stir in ⅓ cup sugar and cool the blended strawberries over ice water. Package in moisture-vaporproof, liquid-tight containers and freeze. Makes about 2½ cups.

Tomato Purée. Wash 2 pounds tomatoes and cut them into quarters, discarding any green or overripe spots. Bring them to a boil, cook for 3 minutes, and drain lightly. Put tomatoes in the glass container of a blender, cover, and blend for about 10 seconds, or until smooth. Strain the blended tomatoes, stir in 1¼ teaspoons salt, or salt and other seasonings to taste, and cool over ice water. Pack the blended tomatoes into moisture-vaporproof, liquid-tight containers and freeze. Makes 2⅔ cups.

FREEZER JAMS

No-cook jams are easy to prepare, and retain a wonderfully fresh fruit color and flavor.

Simply combine ingredients and let stand at room temperature until gelled. If they are to be kept only 2 to 3 weeks, you may store them in the refrigerator. Otherwise, store them in the freezer.

If, at the time of serving, uncooked jams are stiffer than desired or if "weeping" has occurred, a small amount of stirring will soften or blend them.

Strawberry jam

> 2 cups finely mashed or sieved strawberries
> 4 cups sugar
> ½ cup liquid pectin

Combine berries and sugar. Let stand about 20 minutes, stirring occasionally. Add pectin to fruit mixture and stir about 2 to 3 minutes. Ladle quickly into jelly glasses or freezer containers. Cover *at once* with tight lids and let stand at room temperature 24 to 48 hours, or until gelled. Freeze. Yield: about six 8-inch glasses.

Black raspberry jam

Same as for STRAWBERRY JAM.

Cherry jam

Same as for STRAWBERRY, except sour cherries are pitted and put through a food chopper before measuring.

Peach jam

Same as for STRAWBERRY, except 1 teaspoon powdered citric acid is added to the finely mashed peaches.

Apricot jam

Same as for STRAWBERRY, except 1 teaspoon powdered citric acid is added to the finely mashed apricots.

Red raspberry jam

Same as for STRAWBERRY, except increase sugar from 4 cups to 6 cups.

Blackberry jam

Same as for STRAWBERRY, except increase sugar from 4 cups to 5½ cups.

Grape jam

Same as for STRAWBERRY, except crushed grapes are put through a food mill or pressed through a sieve before measuring, and sugar is increased from 4 cups to 6 cups. For spiced grape butter, add ¼ teaspoon cinnamon and ¼ teaspoon cloves to sugar and fruit mixture before letting it stand.

CHAPTER 7

Freezing Eggs and Dairy Products

EGGS

Eggs freeze perfectly—in fact, you cannot tell frozen eggs from fresh after as long as 6 to 8 months' storage. They should be strictly fresh before they are frozen, for, once again, the frozen product is only as good as the original.

Eggs are usually scarce from November through March. When they are plentiful and reasonable in price, they are a most economical product to store in your freezer.

Don't freeze large quantities of eggs in one container unless you know that the amount will be entirely used when it is removed from the freezer. Package eggs in amounts needed for specific recipes and cooking uses. You are well aware of your family's favorite dishes requiring eggs, so you will want to be prepared to take from your freezer just 3 whole eggs for that special chocolate cake, 5 egg yolks for a custard or a sponge cake, 8 egg whites for an angel food. If you are fond of cream puffs, you will want several packages of 4 whole eggs, and so on.

Eggs cannot be frozen in their shells, as the expansion during freezing would crack them. After being removed from the shells, they may be frozen whole or separated into yolks and whites.

Whole eggs and egg yolks must be lightly beaten and mixed with a small amount of salt or sugar. The sweetened eggs should be used for cakes and custards, salted ones for omelets, mayonnaise, et cetera. But the amount of salt added would be imperceptible in any dish and most baked products and sweet dishes of all kinds are improved by the touch of salt. So if you use salt in all frozen eggs, you can use them any way you please. When a recipe calls for a pinch of salt, simply eliminate it from the ingredients when using frozen salted eggs.

Whole eggs

Wash egg shells and break each egg into a cup before combining in a bowl, so it can be discarded if it is not strictly fresh. Beat egg with a fork, or a rotary beater, just long enough to combine thoroughly the yolk and the white, but without beating air into it. Stir in 1 teaspoon salt or 1 tablespoon sugar or corn syrup for each 2 cups of mixed whole eggs. It will take about 5 whole eggs to make 1 cup.

Separated eggs

Wash egg shells, break each egg carefully, and separate the yolk from the white. Remember that even a speck of the fat egg yolk left in the whites will prevent them from being beaten into a thick, staple foam. Should a speck of yolk fall into the whites, lift it out with the sharp edge of a broken egg shell.

Yolks. Beat egg yolks lightly with a fork, or rotary beater, until they are thoroughly mixed, but be careful not to beat air into them. Stir in 1 teaspoon salt or 1 tablespoon sugar or corn syrup to each cup of yolks. It will take about 14 yolks to make 1 cup. Strain egg yolks through a fine sieve and skim off any air bubbles from the surface before freezing, to prevent a crust from forming.

Whites. Egg whites do not coagulate when they are frozen and they need no mixing nor any addition of salt or sugar. Simply pour them into a container leaving ½ inch at top for expansion, label, and freeze. It will take about 8 egg whites to make 1 cup. When they are thawed, they beat to a volume that is equal to that of the fresh product.

HOW TO PACKAGE EGGS
FOR THE FREEZER

Eggs may be frozen in small cellophane bags, each bag containing the number of eggs for a specific use, and several bags may be packed into a carton. Or the eggs may be frozen in leakproof wax-lined cartons, leaving ½ inch head space for expansion. But the most convenient method is to freeze eggs in plastic ice-cube trays. One whole egg, mixed white and yolk, or 2 egg whites, or 2 or 3 mixed egg yolks, can be frozen in each cube. Once frozen, they can be taken from the tray and packaged in a long, thin bag of heat-sealing moisture-vaporproof material. Use a lukewarm curling iron and seal directly across the bag, separating each frozen egg cube. In this way, a cube or two, depending on how much you need, may be snipped off with a pair of scissors and the bag returned to the freezer.

Label clearly

Label each package of eggs with the amount, whether mixed with salt or sugar, the date, and proposed use: EGG WHITES, 1 CUP FOR ANGEL FOOD: 4 EGG YOLKS WITH SUGAR FOR CUSTARD, et cetera.

USING FROZEN EGGS

Let eggs thaw in the unopened package in the refrigerator or at room temperature. Small amounts of eggs packaged for specific cooking purposes will thaw in 30 minutes at room temperature. In an emergency, eggs packed in water-tight packages may be defrosted quickly in a bowl of lukewarm water.

Use defrosted whole mixed eggs and yolks promptly. Egg whites will remain fresh in the refrigerator for several days.

Use whole eggs in omelets, scrambled eggs, custards, ice cream, cakes, breads, pancakes, fritters, waffles, croquettes, and cream puffs.

Use egg yolks in spongecakes, custards, sauces, and mayonnaise.

Use egg whites in meringues, icings, angel food and other white cakes, candies, cookies, sherbets, and desserts.

EQUIVALENTS

3 tablespoons mixed whites and yolks	1 egg
2 tablespoons whites	White from 1 egg
1 tablespoon yolks	Yolk from 1 egg
1 cup whole eggs	5 eggs

BUTTER

Butter will keep fresh and sweet for many months in your freezer. Sweet butter will keep for a year. Salted butter should not be stored for longer than 6 months, since the salt speeds up the development of rancidity in any fat.

Freeze butter in its original carton and overwrap with moisture-vaporproof paper.

CHEESE

Cheese of all kinds freezes well, and may be kept from 4 to 6 months in the freezer. The quality of soft cheeses that are purchased at the exact degree of ripeness to suit your palate will retain this perfect stage and the flavor and texture are not affected. Blue cheese or Roquefort that has been frozen is apt to be more crumbly than fresh.

Cut cheese into family-size portions and wrap in moisture-vaporproof paper so that the cheese will not dry out or transfer its flavor to other foods.

Cottage cheese

Cottage cheese uncreamed and of good quality will keep well in the freezer for 3 to 4 months. Package it firmly in moisture-vaporproof cartons, pressing out as much air as possible and leaving ½ inch head space for expansion. Freeze immediately. Thaw in the refrigerator and add cream, if desired, at the time of serving.

Cream cheese

Cream cheese may be frozen if blended with heavy cream to a thick sauce consistency. Use for dips or "frosting" on sandwich loaves.

CREAM

Cream separates during freezing and is not suitable for table use, nor does frozen cream whip as well as fresh. It may, however, be used for ice cream, custards, and for cooking.

Cream to be frozen should contain from 40 to 60 per cent butterfat, and the more butterfat it contains the better it will freeze. Freeze in liquid-tight, moisture-vaporproof containers—allowing 1 inch head space for expansion during freezing—and freeze promptly. Cream should not be stored longer than 4 months.

Frozen cream should be defrosted slowly in the refrigerator.

ICE CREAM

Both homemade or commercially made ice cream and sherbet can be stored in the home freezer for several months to make quick and nourishing desserts. High-quality ice creams made from pasteurized cream and milk retain their flavor for 2 months. Those made from high-fat-content cream remain smooth in texture longer than those made from light cream or milk.

Commercially made ice cream and sherbet can be stored in the original container and overwrapped with moisture-vaporproof paper, or may be purchased in bulk and repacked in smaller moisture-vaporproof containers.

Chocolate-coated ice cream on sticks makes a quick and amusing dessert for grownups as well as children, and can be eaten directly from the freezer.

Homemade ice cream is the perfect way to use up a supply of cream, rather than freezing the surplus supply of cream itself. Use a recipe calling for a large percentage of heavy cream and a stabilizer such as egg yolks or gelatin. Make it in a hand- or electrically-turned ice-cream freezer so that it will not become grainy during storage (see Index).

Ice cream molded into colorful shapes and *bombes* can add that special touch to special occasions. Ice cream molds in the shape of hearts, bells, shamrocks, Easter bunnies, Christmas trees, and many others can be purchased from your local dairy, wrapped, and stored in your freezer for holiday parties. Or you may be able to find molds in a variety of shapes and freeze your own. Parfait and *bombe* molds are available in better house-goods stores across the country. And a little imagination will go a long way. Those silver-foil Christmas bells used for decoration may be packed full of ice cream and frozen. When solid, the foil can be torn away from the ice cream bell, and the ice cream wrapped and stored for future use.

Ice cream or ice cream combined with cake is an excellent quick dessert to store in your freezer (see Index).

Index

Almond balls, 150
Anchovy and Roquefort fingers, 9
  sandwich roll-ups, 7
Angel food cake:
  freezing, 134, 135
  ice-cream ribbon, 177
Appetizers, 3–16
  anchovy sandwich roll-ups, 7
  bacon and cheese, 10
  bacon and liver roll-ups, 6
  bacon roll-ups, 6
  baked cheese straws, 4
  biscuits, tiny, 4
  bologna rolls, 7
  canapés, 8–10
  cheese sandwich roll-ups, 7
  chilis rellenos con questo, 15
  Chinese egg rolls, 10–11
  clam and cheese canapés, 9
  cocktail balls, 8
  crab-meat canapés, 10
  crab-meat rolls, 11–12
  cream puffs, 4
  crêpes de fromage, 13
  curried cheese canapés, 9
  deviled sardine canapés, 9
  dips, 3
  eggplant, 14
  first course, 10–16
  ham deckers, 7
  liver and bacon roll-ups, 6
  meat rolls and deckers, 7
  mushroom turnovers, 4–5
  Parmesan canapés, 9
  pastry, 4–5
  petits choux, 164
  pigs in blankets, 6
  piroshki, 5
  quiche Lorraine, 12–13
  ratatouille, 98–99
  Roquefort and anchovy fingers, 9
  salami deckers, 7

  salmon and cheese canapés, 8
  sandwich roll-ups, 6–7
  spiced meat balls, 8
  storing time, 3
  stuffed grape leaves, 16
Apple(s):
  apricot tart, 157
  baked, 308
  compote, 308
  for pie, freezing, 307
  juice, 318
  sauce, 307–8
  tart tatin, 157–58
Apricot(s):
  freezing, 308
  jam, 323
  juice, 319
  purée, 320; blended, 321
Ascorbic acid, use of, 304
Asparagus:
  au gratin, 274
  freezing, 271, 273–74
  frozen:
    cooking, 272
    -fresh equivalent, 217
  polonaise, 274
Avocado:
  pineapple ice, 309
  purée, freezing, 309

Baby foods, freezing, 298
Bacon:
  and cheese canapés, 10
  and liver roll-ups, 6
  freezing, 223
  roll-ups, 6
Baked:
  Alaska, 175–76
  apples, 308
  beans, 93–94
  cookies, freezing, 147–48